C0-AMN-733

DATE DUE

# Political Development and Social Change in Libya

# Political Development and Social Change in Libya

**Omar I. El Fathaly**
Arab Development Institute

**Monte Palmer**
Florida State University

**LexingtonBooks**
D.C. Heath and Company
Lexington, Massachusetts
Toronto

DT
236
F37

# 5706516
DLC

3-3-81 JH

**Library of Congress Cataloging in Publication Data**

el fathaly, Omar I
   Political development and social change in Libya.

   Includes bibliographical references and index.
   1. Libya—Politics and government—1969-
2. Libya—Social policy. I. Palmer, Monte, joint
author. II. Title.
DT236.F37                 309.1'61'204                 77-713
ISBN 0-669-01427-3

*Copyright © 1980 by D.C. Heath and Company*

All rights reserved. No part of this publication may be reproduced or transmitted in any form or by any means, electronic or mechanical, including photocopy, recording, or any information storage or retrieval system, without permission in writing from the publisher.

Published simultaneously in Canada.

Printed in the United States of America.

International Standard Book Number: 0-669-01427-3

Library of Congress Catalog Card Number: 77-713

*To our Wives,*
*Hiba and Princess,*
*with love and appreciation*

32240  PCS  3/81

BT

$22.95

451497

ALUMNI MEMORIAL LIBRARY
Creighton University
Omaha, Nebraska 68178

# Contents

# List of Figures
# and Tables

# Acknowledgments

We wish to express our sincere appreciation to the Arab Development Institute, Tripoli, Libya. We also appreciate the cooperation of the innumerable officials in Libya who have freely given their time. Finally, we would like to express our appreciation to Linda Willis and to Hilal Kachoun for their assistance in preparing the manuscript. We, of course, assume responsibility for all errors in the manuscript.

# 1 The Political Development of Libya: A Framework for Analysis

In general terms, a developed country is one that is able to provide its citizens with a level of goods and services roughly equivalent to the highest level of goods and services available in any other country at that point in time. Indexes of development range from per capita income to various ratios of fuel consumption, roads, telephones, television sets, schools, teachers, students, literacy, and death. Although the specific ranking of a state may vary according to the indexes used, the United States, Britain, France, Germany, the low countries, Scandinavia, Japan, Canada, and the Soviet Union consistently cluster near the top of virtually all development scales.[1] Until the commercial production of oil in 1959, Libya ranked at the bottom of everyone's development scale, regardless of the indicators employed. Indeed, in the words of Benjamin Higgins, Libya was the very prototype of an underdeveloped country.

> Libya . . . is a prototype of a poor country . . . the bulk of the people live on a subsistence level . . . no sources of power and no mineral resources, where agricultural expansion is severely limited by climate conditons, where capital formation is zero or less, where there is no skilled labor supply and no indigenous entrepreneurship . . . Libya is at the bottom of the range in income and resources.[2]

Concepts such as development and modernization imply a transition from one point to another. In plotting the course of such a transformation, development theorists from the era of Tönnies and Weber through more recent analysts, such as Parsons, Khal, Apter, Riggs, Inkeles, Lerner, Sutton, and Sjoberg, have dichotomized human society into antithetical ideal types: the traditional and the modern.[3] States such as Libya, they suggest, begin their national life as traditional entities and, through the efforts of their leaders or the pressure of external events, or both, they move with varying speed in the direction of an idealized modern society. No suggestion is implied, of course, that modernization or development will ultimately be achieved or even that much progress will be made in the direction of modernization. Since Libya did begin its statehood under very traditional circumstances, and since its revolutionary leaders do aspire to transform Libya into a totally modern entity, a brief review of the standard traditional-modern dichotomy may provide some idea of the distance the leaders must cover.

1

The antithetical nature of the traditional-modern dichotomy, it is important to note, permeates virtually all levels of social analysis, and the path from one to the other is torturous, indeed. Traditional societies, for example, are said to be predominantly rural; modern societies are predominantly urban. Traditional societies are predominantly illiterate. Modern societies, in addition to being literate, are characterized by near universal education. Communications in traditional societies are in the form of oral, face-to-face contacts. Communications in modern societies are media-intense.

The social structure of traditional societies is based upon the extended family, which bears primary responsibility for nurturing individuals into adulthood, shaping their basic values to conform with the needs of society, determining their occupations, selecting their spouses, defining their recreational groups (mainly relatives), caring for them in time of illness or old age, and providing protection from external enemies. And, since most extended families bear collective responsibility for the behavior of their members, they are also responsible for rigidly policing behavior in an effort to minimize interfamily conflict.

The social structure of modern societies is a highly differentiated network of specialized socioeconomic and political units which reach their apex in the state. It is the state, not the extended family, that bears ultimate responsibility for meeting the individual's various needs, and it is the state that shapes the fundamental values of the individual.

Traditional societies are characterized by poorly differentiated, agrarian, family-based, barter economies which neither utilize nor generate innovative technology and which seldom provide goods and services beyond the level of bare subsistence. Modern societies are characterized by highly differentiated, industrialized market or command economies dominated by "public" corporations which utilize and generate innovative technology and which create a surplus of goods and services sufficient to provide most members of society with a standard of living much higher than mere subsistence.

The political systems of traditional societies are similarly characterized by rudimentary organizational structures dominated by family-based, tribal chieftains who justify their authority on the basis of lineage, religion, or tradition, and who, either individually or with the assistance of close relatives, perform both the input functions of interest articulation and interest aggregation (reading the masses) and the output functions of rulemaking, rule application, and rule adjudication.[4] The political systems of modern societies, in contrast, are characterized by complex, highly differentiated organizational structures dominated by elites selected predominantly on the basis of achievement. Most political functions, including interest articulation, interest aggregation, rule making, rule administration, and rule adjudication, are performed by specialized units. Mass political participation in traditional societies is minimal; mass participation in modern societies is intense.

Finally, traditional cultures, including their religions, traditions, myths, norms, and mores, justify established social, economic, and political patterns as the will of God or other supernatural forces and reinforce the operation and perpetuation of the traditional social order by stressing the values of passivity, fatalism, and conformity. Modern cultural systems also justify established social, economic, and political patterns on the basis of supernatural appeals to God, dialectical materialism, or national destiny, but, in contrast to traditional cultures, are said to stress political participation, achievement, creativity, nationalism, and other values essential to the operation and perpetuation of modern economic and political systems.

Since human behavior tends to be shaped by the individual's structural and cultural milieu, traditional individuals, reflecting the values of traditional cultures, are generally characterized as passive, fatalistic, conformist, and noninnovative.[5] Modern individuals, in turn, are said to have a far stronger sense of human volition; to be more aggressive, more innovative, and to be imbued with what David McClelland has termed "achievement motivation."[6] Moreover, because of their geographic isolation and general illiteracy, traditional individuals are said to be intensely superstitious or religious. Modern individuals, because of greater exposure to information, tend to be less religious.

Similarly, traditional individuals, reflecting the pervasive role of the extended family in the structuring of their lives and the shaping of their identity, are said to be particularistic and parochial. Kinship obligations ethically supersede moral obligations to the state or other groups. Loyalty to the state, if awareness of the state exists at all, is minimal. Modern individuals, by contrast, are said to be universalistic. Kinship obligations are regularly superseded by occupational, political, and social obligations. Merit and the maximization of personal advantage outweigh kinship ties in the selection of employees and associates. The state rather than the family is the terminal focus of individual loyalty. Nationalism is pervasive.

Since the ethical value hierarchy of traditional individuals places obligations to the family above obligations to other groups, conflicts among families in traditional societies tend to be intense. Distrust of nonkinship groups tends to be pervasive. The breadth of political and economic networks in modern societies, by contrast, demands a broader, nonkinship foundation for interpersonal trust and interaction. In much the same manner, traditional individuals are said to be atomistic; to be concerned only with their own immediate needs and to have little concern for the needs of others. Modern individuals, in turn, are said to manifest much more concern for the community as a whole.

Without entering a methodological debate over the utility of dichoto-mizing societies into two ideal types, we can say without hesitation that the Kingdom of Libya, on the eve of her independence in December, 1951, closely approximated the model of a traditional society presented.[7] We can also say without hesitation that Libya's revolutionary leaders have set as their objective the transformation of Libya into a society every bit as modern as the United States, Japan, or the Soviet Union. The distance they must cover, accordingly, is great, indeed.

In line with our previous comments, the objectives of this book are (1) to delineate the problems Libya's modernizing leaders must overcome if they are to achieve their goals of rapid political and economic moderniza-tion, (2) to describe and assess their efforts to overcome these developmental problems, and (3) to chart the course that remains if the elusive goal of modernization is to be attained.

As a first step in analyzing the problems and progress of Libya's poli-tical modernization, the primary objective of this chapter is to outline what we feel are the key elements in the development process.

## The Elites and Development

The rapid modernization of any society is dependent upon the interaction of a bewildering array of economic, social, and political variables. Few var-iables, however, are more important to the modernization of a state or society than the structure and behavior of its dominant elites.[8] The ruling elites, after all, set the tone of the development process. They allocate re-sources and determine which direction development is likely to take. All things being equal, an elite committed to the value of economic develop-ment is far more likely to stimulate economic development than an elite that is equivocal vis-à-vis the value of economic development or an elite who opposes development as a threat to its own status and survival.

Judging the ability of an elite to either facilitate or retard the modern-ization process, of course, requires an extensive inquiry into a society's elite structure and the values and behavior of its members. One obvious question, for example, concerns the operational definition of the elite. Other pertinent questions involve the delineation of elite values as well as their intensity and cohesiveness. Just how much does the elite value modernization? How does it conceptualize modernization? What are the major values competing with modernization? Are elite values cohesive, or do radically divergent value orderings exist within the elite? Because the role of the elite is so central to the development process, a sizeable portion of our analysis of political development in Libya will be devoted to answering these questions as they relate to Libya's revolutionary leaders.

Regardless of how intensely an elite may wish to modernize its society, however, wishing will not make it so. At minimum, the ability of an elite to modernize its society depends upon its capacity to (1) control the human and material resources of the state (2) mobilize those resources toward its modernizing goals, and (3) cope with the political stress and dislocation accompanying the modernization process.[9] Control, as we shall use the concept, refers to the absence or minimization of strikes, riots, separatist movements, armed insurrection, and other forms of political violence. Just how much violence a regime can manage and still be said to have control of its population and territory is an empirical question and clearly varies from country to country. As recent events in Iran and Lebanon demonstrate, however, an inverse relationship clearly exists between the levels of domestic violence and the administrative and economic capacity of a state.

Development, however, involves more than the ability to control the human and material resources of a society. Elites who have controlled their societies solely by coercion or by keeping their populations in a state of ignorance and social fragmentation have often ruled the least economically developed societies in the world. The challenge confronting Libya's revolutionary elite is to remain firmly in control of its society and simultaneously mobilize the citizens to actively work in support of its modernization goals.

Mobilization, as we shall use the term, has both structural (institutional) and behavioral dimensions. It includes making the people want to become involved in the development process, and also includes providing the structures and institutions necessary to harness their energies and channel them into the desired areas. As we shall see in the ensuing chapters, the greatest challenge to Libya's revolutionary elite during its first decade lies in the area of mobilization, in both its organizational and motivational dimensions.

Yet, a third problem confronting modernizing elites is the necessity to cope with the changes and turmoil unleashed by the mobilization process. As people do become involved in the modernization process—as they become more educated, more urbanized, and more exposed to the mass media—they tend to place an increasing array of demands upon the government. Material expectations for better standards of living or demands for greater political participation often increase more rapidly than can be handled by existing political and economic institutions, a situation that often leads to frustration and conflict, and a situation which, if left unchecked, may threaten the elite's ability to control its population.[10]

The ability of a dominant elite to control and mobilize the masses and to cope with the tensions and conflict of social change depends ultimately upon its ability to induce the masses to behave in the desired manner. In this endeavor, elites possess three fundamental means of manipulating the masses: symbolic, economic, coercive.[11] Symbolic manipulation refers to the

ability of the elite to symbolically persuade the masses to support its programs on a voluntary basis because the masses believe it is the proper thing
to do and because they believe the elite has their best interest at heart. Or,
elites can manipulate the masses by granting or withholding material rewards. Or, they can manipulate them through actual or threatened coercion. Most elites, it is probably fair to say, employ all three means of mass
control and mobilization. Nevertheless, it is also fair to say that the dominant elites of economically developed societies rule primarily through the
manipulation of symbols, whereas the leaders of most developing areas rely
far more heavily upon coercion. The greater the ability of an elite to manipulate the masses on the basis of symbols, the greater its likelihood of achieving objectives. A central theme in much of our analysis will thus be the revolutionary elite's drive to build a base of symbolic support within the Libyan
population.

**The Masses and Development**

If the political development of a state is influenced by the values and resources of the elite, it is also profoundly influenced by the attitudes and behavior of the masses. It is, in the final analysis, the masses who must execute elite decisions. Quite clearly, the more mass values conflict with elite
values, the more difficult the task of mobilizing the masses in support of
elite values will be.

   In the Libyan context, several dimensions of mass behavior have
proved to be problematic. Some are manifestly political. Others are dimensions of broader social behavior that tend to tie Libya to its traditional past.
The concepts surveyed forthwith are of particular relevance to our later
analysis.

*Nationalism, National Identity, and National Integration*

The more members of a society are aware of themselves as members of a
nation and the more intense their sense of national awareness, the more
readily they can be symbolically manipulated by appeals to sacrifice and
work for the good of the state.[12] Such nationalistic appeals are the standard
fare of the propaganda agencies of virtually all states and require little elaboration. What does require elaboration is the difficulty of separating nationalistic symbols from ethnic and religious ones. Many leaders in the developing areas rely heavily upon religious and ethnic appeals to elicit mass
displays of emotional support, yet such appeals have little use in controlling
or mobilizing the masses when religious or ethnic issues conflict with the

modernization goals of the state. Thus, in weighing the ability of a dominant elite to use nationalistic appeals as a means of mobilizing the masses to support modernization objectives, it is necessary to examine the extent to which all of the state's major religious, ethnic, and economic groups are integrated into a common political community, and the extent to which loyalty to the state takes priority over loyalty to various parochial groups. Clearly, the more the diverse population segments of a state have been welded into a common political community, the more effective the nationalistic appeals of the elite are likely to be in mobilizing that population. By whatever measures one would care to use, Libya, on the eve of its revolution, did not form an effective political community.

## Legitimacy and Institutionalization

The more the citizens of a state value their political institutions or leaders—the more intensely they feel that existing political institutions are crucial to their own security, beliefs, material prosperity, and general well-being—the more readily they can be controlled and mobilized through the use of symbolic appeals by the dominant elites—and the more tolerant (easily controlled) they are likely to be vis-à-vis the stress and tensions that generally accompany rapid social and economic change.[13]

In many developing areas, leaders may be perceived as legitimate by large segments of the population who, nevertheless, possess little faith in the formal political institutions of the state. Although the legitimacy of the leader provides a means of symbolically mobilizing the masses, the legitimacy of the government often remains contingent upon the survival or continued popularity of a single individual. Should that individual fall from grace, the political system might well be thrown into turmoil and a new set of elites would be forced to begin anew the process of building a base of mass support. Such a situation is clearly antithetical to the objectives of political or economic development. Accordingly, the more institutionalized the political institutions of a state, the more likely they are to survive the vicissitudes of social and economic change. The later chapters of our analysis of political development in Libya focus specifically on the efforts of Libya's revolutionary leaders to institutionalize the revolution.

## Mass Demands, Expectations, and Politicization

The ability of an elite to control the masses and to mobilize them in support of its modernization goals would also seem to be profoundly influenced by the type, intensity, and cohesiveness of the demands the masses place upon the political system and its leaders.[14] The more politicized the population, that is to say, the more individuals look to the government to satisfy their needs, the more unfulfilled demands are likely to be translated into direct political action. Problematic also, particularly in situations of rapid socioeconomic change, is the tendency for demands to escalate more rapidly than the government's capacity to meet them, a process commonly referred to as the revolution of rising expectations.[15] The political conflict resulting from such spiraling expectations is one of the primary reasons why many political leaders who have attempted to rapidly mobilize their societies in pursuit of rapid economic development, have found themselves embroiled in bitter political conflicts, conflicts that almost invariably spill over into the economic arena and result in economic stagnation. In the years following the discovery of oil, the demands of the Libyan population for an ever-increasing array of goods and services escalated far more rapidly than the monarchy's capacity to meet them. Those demands, of course, were inherited by the revolution. Also problematic from the perspective of Libya's revolutionary leaders, was the fact that different segments of the population appeared to have different demands. The urban workers, for example, demanded greater economic benefits; the rural areas demanded preservation of religious and tribal values, regardless of their impact upon economic development; the new middle class and the new generation of students demanded greater roles in Libya's political life. The more varied the pattern of demands facing an elite, of course, the greater the probability becomes that important segments of the population will be dissatisfied and will resort to violent political action to rectify their grievances.

*Supports: General Behavioral Predispositions*

It is ultimately the Libyan masses, as suggested previously, that must execute the revolution's development projects, and it is the Libyan masses that must operate the economic and political systems in a manner capable of meeting popular demands. It thus becomes crucial to examine the type, quantity, and quality of supports the Libyan masses can contribute to the execution of elite objectives. Attitudinal supports relating to legitimacy and nationalism were discussed previously and need little further elaboration at this point.

An even more crucial question, at least in our view, concerns the productive and administrative skills of the masses. What can they do? The economic, political, and social modernization of a society requires an enormous pool of administrative and technical talent, the development of which may take generations. The smaller the technical resource pool available to an elite, the more difficulty it will have in achieving its goals and in meeting mass demands.[16] Analyzed in these terms, the support pool inherited by the revolution was meager, indeed.

Moreover, underlying all the manifestly political attitudes and behavior patterns surveyed earlier is a variety of general behavior patterns introduced in our earlier discussion of traditionalism and modernity. Traditional societies, such as Libya, tend to be characterized by fatalism and the near absence of innovation; by intense religiosity, low empathy, and high levels of interpersonal and intergroup distrust; by intense particularism, atomism, or the absence of civic responsibility; and by clear tendencies to confer status and select leaders on the basis of ascriptive values, such as lineage, age, or religiosity, rather than on the basis of achievement or merit. The impact of such attitudes and behavior patterns upon political and economic development can be truly devastating. It is difficult for individuals to direct all their loyalty to the family or tribe, for example, and still be mobilized by appeals of nationalism or regime legitimacy.[17] In reality, individuals who direct the totality of their loyalty to parochial groups may possess little awareness of the state, or may consider it to be of little personal value. Indeed, they may well view the state and its centralized political institutions as a threat to the maintenance of family, tribal, or other parochial values. Also, the more family and parochial loyalties that take precedence over loyalty to the state, the more members of the bureaucracy and other government agencies are likely to use their official positions to further family and parochial interests rather than the interests of the state. Clearly, the more such particularistic behavior pervades government operations, the less likely it becomes that government agencies will be in a position to build legitimate support, and the more difficult the modernization process is likely to become. It is truly difficult to ask others to identify with the state and its political institutions when the representatives of the state who interact with the masses on a daily basis are primarily concerned with serving the interests of specific groups. This being the case, it should come as little surprise that the first target of the revolution was the destruction of Libya's tribal system.

Similarly, if a majority of the population defer to leaders selected on the basis of ascriptive values such as lineage or age, it may be difficult for modernizing leaders to establish their own legitimacy. Moreover, it might also be hypothesized that traditional tribal and religious elites are very much aware of the fact that their authority resides in the preservation of the tribe and religion, and that they would use their authority with the masses to resist any modernization programs that might lead to aggrandizement of the state and the political system at the expense of the tribe or other parochial institutions. This hypothesis is examined in chapter 5.

The intense levels of interpersonal and intergroup distrust that tend to characterize traditional societies would seemingly make it difficult for modernizing leaders to build an integrated political community in which individuals would set aside parochial conflicts and work for a recognized common good. The greater the intensity of intergroup conflict, the greater the probability that regime efforts would be judged in we-they terms, with programs designed to aid one segment of society automatically triggering the resentment of its opponents. Building legitimacy or symbolic resources in such an environment would be problematic at best. Moreover, economic development is a complex and pervasive goal that requires broad areas of mutual cooperation, communication, and coordination. The more intense the levels of interpersonal and intergroup distrust in a society, the more difficult such communication and coordination become. Rather than viewing civil servants and development technologists as neutral agents of the political system, the masses might tend to view them as members of opposing groups with a specific axe to grind. The long tradition of particularistic behavior and group conflict in Libya provides a clear precedent for such expectations.

Perhaps the most visible characteristic of traditional societies is their intense religiosity. Religiosity, as we will see shortly, is certainly a characteristic of Libya. Religion, of itself, of course, is difficult to classify as either facilitative or obstructive to social and economic modernization.[18] On the facilitative side, Max Weber's *The Protestant Ethic* suggests that religious values stressing achievement and the accumulation of capital can serve as a profound stimulus for economic growth.[19] Similarly, in societies where national symbols are poorly developed, religious symbols might well be adopted by a modernizing leader as a means of legitimizing his position and mobilizing the masses in support of modernization and change. Nasser's program of Islamic socialism provides an excellent example of an effective merging of religious and modernizing values. On the negative side, the religious values stressed by most religious elites, and particularly the local holy men, tend to be the values of resignation, fatalism, and subservience to the ascriptive selection of elites, values that are clearly antithetical to the modernization process. The situation in revolutionary Libya presents an interesting study in this regard, for Colonel Qadafi has utilized religious symbols to legitimize his position and has been a staunch defender of the Islamic faith. Our data, however, suggest that Islam as practiced by the local holy men does, indeed, obstruct modernization. The logical outcome of this situation has been a call for "Islam without priests," a subject discussed at length in later chapters.

The ability of a leader to control and mobilize the members of society, then, depends to a large extent upon fundamental cultural patterns as well as upon the manifestly political attitudes of his constituents. If mass attitudes and behavior are not conducive to modernization, little real development is likely to occur until such attitudes have been substantially modified. Attempts to modify the political and economic behavior of Libya's population, as we will see throughout our analysis, has become the foremost preoccupation of Libya's revolutionary leaders. It is upon their success in this endeavor that the fate of the revolution will ultimately rest.

## *Institutions: Linkage Mechanisms and Penetration*

If the modernization process is dependent upon elite values and the ability of the masses to execute those values, it is also dependent upon the quality of organizational mechanisms available for linking the masses to the elite and for harnessing the masses to elite goals.[20] It is difficult, for example, to coerce the mass without a viable police and military apparatus. It is difficult to build legitimacy and popular support through the distribution of a society's economic resources and to supervise complex modernization projects without a viable bureaucracy. It is difficult to speak of the institutionalization of legitimate political institutions when national political institutions either fail to exist, or change their shape on a routine basis. It is difficult to accurately assess mass demands and to maximize mass support without an effective linkage mechanism such as a political party. It is difficult to shape or alter mass behavior patterns without an effective education and media apparatus capable of executing complex socialization and resocialization programs. In short, it is difficult to control and mobilize the masses unless the elite has the organizational capacity to reach them on a direct and regular basis.

All of this may seem obvious, but the fact remains that most developing areas lack the organizational capacity to control the masses and to mobilize them in support of modernization efforts. This situation was certainly true of Libya on the eve of its socialist revolution. National political institutions were largely discredited. The bureaucracy was in shambles. Political parties existed only in embryonic stages and were limited to the urban areas. The military establishment was divided. All of the institutional requisites for the modernization of Libya, then, were missing. The revolutionary regime did not initially possess the organizational capacity to mobilize the population or to create institutions capable of acquiring sufficient legitimacy (institutionalization) to survive the stress and turmoil of the modernization process. Such an organizational capacity would have to be built largely from scratch, based on a population that possessed most of the traditional behavior patterns just summarized.

## Format of the Book

Our analysis of political modernization in Libya adheres to the preceding framework as faithfully as possible within the limits of our data. Chapter 2, for example, attempts to provide an integrated picture of social, economic, and political life in Libya as it existed prior to the revolution.

Chapter 3 begins the direct application of the conceptual framework to the analysis of political modernization in revolutionary Libya by describing the events of the revolution and by analyzing the structure, values, and cohesion of Libya's new modernizing elite.

Chapter 4, in turn, describes the means used by the Revolutionary Command Council (RCC) to meet the first prerequisite of political modernization: the ability to control the human and material resources of the state. This process, it should be noted, was not a particularly smooth one.

Chapters 5, 6, and 7 focus on the second prerequisite of the modernization process: the ability to mobilize the population of the state in support of the modernization goals of the regime. Libya's revolutionary leaders tried three radically different approaches to modernization during the revolution's first decade; three chapters were required to do these efforts justice.

Chapters 8 through 10 describe the mobilization programs outlined for the revolution's second decade, programs that have initiated Libya's transformation into a socialist state governed by a system of direct popular democracy.

Finally, chapter 11 summarizes the progress and continuing problems of political modernization in Libya, paying particular attention to the ability of the revolutionary leadership to establish political institutions capable of coping and adjusting to the stress and tension generated during the process of rapid social and economic change.

## Sources of Information

In pursuing our analysis, we have attempted to survey virtually all of the books, dissertations, articles, and other secondary resources relating to Libya available in the United States and Libya. The overwhelming majority of the information provided in the book, however, is based on primary sources. These sources include: (1) an intensive attitudinal survey of 10 percent of the population of Zawia province, (2) in-depth interviews with a full range of local leaders, including tribal chiefs and several varieites of local administrators generated by the rather cataclysmic shifts from one mode of mass mobilization to another, (3) in-depth interviews with leading officials of the monarchy and the republic, and (4) an endless array of newspaper and public documents, the majority of which were available only in the Arabic language.

Although specific methodological materials will be provided in the context of the discussion or elaborated in footnotes, this is probably the easiest point at which to describe the 1973 survey of Zawia province in as much as survey data are referred to throughout the book, and repeated methodological references would become tedious.

The initial draft of the survey instrument was developed in the United States in English. Later it was translated into Arabic and pretested at the University of Libya at Benghazi. An interview team of forty-nine students from the University of Libya and the Zawia Teacher's Institute were given one week of training. After the training sessions, the interviewers were divided into teams based primarily on their common tribal origins. It was felt that the refusal rate would be high if the interviewers were not native to the area in which the interviews were to take place. It was also necessary to provide each interviewer with a letter of authorization from the minister of interior. Such letters were particularly important in gaining the cooperation of municipal officials.

The general survey contained four distinct subsamples: municipal and provincial officials (n = 21), popular committee members (n = 60), tribal leaders (n = 10), and the general public (n = 576). The sample of public officials included the mayors, deputy mayors, and the department heads of the seven municipalities of Zawia province. The popular committee sample included municipal-level popular committee directors and deputy directors in Zawia province and a random sample of popular committee members.

In selecting respondents for the approximately 570 public interviews, a quota was assigned to each of the seven municipalities in the province based on their populations. Within each municipality, respondents were selected by using a stratified random sample. Since every municipality was divided into zones headed by a zone administrator, the head of the interview team contacted the mayor of the municipality to identify the zone administrator. The zone administrator, in turn, provided information on the total number of people in the zone and the geographic locations within the zone of major social groups, such as government employees, small businessmen, farmers, and bedouins. The zone random sample was clustered within each of these major social groups, as no documentation existed that would allow random identification of geographic areas within zones. The sampling strategy was to identify major social and geographic clusters (government officials at work, farmers on their farms, small businessmen in their shops, and bedouins in their geographic areas) and randomly select a quota from each cluster. The size of the sample from each of these clusters was based on the zone administrator's estimate of the relative size of the group in the zone.

One way to check the accuracy of a sample is to examine the extent to which its demographic characteristics correspond to known demographic characteristics of the population. In this regard, the public sample was drawn from the male population nineteen years and older. Females were excluded because they participate in the political process at very low rates (an estimated 3 percent turnout at the last provincial election), and when they do participate they usually follow the pattern of their husbands or fathers. Males under nineteen were excluded because they were under the legal age for electoral participation. The proportion of males nineteen and older in the sample corresponded quite closely to the proportion in municipalities of Zawia. The largest discrepancy was in Zahra (11 percent in the population and 16 percent in the sample). In the remaining six municipalities, the difference was not greater than 3 percent. Zawia province, with 24 percent of the population male and nineteen years and older, corresponds closely to the 27 percent figure for the entire country.

To ascertain the reliability of the questionnaire, responses to three Likert-type items of similar content were examined for the percentage of response incongruence. Extreme response incongruence (shifts of more than one position) totaled less than 4 percent among the public respondents. Extensive shifting, however, did occur among adjacent positions, a fact in large measure explained by the slightly different emphasis of the items involved in the reliability correlations. Virtually no response incongruence occurred among the more specialized subsamples in reference to items of similar content. Content validity was the major validity control used in the study. The validity of the questionnaire was also ascertained by extensive pretesting in Libya and through the evaluation of the questionnaire by a panel of Libyan scholars and administrators. Ambivalent items were either deleted or revised.

It should be noted that all interviews were conducted in the strictest confidence. Accordingly, no footnote references have been made to names, dates, or interview subject matter. Unless citations exist to the contrary, material presented in the later chapters may be assumed to be based on interview data. We saw little use in making footnote references only to indicate that the information provided was the result of confidential interviews.

Finally, we have adopted the policy of footnoting only extensive extracts of Colonel Qadafi's speeches, sayings, and writings. Briefer references are paraphrases of themes stressed by Qadafi and the members of the Revolutionary Command Council over extended periods of time and find reference in the longer quotations.

# 2 Libya: The Historical, Economic, and Social Milieus

It is difficult to analyze the problems confronting Libya's revolutionary leaders as they embarked upon the task of transforming Libya into a modern state without at least some knowledge of the historical, economic, and social milieus in which they were to operate.

Independent Libya came into existence in 1951, following several centuries of Ottoman control, three decades of Italian occupation, and almost a decade of British and French administration. The Libyan Arab Republic, known as the kingdom of Libya until the Socialist revolution of 1969, consists of three states, having a combined area of about 680,000 square miles. As such, Libya is the fourth largest state in Africa, and possesses a total population of just over 2.5 million people.

## The Political Environment

### The Making of a State

Libya became an independent state under the auspices of the United Nations on December 24, 1951. Libya was divided into three states or provinces: Cyrenaica (Benghazi) in the east, Tripolitania (Tripoli) in the west, and Fezzan in the south. When the Italian occupation was replaced by the British military administration, the British authority promoted the idea of independent Cyrenaica under "Emir" Idris, who had been proclaimed emir of Cyrenaica in 1921. No decision was made concerning Tripolitania or Fezzan. In debates in the House of Commons, Anthony Eden, the secretary of state for foreign affairs, acknowledged that "his Majesty's Government is determined that at the end of the war [World War II] the Senussi [the king's family, tribe, followers] of Cyrenaica will in no circumstances again fall under Italian domination."[1]

On behalf of Cyrenaica, Omar Mansur al-Kikhya, the most notable Cyrenaican leader after Idris, addressed a letter to Sir Edward Grigg, the British minister of state in Cairo, asking the British to recognize Idris as the emir of Cyrenaica, to recognize Cyrenaica as an independent country, and to assist Cyrenaica militarily, economically, and administratively. In return, Great Britain was to be given the right to station forces on Cyrenaican territory, and Cyrenaica was to be an ally of Great Britain.[2] On the same day,

15

Idris endorsed al-Kikhya's proposals in a letter to Sir Grigg assuring that the proposals conformed "with our desires and the desires of our Cyrenaican nation."[3]

Tripolitanian leaders, with only meager cooperation of Fezzanan leaders, were trying to join Idris and his followers in a united front to make demands upon the British. Tripolitania recognized the leadership of Idris but objected to the idea of an independent Cyrenaica, proposing instead a unified country. Al-Kikhya rejected Tripolitania's proposals.[4]

With the signing of the Italian peace treaty in 1947, the fate of Libya and the other Italian colonies was left in the hands of the big powers and the United Nations. The Italians also renewed their claim of sovereignty over Libya. Great Britain, ignoring its pledges of independence made to the Libyans, joined Italy in the Bevin-Sforza Plan, named for Ernest Bevin and Count Carolo Sforze, the British and Italian foreign ministers. The plan suggested giving the United Nations trusteeship over Tripolitania, Cyrenaica, and Fezzan with Italy, Great Britain, and France, respectively, serving as trustees.[5] The Libyan public responded violently with general strikes and demonstrations protesting the trusteeship plan, and the plan was ultimately rejected.[6]

The alternative plan of immediate independence was adopted by the General Assembly, and the process of making a new state began under the guidance and supervision of the United Nations. The Libyan leaders, although recognizing the leadership of Idris, still differed as to the shape and position of their future state. One group, preferring a unitary government with more ties and cooperation with the Arabs and less with the West, was organized by the National Congress party under the leadership of Bashi al-Sa-dawi. A second group, led by Idris and the Independence party, sought a federal form of government and close relationships and allies in the West, especially with the United Kingdom and United States. The outcome of an election favored the second group. The federal form of government was ultimately established, with the king's most loyal supporters being appointed to key positions of federal and provincial leadership.[7]

*The King*

Mohammed Idris El Senussi, the first king of the new kingdom of Libya, was born on March 12, 1890, in the remote oasis of Jaghbub, to an extremely religious family. His grandfather had founded the Senussi religious order which preached a return to the Islamic rituals and teachings as embodied in the Koran. Idris was educated in Islamic law and theology in the secluded Koranic school of Jaghbub.

Idris became a leader within the hierarchy of the Senussi order, and he enjoyed great prestige and power among tribal and religious groups, especially in the eastern part of the country. His political leadership derived from his role as a religious leader. Also, in his exile in Egypt, he was surrounded by other leaders and notable people who had fled the country during Italian occupation and who trusted and respected him for his family ties, religious background, and personality.

After the making of the state, the constitution granted the king broad powers: "the executive power shall be exercised by the king within the limits of the constitution" (Article 42), and "legislative power shall be exercised by the king in conjunction with Parliament" (Article 41). He opened and closed parliamentary sessions . . . the king may issue decrees . . . which shall have the force of law . . . " (Articles 62,64). He created and conferred titles; namely, the prime minister, diplomatic representatives, and senior officials, and could remove them from office at any time (Articles 71-74). He appointed the members of the senate (Article 94). He was the supreme commander of all the armed forces and had the power to declare war, conclude peace, and enter into treaties which he ratified after the approval of Parliament (Articles 65-69). The king, as "supreme head of the state," was "inviolable" and "exempt from all responsibilities" (Articles 58-59).[8]

Idris devoted most of his energy to religious and tribal matters, and supposedly regretted the need to spend so much time on affairs of state.[9] Neither willing to delegate authority or to trust others to run the state, he impeded even the most able people of his administration in executing the duties of their posts. The king was confused and reluctant in his political stands, and he rarely expressed support for any specific programs or took a clear-cut position on public issues.[10]

Although King Idris expressed devotion to the nation as a whole and publicly eschewed any thoughts of his own regional and personal interests, he privately confessed different feelings to the American ambassador in Libya. Mr. Villard wrote: "I had many teas, as well as luncheons with King Idris during the two and a half years I resided in his realm. The unfailing subject of interest to him was the past, present, and future of Cyrenaica. Uppermost in his mind was the rebuilding of Benghazi."[11]

While the country was suffering from poverty and lack of funds, the king's government kept moving between two capitals, and later three, mainly to keep the balance of regional influence and interests. The king spent funds generously on matters related to religion or promoting his family's history and image: the Islamic University (University of Mohammed Iben Ali El Sannussi) in Beida, and the building of the new (third) capital Beida, where some of his family resided or were buried. Beida has been described by one writer as "the Brasilia of Libya, built from nothing to nothing."[12]

The king emphasized Libyan-Arab brotherhood and solidarity, but unless he was under tremendous pressure, his words seldom went beyond lip service. He blocked Libyan membership in the Arab League until 1953, and he generally fell short of showing any positive support to the Arabs in the Middle East, even when it was to his advantage to do so. Instead, the king consistently pursued strong relationships with the West.

The Royal Diwan, headed by loyal but traditional leaders, tended to filter whatever information reached the king. Thus, the Royal Diwan gained tremendous power in running state affairs and contributed greatly to the instability of the political system. The Royal Diwan controlled many things that the king did not care to run or never heard about. Its leadership was a clear representation of power for tribal, familial, and religious elements in Libyan politics.

*The Cabinet*

Within a brief period, the federal system and the policies of the king led to crises in government. Clashes of authority broke out between federal and provincial politicians a few months after independence. A quarrel within the royal family, lack of coordination among the four governments in the region, and deeply conflicting regional interests contributed to internal disunity and the political instability of the country. The first government was brought down and Muntasir, the first prime minister, was forced to resign before the end of 1953 even though the king did not accept his resignation until February, 1954.[13] The new cabinet, under the premiership of Mohammed al-Sakisli, fell within two months as a result of conflict over the authority, jurisdiction, and legal boundaries of the various government agencies.[14]

The third cabinet, with Mohammed Bin Halim as premier, survived for thirty-seven months, with five cabinet reshuffles. Bin Halim faced tremendous regional conflicts and power struggles between his office and the Royal Diwan. Successor Abdu-al-Majid Kubar's cabinet was brought down in 1960, after forty months in office, as a result of corruption and financial scandal. Kubar was succeeded by Mohammed Bin Othman, who tried to restore public confidence in government and to seek harmonious relationships between his government on the one hand, and the Royal Diwan on the other.[15]

Bin Othman's cabinet survived until 1963, when it was replaced by Muhiaddin Fekini's cabinet, whose constitutional changes transformed the country from a federal to a unitary form of government. Fekini was faced with public demands to renegotiate the British-American-Libyan treaties. Clashes between demonstrating students and the powerful Cyrenaica Defense Force (CDF) in Benghazi brought to a head the issue of cabinet authority versus Royal Diwan authority. The CDF eventually fired on the students, forcing Fekini to resign.[16]

The liberally educated and progressive Fekini was replaced by the conservative Muntasir (his second term), who stressed stability based on discipline and public order. Poor health was Muntasir's valid reason for resigning in 1965, when he was named head of the Royal Diwan. Husayn Maziq was appointed Muntasir's successor. Maziq had had a long career in government service and had served as foreign minister under Muntasir. Even though his education was very limited, he proved to be intelligent and hardworking. Maziq met with violent demonstrations from the public and sharp attack from the opposition over two issues: Libyan failure to assist its Arab brethren in the 1967 Arab-Israeli War and his decision to resume oil shipments to Western Europe. He was forced to resign on July 1, 1967.[17]

Abdulgader al-Badria was named prime minister and served for only five months, to be replaced by Abdulhamid al-Bakkush, a thirty-five-year-old lawyer. Bakkush tried to balance his cabinet with conservative-liberal members, appeal to the newly powerful young educated groups, and at the same time keep peaceful relationships with the Royal Diwan and the old traditional leaders. But he was faced with accusations of corruption and favoritism. His governing approach antagonized the older generation and their leaders, and he was tolerated for only eleven months.[18] At the end of 1968, Bakkush was replaced by Wanis al-Gaddafi, a veteran of many previous cabinets. His main interest was the implementation of administrative reform, but the short period of time he spent in office before the revolution of September, 1969, prevented his plans from unfolding.[19]

During this period of seventeen years, there were eleven cabinets (averaging eighteen months per cabinet), with thirty-two reshuffles (averaging six months each), and a total of 101 cabinet members in office. Counting each of the appointments of cabinet members who were appointed more than once, the total comes to 141 ministers. The ministers rarely had time to familiarize themselves with the issues of their posts, or to develop future plans and strategies for their departments. They were always under the threat of being dismissed or reshuffled. Most of them were there to get for themselves everything they could in the shortest period possible.

As far as quality is concerned, the great majority of these cabinet members were incapable of handling the fundamental issues of their posts. They were chosen either to balance regional interests, or for their past and present support of the king. They were also chosen not for qualifications and skills, nor political ideology and experience, but for the family, tribal, and religious influence they represented. These elements declined in number in the second half of the monarchy, with technocrats and bureaucrats playing a growing role in the management of the country.[20]

The premiership was dominated by traditionally powerful families or tribal members. Of the eleven prime ministers, seven were influential tribal leaders, three were members of influential families, three were university graduates, two had moderate administrative experience, and all but one had supported the Senussi family or demonstrated loyalty to the king himself prior to their appointment.

Under growing public pressure resulting from the socioeconomic changes of the oil boom and exigencies arising from the regional and international environments, the government was faced with more demands than it could cope with. The political and administrative scene in the country deteriorated, and the last days of the monarchical regime were marked by corruption, nepotism, maladministration, and fiscal dishonesty.[21]

The cabinet was controlled by the king via his control of the prime minister. The frequent reshuffling of officeholders promoted ministerial instability and effectively prevented individuals from consolidating their influence.[22] The Parliament was also controlled by the king through his control of the elections. In the seven elections held in Libya (1952, 1955, 1960, 1964, 1965, 1967, and 1968), the government exercised substantial control over certification of candidates and results. This was done mainly to secure the success of government candidates.[23] The tribal and parochial nature of Libyan society fostered voting on grounds of personality or on family or tribal connections, rather than on national issues or even local issues,[24] although such tendencies were less marked in Tripoli and Benghazi.

Bureaucracy also posed a severe problem to the Libyan political system in the period 1952 to 1969. It represented only regional and group interests and was a prototype of maladministration. Before the adoption of a unitary form of government, Libya had been ruled by four governments. In addition to the federal government which moved between three capitals, there were three provincial governments with an average of eight ministers each. Tripolitania and Cyrenaica each employed more civil servants than the federal government. Each province followed its own policies without regard to the national federal policies—an extravagant, cumbersome, and inefficient arrangement, unmatched in similar conditions anywhere.[25]

## The Economy: 1951-1969

A study of the Libyan economy under the monarchy can be divided into two periods: pre-oil 1951-1960, and post-oil 1960-1969.

At the time of its independence, Libya was one of the poorest nations in the world, with a per capita income of less than $30 per year in 1951 and $100 per year in 1960. It was a prototype of a poor country "in the bottom of the range in income and resources," as Professor Higgins described it.[26]

Over 70 percent of the labor force was engaged in agricultural and animal husbandry activities, which accounted for about 30 percent of the gross domestic product (GDP). Ironically, by the early 1970s, agriculture accounted for only about 3 percent of the GDP and absorbed only about 30 percent of the labor force.[27] Of its vast area, only 5 percent was considered economically useful, and around 1 percent was regarded as adequate for permanent cultivation. Because of the scarcity of ground water, the unreliability of rainfall, and the poor irrigation of production methods, ahd 1 percent was not economically utilized. The economic value of human resources, the known mineral resources, the available capital for development, and the climatic conditions were too poor to generate growth or provide any prospects for industrialization beyond certain traditional handicrafts.

These conditions gave little hope, if any, for Libyan economic and social development. To some experts, Libya was almost a hopeless case.[28] International donors participated in programs for technical and financial aid, and until the discovery of oil in 1959, Libya was greatly indebted for its economic and political viability to the United Nations and certain Western and Middle Eastern nations.[29]

The bleak picture of the first period changed rapidly and drastically with the oil discoveries in 1959. The outstanding characteristics of the Libyan economy in this period were the transformation from a stagnant to a rapidly growing economy and the predominance of the oil sector. Within eight years of the first oil shipment, Libya became the world's fourth largest exporter of crude oil, a rate of growth unknown anywhere in the industry's history.[30] Eventually, this dramatic change was reflected in the government budget and national economy. Surprisingly, within a few years, Libya moved from the status of a capital-deficit nation to a capital-surplus nation, from an aid recipient to an aid extender.[31] The increase in oil revenue and its ratio to total revenue, accompanied by an unfortunate decrease in other sectors of the economy, especially agriculture, are portrayed in table 2-1.

Libya's society, administration, and economy were unprepared to utilize and absorb the new wealth. One effect of oil production on the economy was the rapid wave of one-way migration from the rural areas to urban centers, a migration that resulted in crowded urban centers and deserted farmland in many parts of the country.[32] As a result of increased urban population and increased per capita income, there was a sudden increase in the demand for food and agricultural products. This situation, given a healthy economy, could have been a strong stimulus to agricultural production. However, the low state of technological development in agriculture and the increasing cost of labor have resulted in reliance on agricultural imports, which increased over threefold during the sixties.[33]

"Libyan agriculture," according to one source, "was left to stagnate in its low level of development, and the consumer turned to the world markets

**Table 2-1**
**Libyan Total Revenue and Oil Revenue**

| Year | Total revenue (US Millions of dollars) | Oil Revenue as Percentage of Total Revenue |
|------|------|------|
| 1962 | 86.698 | 7.8 |
| 1963 | 121.050 | 20.0 |
| 1964 | 212.918 | 37.6 |
| 1965 | 289.027 | 63.6 |
| 1966 | 423.360 | 66.6 |
| 1967 | 1,080.912 | 83.4 |
| 1968 | 838.320 | 76.5 |
| 1969 | 1,205.904 | 77.4 |
| 1970 | 1,491.840 | 82.0 |
| 1971 | 1,853.177 | 84.9 |
| 1972 | 2,840.076 | 88.4 |
| 1973 | 2,459.772 | 85.3 |
| 1974 | 8,619.240 | 95.3 |
| 1975 | 6,999.290 | 95.1 |

Source: Volume 14 of Annual Report: Bank of Libya, Tripoli, 1970; Volume 17 of Annual Report: Bank of Libya, Tripoli, 1975; Volume 20 of Annual Report: Bank of Libya, Tripoli, 1975, pp. 114-116.

for the purchase of his daily food. . . . At the beginning of oil exploration the total value of imported food and food produce was about $1,700,000. By 1969 it was $95,000,000." At the same time, agricultural exports had declined from a value of $4,180,000 in 1956 to "$2,040,000 in 1961, and to only about $108,800 in 1968. . . . The last figure was not enough to pay for Libya's import of food for one-third of a single day."[34]

The term rentier state has been applied to nations with economic situations similar to that of Libya. Rentier states are those which receive revenue from their raw material production under circumstances that do little to stimulate their overall economic development. Other production is very insignificant. H. Mahdavy, in applying the rentier state model to Iran,[35] showed that the danger facing rentier states is that, although some of their natural resources are being fully developed by foreign concerns and subsidized government expenditures, most of the population may remain in a backward condition, and the most important factors for long-term growth may receive little or no attention at all.

This dangerous situation fits Libya precisely. The International Bank for Reconstruction and Development (IBRD) mission to Libya reported in 1960 that the discovery of oil did not provide an easy or complete solution to the problems of economic development.[36] Robert Mabro applied the rentier state model to Libya and showed that Libya had become a wealthy rentier state in which the economy remained dependent and underdeveloped. Government expenditures and development programs became totally dependent upon oil revenues. Consumption patterns became geared to the use of imported commodities. There were no links between the proceeds of production, effort, and incentive. The rentier state can achieve dramatic rises in per capita income without going through the social and organizational changes usually associated with the processes of economic growth.[37]

The monarchy dealt with the abundant petro-money by allocating 70 percent of it for development. Accordingly, the first five-year plan was drawn in 1963 and concentrated on building the foundation of economic development by stressing infrastructural projects. The plan allocated $746,000,000 and was increased to a total of $1,234,000,000. In 1968, the plan was extended for the fiscal year 1968-69 to permit adequate preparation of the second plan and, at the same time, to give the administration another year to complete the unfinished projects. The first plan and its extension demonstrated, among many other things, the shortsightedness and poor planning and management capabilities of the government agencies.

Libya, according to Higgins, had become a prototype once again: no longer of a poor country, but one of unbalanced growth. R. Mabro argued that there were essentially two ways in which Libya could use its oil to overcome the awesome disadvantages it had carried through history. One was to get more out of its oil by maintaining reasonable rates of oil extraction. This would prolong the life of oil resources in order to buy more time for development. The other way was to concentrate on developing Libya's human capital as the sole key to real development.

**The Social Environment**

Libyan society under the monarchy conformed closely to the model of traditional society outlined in chapter 1. The basic units of Libyan society are the extended family, clan, tribe, and village, with some modification of this arrangement in urban centers.

The typical Libyan family consists of father, mother, single and married sons, unmarried daughters, grandparents, grandchildren, uncles, aunts, and cousins. The father or oldest male is usually the top authority in the family. (Adult status is usually bestowed on fathers.) Sons carry on the name of the family and return to the father's house. Daughters keep their original family name but belong to their husband's family as long as they are married.

The individual in a traditional society such as Libya's subordinates his personal interests to those of his family and considers himself to be a member of a group whose importance outweighs his own.[38] Since the individual is identified with his family, his good or bad deeds bring collective fame or shame to the family and to the tribe. It is the family unit that integrates virtually every aspect of the individual's life: social, economic, and political. It is the family "which socializes the individual into his culture and which bears primary responsibility for his adherence to social norms."[39]

Family membership is also a requirement, in most cases, for membership in larger units such as clans and tribes. The family, as well as the clan and the tribe, functions as the educational, economic, and security-providing organization for its members. The high degree of collectiveness and solidarity cannot be matched in any modern organization. In return, the individual has to obey, respect, and preserve the rules and traditions of those social units.

Related families make up the clans and tribes. Usually, leadership of the tribe belongs to the head or members of the most powerful family within the most powerful clan, although occasionally the formal leader (sheikh or chief) of the tribe may be a member of a less powerful family who is backed by prominent families.

The power, prestige, and influence enjoyed by families in the social structure come from multiple sources: (1) birth, that is, descent from leaders or reputable families, even after the disappearance of the original leaders, (2) individual or collective wealth, (3) size of family, clan, or tribe, which brings security and support, (4) religiousness, courage, and generosity of the individual or the related group, (5) political or administrative position, and (6) power and prestige associated with the professional stature of lawyers, doctors, judges, and others, whose professions require a high level of education.[40]

The idea of family influence had been utilized by the national leadership as a source of control and mobilization, and functions as a link between national authority and citizens. The so-called *ayan* ("notables"), *wujaha* ("influentials"), or *abna-el-ayelate* ("the sons of predominant families"), took the roles of leadership in Libyan society from the period of Ottoman control up to the 1969 revolution.

## The Hierarchy of Traditional Authority

Decision making in a traditional society like Libya's is highly authoritative. Heads or chiefs of social units, in consultation with some of the elders in those units, make the decisions. Kinship and unit solidarity provide the support of the rest of the unit members necessary to carry out those decisions. Failure to carry them out would threaten the solidarity and communal brotherhood, an eventuality that would challenge the very existence of the traditional individual.

The same roles of hierarchy, kinship, and collective solidarity are at play in the selection of leaders in traditional Libyan society. Within the basic social unit, the family, all authority and leadership belong to the father, grandfather, or eldest son. These authorities demand absolute loyalty from family members. To act contrary to familiar leadership is to commit treason and is treated as such. The decisions of the leaders must be respected and carried out by all the members.

In the second unit, the clan, leadership is based on the prestige, reputation, and economic and social status of the family. A family that scores high on these ascriptive factors has greater power and influence, as well as a more favorable chance to assume the leadership of the clan. Selection of leadership in the third unit, the tribe, is subject to the same conditions, except that at this level the family that assumes the position of leadership builds reputation and power for the whole clan to which it belongs. Likewise, special status will rest on a tribe when one of its families assumes the leadership of the village, town, or region. Thus, collective identity of the family extends to the tribal level.

A family that has assumed a position of leadership on any level will find it hard to change its role or degrade its status. The inheritance of family status will continue from one generation to the next, preserving the reputation for a very long period of time. The fact that "several families controlled the country and determined the destiny of its people throughout the period of 1952 to 1969, then, was a logical result of the structure of Libyan society."[41]

Wherever there is competition for leadership or political position among tribes, the support for the candidates will split along tribal lines. The saying *weld kapeletna* ("the son of our tribe") will be the slogan of the supporters. *Weld bladna* ("the son of our village") will be the slogan when the range of competition is wider. *Weld ayla,* or *bate* ("the son of family") implies more or less certain qualifications, such as respectability, trustworthiness, righteousness, courage, religiousness, wealth, and membership in a highly reputable family and tribe. Education, ability, and effectiveness are virtually invisible to the electorate.

## Religion

Standing next in importance to the traditional units of family, clan, and tribe, religion is another variable that significantly affects the structure, values, and attitudes of Libyan society. It is a primary unit of loyalty and identity.

A religious title has its own connotation within the society. The *mufti* ("juris consult," or the top of the religious hierarchy) "held the highest honorary religious position in the country."[42] *Kodat* ("judges"), connected in the public mind with religion, enjoy exceptional privileges in the community. *Fakih* and *shaikh* ("religious teacher") were titles given to individuals exceptionally knowledgeable and wise in religious and general affairs. *Ulama* ("most knowledgeable," or "scientist") is a title given to the most erudite individuals, mainly in religious sciences and Islamic teachings.

The religious institutions and their leaders have played important roles in the social, educational, and political life of the country and its people. This role has a deep-rooted background, starting from the Ottoman occupation and continuing up to very recent times. The most notable and prolonged effects of religion have been on the leadership and institutions that regulate society. The judicial system, and many special and important political committees and advisory councils, for example, were dominated by notable religious leaders.

Throughout Libya's history and particularly under the monarchy, religion became a political symbol of crucial importance in controlling and mobilizing the masses. Religion, for example, was central to Arab League efforts to motivate the Libyan public to demand independence from the United Nations commission. A *fatwa* ("declaration") was published, insisting that "voting for other than independence would be against religion."[43] As another example, the leaders of the National Congress party in making their bid for national leadership on the eve of Libyan independence in 1951 appealed to the masses, saying that their party was the true Islamic party. They stood for the unity of Islam and against federalism (the program of opposition), which was for the division of Islam and yielding to the infidels.[44]

There was an inevitable association between family prominence and religious leadership. The fact served to intensify the concentration of religious leadership within small groups of families throughout the country. The strong role of religion in a traditional Islamic society like that of Libya has produced a society with special features. Conservative attitudes have been predominant in every respect. Values and behavior have been a function of religious background and attachment; hence, evaluation and acceptance of innovation and change have been subject to religious beliefs and notions. Libyans have looked to the Koran as a source of and guide for right action. The supreme laws have been the laws of God, which determine people's relations with each other and with God.

## Demography: Education and Urbanization

Throughout the Ottoman period, the only centers of learning were religious institutions, located in only a small number of cities in Libya. Education was available to only a few individuals whose families recognized the value of education or had economic conditions that allowed the children to be spared from working. The quality of education available, and the length of time one could spend as a student, were limited. The student could be trained as a teacher of the Arabic language or religious science, or as a *kadisharia* (judge of Islamic jurisprudence).

During the Italian occupation, religious education continued to be the major type available. More Koranic schools were opened through private efforts, but instability of the region and severe economic conditions prevented this already inadequate system of education from flourishing. Secular schools were also opened in a few urban centers during this time. The policy of the colonial administration was to restrict the number of Libyans educated beyond the primary stage, and all teaching was conducted in Italian.[45] The handful of Libyans who wanted to seek further education had to travel to Egypt, where they could continue mainly in Arabic literature and religious science, or to Italy and a few other regions for study in more secular fields.

The British administration put more emphasis on secular education and established vocational schols separate from religious educational institutions. The new schools, still inadequate, with meager resources and teaching staffs, served only residents of urban centers.

In general, the society was untouched by education, and even years after independence, "more than ninety percent of the population were illiterate and only a handful of Libyans had been given an opportunity to study at a university or to qualify for a recognized profession."[46] During the first decade of independence, severe economic problems, regional conflict of interests, and poor management of the available resources severely handicapped the development of a sound education system. On the eve of independence, of a total enrollment of 32,741; only 537 students were attending secondary and technical schools. There were no girls enrolled in secondary schools, and there were no female primary school teachers. The number of secondary school teachers totaled twenty-five, and only fourteen Libyans held university degrees from European and Egyptian universities.[47] Finally, not until 1959 were the first university degrees awarded to a graduating class of thirty-one by the only Libyan university.[48]

The discovery of oil at the beginning of the 1960s brought a radical change in the Libyan economy and eliminated the economic obstacles to education. Since then, educational facilities have greatly expanded, schools have been built in rural and remote areas, more colleges have been established in the University of Libya, and more vocational schools and training centers have been instituted.

During the monarchy, education was influenced by religious elements more than in any of the previous periods. The fact that King Idris owed his political power to his religious background and leadership was an important factor in his reactivation of existing religious institutions and the development of new ones. Even with relatively large expansion, however, the educational system did not meet the country's need for trained technical, managerial, and skilled personnel.[49]

The Libyan population remained predominantly rural during the monarchy, but the nation was changing rapidly. The urban population represented 22 percent of the total in 1954, 27 percent in 1964, and an estimated 35 percent in 1972. According to population projections by private consultants, the urban population will have increased by more than 52 percent between 1969 and 1979.[50]

The recent urbanization in Libya has consisted of rural emigration to the two main urban centers, Benghazi and Tripoli, whose annual population growths have been reported as 7.0 and 6.5 percent, respectively.[51] This migration resulted from the anticipation of higher wages and immediate cash, and the lack of modern life facilities (education, communication, health, and services) in the rural areas.

This one-way movement led to a deterioration of the already deficient agricultural sector and aggravated the conditions of housing, transportation, and other services which were already deficient in meeting the needs of the original city dwellers.

**Mass Behavior**

In demographic and economic terms, Libya had clearly moved away from the classic model of a traditional society presented in chapter 1. The majority of the population had become at least semi-urbanized. Education, at least among Libya's youth, had become pervasive. Media exposure, at least in terms of radio, had become almost universal.

From a theoretical as well as a practical perspective, an interesting question arises concerning the impact of urbanization and media exposure on the presumed traditional attitudes of the Libyan masses. As mentioned earlier, urbanization had been both recent and rapid. Also, the discussion of Libya as a rentier state indicated that Libyans had not been deeply involved in the economic development of their country. Although they were the benefactors of a wealthy economy, they had not been its creators. Just how traditional was the Libyan population, and just what had been the impacts of urbanization, media exposure, and education on the transformation of traditional behavior patterns? Were Libya's revolutionary leaders dealing with a predominantly traditional, transitional, or modern population, or a combination of all three types?

If the preponderance of the Libyan population continued to manifest the values associated with the traditional structure of Libyan society outlined in chapter 1, their behavior would clearly manifest intense levels of tribalism, religiosity, particularism, fatalism, interpersonal distrust, atomism, and other traditional patterns. Empirical data relating to the traditionalism of Libya's citizens during the early years of the revolutionary era were provided by our 1973 survey of Zawia province. One of the hypotheses of the survey was that most Libyans would, indeed, manifest such traditional behavior traits.

As a first step in testing this hypothesis, questionnaire items relating to religiosity, particularism, fatalism, interpersonal distrust, and atomism were factor analyzed to ascertain whether they actually represented discrete behavior patterns or whether they were all merely facets of singularly underlying behavior dimensions labeled traditionalism.[52] The factor analysis indicated that the five categories represented independent behavior dimensions. The items with the strongest loading in each cluster were then combined to form, respectively, a religiosity, particularism, interpersonal distrust, and fatalism scale. A single questionnaire item loaded on the atomism factor, thereby precluding the development of an atomism scale.

*Religiosity*

The religiosity scale consisted of two items, the percentage distributions for which appear in table 2-2. The intensely religious category of the religiosity scale consisted of individuals who prayed at the mosque every day and who described themselves as being at least very religious, or individuals who described themselves as being extremely religious and prayed at the mosque at least twice a week. The religious category included individuals who, at minimum, described themselves as being extremely religious and prayed at the mosque at least once a week or who described themselves as being somewhat religious and prayed every day. The least religious category consisted of individuals who indicated they were not religious and prayed at the mosque once a year or less.

If religiosity were defined simply as being somewhat religious and praying at the mosque at least once a week, virtually all of the Zawia sample would have fallen into the religious category. The influence of religion in Libya, then, is clearly pervasive. If religion is antithetical to modernization, as some theorists suggest, the transformation of Libyan society facing Libya's revolutionary leaders would be a difficult task indeed.

It is interesting to note, however, that Colonel Qadafi is himself a devoutly religious individual who has placed the glorification of Islam on par with the economic modernization of Libya. While attempting to crush the tribal system and radically transform mass behavior patterns, he has elevated Koranic strictures to the status of national law. Also, as we will see

**Table 2-2**
**Religiosity among Libyans**
(*percentages*)

| Are you a religious man? | |
|---|---|
| Extremely religious | 10.6 |
| Very religious | 42.7 |
| Somewhat religious | 45.2 |
| Not religious | .9 |
| Do not know | .5 |
| | (n = 564) |
| **How often do you pray in the mosque?** | |
| Every day | 26.4 |
| Twice a week | 17.7 |
| Once a week | 46.9 |
| Once a month | 3.3 |
| Once a year | 1.9 |
| Never | 3.8 |
| | (n = 572) |
| **Religiosity scale** | |
| Intensely religious | 41.4 |
| Religious | 23.3 |
| Moderately religious | 30.0 |
| Minimally religious | 5.3 |
| | (n = 563) |

shortly, the revolution has chosen to work within the fold of Islam, stressing the many facets of the Islamic religion that are compatible with modernization and socialism.


*Particularism*


The particularism scale consisted of the two items indicated by the factor analysis that best reflect internal group solidarity and hostility toward individuals beyond the immediate confines of the respondent's family or religious groups. The results of a third item relating to particularism, suggested by the factor analysis as reflecting other dimensions of traditional behavior in addition to particularism, have also been included in table 2-3. It has not, however, been included in the particularism scale.

In general, the intense category on the particularism scale consisted of those individuals who interacted with individuals outside the family less than once a week, and who, in a more general sense, were wary of individuals who rejected prevailing religious norms. The least particularistic individuals were those who interacted several times a week with people out-

**Table 2-3**
**Particularism among Libyans**
(*percentages*)

| | |
|---|---|
| About how frequently do you get together in the evening with people outside your family? | |
| About once a month | 24.4 |
| About once a week or a few times a month | 35.4 |
| Several times a week | 24.4 |
| Almost every evening | 15.7 |
| | (n = 573) |
| How true is the statement religious people are the most truthful, respected, and friendly people in the community? | |
| True for all religious people | 22.2 |
| True for most | 48.2 |
| True for some | 28.8 |
| True for none | .9 |
| | (n = 573) |
| People outside the family cannot be trusted at all. (not included in particularism scale) | |
| Strongly agree | 8.9 |
| Agree | 27.1 |
| Disagree | 45.7 |
| Strongly disagree | 18.3 |
| | (n = 573) |
| Particularism scale | |
| Intensely particularistic | 27.1 |
| Particularistic | 28.5 |
| Minimally particularistic | 21.9 |
| Nonparticularistic | 22.6 |
| | (n = 572) |

side the family, and who were willing to tolerate deviance from prevailing norms. Since 56 percent of the respondents fall into the intensely particularistic or particularistic categories, one can only conclude that Libya clearly remains a family-centered particularistic society. The data thus reflect that the Revolutionary Command Council's mobilization goal of transforming Libya into an intensely nationalistic political community in which loyalty to the state supercedes parochial attachments would clearly encounter mass resistance.

## Atomism

As noted previously, only one of the questionnaire items loaded on the factor we have chosen to label atomism, thereby precluding the development of an atomism scale. Our one indicator of atomism was a request for respondents to agree or disagree with the highly atomistic proverb, the text and percentage distributions for which appear in table 2-4. On the basis of their responses to this single item, Libyans do not appear to be excessively atomistic.

We would suggest, however, that our single measure of atomism was particularly stringent, and that the fact that 18 percent of the respondents were willing to agree with a proverb suggesting that only their horses require grass is, in itself, an interesting finding. In this regard, two additional points are worthy of note. First, the coefficients provided in table 2-8 indicate that atomism as measured by our single item was far stronger in the rural areas than in the more urban areas. Second, Libyan administrators interviewed in our survey indicated repeatedly that the lack of civic consciousness and civic responsibility among the Libyan public was profound. Their comments in this regard are discussed in chapter 5. At the very least, the subject of atomistic attitudes, including a lack of civic concern, is clearly worth further study.

*Fatalism, Interpersonal Distrust, and Tribalism*

The fatalism scale was similarly based upon the respondents' acceptance or rejection of standard proverbs. As shown in table 2-5, respondents were asked to choose between contrasting sets of fatalistic and nonfatalistic proverbs. The fatalism scale ranged from two (complete agreement with both fatalistic proverbs) through four (complete agreement with both nonfatalistic proverbs). Our respondents manifested clear fatalistic tendencies, with approximately 58 percent of the sample indicating complete agreement with both fatalistic proverbs. The members of our sample, thus, manifested little

**Table 2-4**
**Atomistic Attitudes among Libyans**
(*percentages*)

What do you think of the familiar saying,
"Oh God there is nobody but myself and
that after my horse, there is no need for grass"?

| | |
|---|---|
| Strongly agree | 5.1 |
| Agree | 12.5 |
| Disagree | 38.7 |
| Strongly disagree | 43.7 |
| | (n = 573) |

**Table 2-5**
**Fatalism among Libyans**
(*percentages*)

| | |
|---|---|
| Place a check mark beside one of the following two proverbs with which you agree. | |
| Nothing happens without the will of God. | 67.6 |
| (God says) If man tries, I will help him. | 32.4 |
| | (n = 574) |
| Place a check mark beside one of the following proverbs with which you agree. | |
| Livelihoods are divided by God. | 80.5 |
| The poor man is responsible for his own poverty. | 19.2 |
| | (n = 574) |
| Fatalism scale | |
| Intense fatalism | 58.2 |
| Moderate fatalism | 32.2 |
| Low fatalism | 9.6 |
| | (n = 572) |

in the way of the initiative or innovative thrust that would be crucial to the success of all phases of the RCC's mobilization efforts.

The interpersonal distrust scale was based upon responses to three items, as shown in table 2-6. As hypothesized in the earlier discussion, manifestations of interpersonal distrust were clearly evident among members of our sample. This fact, too, would pose difficulties for the RCC's mobilization efforts which require a high level of interpersonal cooperation and tolerance.

The questionnaire also contained several items relating to tribalism, the text and percentage distributions for which appear in table 2-7. All tribal items reflect intense tribalism among Libyans. The fact that the tribal system had been abolished by the government prior to the survey, however, resulted in a nonresponse rate of almost 40 percent for the tribalism items, making the data difficult to interpret. Because of the high nonresponse rate, the tribal items were not scaled. The responses that were received, however, leave us little doubt that tribalism remains very much a part of Libyan life.

*Modernization and Value Change*

Quite clearly, many of the traditional behavior patterns discussed in chapter 1 as being antithetical to political and economic modernization were very much in evidence at the time of our survey in 1973. Particularly important

**Table 2-6**
**Interpersonal Distrust among Libyans**
(*percentages*)

| | |
|---|---|
| Check one of the following which suits your judgement: | |
| Most people can be trusted | 63.2 |
| You cannot be too careful in your dealings with others | 36.8 |
| | (n = 525) |
| | |
| Would you say that most people are more inclined to | |
| help others, or more inclined to look out for themselves? | |
| Help others | 30.1 |
| Look out for themselves | 69.7 |
| | (n = 568) |
| | |
| What do you think of the saying, "If you were not | |
| a wolf, other wolves would eat you"? | |
| Agree | 77.3 |
| Disagree | 22.6 |
| | (n = 576) |
| | |
| Interpersonal distrust scale | |
| High trust | 6.4 |
| Moderate trust | 28.0 |
| Moderate distrust | 48.2 |
| Intense distrust | 17.4 |
| | (n = 517) |

to our objective of delineating the environmental problems confronting the RCC's modernization efforts is the question of what impact education, media exposure, and the recent migration of rural Libyans to the urban areas had on the traditional behavior patterns surveyed. Were the new urban dwellers markedly less traditional than their rural counterparts, or were Libya's new urbanites still traditional country folks at heart?

Table 2-8 displays correlations between each of the five dimensions of traditional behavior surveyed and a demographic modernization scale based upon the urbanization, education, and television variables. Positive correlations indicated a decrease in traditional behavior with increases in education, urbanization, and media exposure.

The coefficients in this table suggest that education, media exposure, and urbanization were each associated with dramatic decreases in particularistic, fatalistic, and atomistic behavior. Given time and increased education and media exposure, the impact of such traditional values as a deterrent to modernization might well dissipate. Interpersonal distrust, on the other hand, remained impervious to all of the demographic indicators. To the extent that past experience is a valid indicator, interpersonal coopera-

**Table 2-7**
**Tribalism among Libyans**
(*percentages*)

| | |
|---|---:|
| If you belong to a tribe, to what extent do you feel loyal and attached to it? | |
| Very attached | 33.2 |
| Attached | 38.2 |
| Somewhat attached | 9.4 |
| Not attached | 19.1 |
| | (n = 319) |
| Do you feel proud to belong to your tribe? | |
| Very proud | 38.1 |
| Proud | 28.8 |
| Somewhat proud | 9.4 |
| Not proud | 23.8 |
| | (n = 320) |
| If you had the change, would you like to drop all tribal identification? | |
| Yes | 41.0 |
| No | 59.0 |
| | (n = 340) |
| If you had the chance, would you like to change to another tribe? | |
| Yes | 19.4 |
| No | 80.6 |
| | (n = 310) |

tion and toleration among Libyans are likely to remain low, regardless of demographic trends.

It is also interesting to note that of the demographic variables employed in the survey, urbanization had the least direct impact on the erosion of traditional behavior patterns. It would appear that the mere fact of urbanization, exclusive of education and media exposure, had little impact on the deterioration of traditional Libyan values. Though becoming urban, Libya's population was not necessarily becoming urbanized. Moreover, excessive urbanization may have had a cluttering effect, placing more strain on Libya's limited bureaucratic resources than they could effectively handle. This would particularly appear to be the case in as much as Libya's increased urban migration resulted less from the rationalization of employment patterns than from the desire of an affluent population to enjoy the amenities of an urban existence.

**Table 2-8**

**Demographic Modernization and Traditional Behavior**

$(n = 576)$

| | Religio-sity | Particu-larism | Fatalism | Inter-Personal Distrust | Atomism |
|---|---|---|---|---|---|
| Demographic scale[a] (education, urbanization, and television exposure) | G = [b] 0.175 | 0.460 | 0.400 | 0.257 | 0.643 |
| Urbanization | 0.097 | 0.293 | 0.247 | 0.398 | 0.646 |
| Education | 0.211 | 0.501 | 0.473 | 0.156 | 0.629 |
| Television | 0.265 | 0.468 | 0.338 | 0.244 | 0.578 |
| Newspaper | 0.284 | 0.556 | 0.488 | 0.157 | 0.684 |
| Age | 0.429 | 0.384 | 0.249 | 0.081 | 0.329 |

Source: Omar I. El Fathaly, Monte Palmer, and Richard Chackerian, *Political Development and Bureaucracy in Libya* (Lexington, Mass.: Lexington Books, D.C. Heath) 1977.

[a]Questionnaire items relating to television exposure, urbanization, and education were combined into a demographic scale. All three items received equal weight. Possible scale scores ranged from 3 through 9, with 3 indicating rural states with no education and no television exposure and 9 representing the highest scores of urbanization, education, and television exposure. Individuals receiving scores of 3 and 4 were considered traditional, individuals receiving scores ranging from 5 to 7 were considered transitional, and individuals receiving scores of 8 or 9 were considered modern.

[b]Gamma Coefficients. All coefficients over ±.200 are significant at the .05 level or beyond. Coefficients were based upon a pairwise deletion of cases.

# 3 Revolution and Revolutionary Elites

Few variables are more important to the modernization of a state or society than the structure and behavior of its dominant elites. It is the elites that set the tone of the development process and it is the elites that allocate the resources necessary for development. Accordingly, the objective of this chapter is to examine Libya's revolutionary elite in terms of its structure, conceptualization of modernization, cohesion, and level of value consensus vis-à-vis modernization. We will also examine the position and stability of elite modernizing values in relation to the overall hierarchy of elite values. As a first step toward analyzing Libya's revolutionary elite, however, it is necessary to describe the circumstances of the revolution.

## Background of the Revolution

During the eighteen years of the monarchy, the king's policies stressed maintenance of his personal control and the perpetuation of Libya's traditional religious and tribal values.[1] Systematic attempts to mobilize Libya's human and material resources toward the goals of rapid socioeconomic modernization were not pursued, nor were serious efforts made to broaden the base of the Libyan political system or to make it more adaptable to the social tensions unleashed as a result of the massive infusion of oil revenues replacing what had been a poverty-stricken dependency on world charity.

The static posture of the king thus produced a situation in which the social and economic modernization of Libya proceeded in spite of the political system rather than under its direction. Growth and change were as erratic as they were sudden. Traditional supporters of the king prospered, often embarking on a variety of pretentious and ill-conceived and uncoordinated projects. Potential adversaries received sufficient material benefits from the regime to whet their appetites, yet never a share consistent with their expectations. As Libya's wealth grew, frustrations increased proportionally. More importantly, the monarchy seemed impervious to change. The king's advisors (Diwan) in 1969 were essentially the same as his advisors at the inception of his reign in 1951. The new groups spawned by the oil boom—students, bureaucracy, army, business community—were largely excluded from effective participation in the political system. The king's personal legitimacy (*baraka*) waned, and gave way to cynicism among all but his staunchest supporters. His support had never been particularly strong in Tripolitania. Libya's democratic institutions had been largely discredited through years of fraud and enjoyed little legitimacy of their own. The bureaucracy, corrupted by the inundation of oil wealth and characterized by inefficiency and haughtiness, had become the object of popular scorn. Surveying the wreckage, the king chastised his supporters for their corruption, yet so feared a revolution that he became their captive.[2] The king, a deeply religious ascetic who served as the center of the entire system, became increasingly isolated. The monarchy had begun to collapse of its own weight.

The revolution of 1969, then, came as little surprise to anyone. The surprise lay not in the revolution, but in its executors. According to rumors, Muhammud Heikal, editor of the Egyptian semi-official *Al Ahram* and Nasser's personal envoy who had been dispatched to Libya to assess the revolution, demanded, "Where is Abdul Aziz?" Heikal referred to Abdul Aziz Shelhi, the second most important officer in the Libyan army after the chief of staff.[3] The Shelhi group had planned a coup d'etat a few days hence, a coup that was to deny the probable accession of the crown prince to power and a coup that was presumably cleared in advance by the Egyptian president. Abdul Aziz Shelhi, as it happened, was under arrest as were virtually all other members of the ancient regime. After considerable delay and much confusion, Heikal was introduced to Captain Muammar Qadafi, a junior officer as totally unknown to knowledgeable Libyans as Nasser had been to knowledgeable Egyptians some fifteen years earlier.

**The Story of the Revolution**

The story of the revolution, recounted in great detail by Libyan radio and television each September 1, is worth describing at this point because it illustrates both the core values of the new Libyan leaders and the rudimentary and unstructured nature of Libyan political institutions under the monarchy. It also stands as a testimony to the profound influence of Gamal Abdul Nasser on the youth of the Arab world and to the effectiveness of his *Voice of the Arabs* as an instrument of revolution and change.

The origins of the Libyan revolution, according to official accounts, can be traced to 1959 when Muammar Qadafi first established a political study cell among students at the secondary school in Sebha, the capital of Fezzan.[4] Approximately fifteen years old and in the early years of secondary school, Qadafi led his group in discussions of Nasser's speeches broadcast by the *Voice of the Arabs* and plotted means of implementing Nasser's Arab revolution in Libya. Nasser's revolution had begun as a military coup and, given the exigencies of the Libyan situation and their humble background, there was little prospect that Qadafi and his group could alter Libyan politics by any means other than a military coup. Accordingly, Qadafi urged members of his cell to enter military college rather than pursue alternate careers. Jalloud, perhaps Qadafi's closest confidant, for example, reportedly had planned to enter medical school, but did alter his plans and entered military college at Qadafi's urging.

As we will see shortly, the hard core of the RCC and the preponderance of its remaining members came from Qadafi's "first" cells in Sebha, and subsequent first cells in Musrata and in the military academy at Benghazi. His apparent psychological domination of members of both the military and civilian branches of his movement began at that time.

Each member of Qadafi's first cell, in time, created his own study cell, referred to as a "second" cell, in which the member would repeat the discussions of the first cell. In the best conspiratorial fashion, members of the second cells were presumably unaware of the composition of either the first cell or the other second cells. Membership in the secondary cells, however, required the prior approval of Qadafi. Most members of the second cells were to form the core of what we refer to as the free officers and the civilian auxiliaries, which will be discussed later in this chapter.

Qadafi's activities at Sebha eventually brought him into conflict with the local authorities, and he was forced to continue his studies at the secondary schools in Musrata, one of the larger urban centers in Tripolitania. In particular, Qadafi was expelled for protesting the king's lack of support for the Arab forces during the continuing Arab-Israeli crisis. The cell pattern was repeated at Musrata, thereby broadening the regional base of Qadafi's group. RCC member Omar Mahasi was associated with the Musrata cell. He, too, was urged to enter the military college rather than pursue a civilian career. Other important civilian auxiliaries were also recruited during Qadafi's schooling in Musrata, the most notable being his close friend, Mohammed Khalil, who was subsequently appointed as the first mayor of Musrata.

Qadafi's group graduated from the secondary school in Musrata in 1963, and entered the military college the same year. Both the military college and the University of Libya were located in Benghazi, a circumstance of some importance to Qadafi's movement, because it brought him into closer contact with dissident elements in Cyrenaica as well as with Nasserite students at the university in Benghazi. The cell pattern was repeated at the military college with RCC members Magareif, Najim, El Kawaldi, El Hamedi, and others entering the movement at this point. The free officers movement, distinct from the nucleus of Qadafi's study cells, was initiated during this period, as was the civilian auxiliary. Qadafi and most of his group graduated from the military academy in 1963-64, assuming junior positions in the Libyan army and, in most instances, receiving advanced training abroad. Qadafi attended the British military academy at Sandhurst for approximately six months.

In spite of their efforts to maintain secrecy, Qadafi's group did not go unnoticed by the king's intelligence. On the eve of the revolution, approximately twelve days before Qadafi's planned date for the revolution and two days prior to the anticipated Shelhi coup, Qadafi and his group received twelve hours notice to report to England for advanced training. Having little alternative, they executed the coup that evening, September 1, albeit in a haphazard fashion that benefited considerably from the fact that potential opponents to Qadafi's coup assumed that Shelhi had decided to move early. The coup first struck the arsenal of the Cyrenaica Defense Force in Beida, the main base of the king's support, and then followed the standard pattern of military coups by occupying the palace of the crown prince, the ministry of defense, and the broadcasting stations at Tripoli and Benghazi. Only at one of the broadcasting stations was minor resistance encountered, with a brief scrimmage resulting in two of the three casualties produced by the revolution. The royal family, members of the Royal Diwan, cabinet ministers, senior military and police officers, and most members of parliament were arrested.[5] The king was out of the country at the time of the coup and accepted exile in Egypt. When the arresting officers awoke Abdul Aziz Shelhi, deputy commander of the Libyan army, to place him under arrest, his initial response at their presence was rumored to be "no you fools, the coup is not tonight."

The success of the coup was abetted by two groups: the free officers and the civilian auxiliaries. The free officers were mainly recruited during the period of Qadafi's military schooling in Benghazi and during his years as a junior officer prior to the revolution. The group lacked any formal structure aside from the fact that it was supportive of change, was receptive to Qadafi's ideas, and expressed a prior willingness to support a coup should one be forthcoming. The free officers were not part of the planning stage. They were, in fact, the last ones to be contacted prior to the coup. They formed the backbone of the revolution during its period of implementation, and they are currently the dominant element within the Libyan army. Thus, although most of the free officers were not overt conspirators in the coup, their participation was essential to its success. Each person subsequently received a certificate from Qadafi establishing his credentials as a free officer. Each had established a personal bond of trust with Qadafi that assured him of having at least minor elite status under the new regime.

The precise role of the civilian auxiliaries in the coup is less easily defined. The civilian auxiliary began in an embryonic sense with the Sebha cells and expanded during the Musrata period. The civilian groups developed in scope and maturity in Benghazi, however, after Qadafi made contact with Nasserite groups at the university there. Civilian supporters from the Sebha and Musrata cells were similar to Qadafi in class background and political orientation, drawing their main political motivation from the *Voice of the Arabs* and Nasser's speeches. Civilian supporters drawn from the University of Libya in Benghazi were more sophisticated in both political and ideological terms, although they, too, possessed a strong Nasserite orientation. The civilian groups also lacked formal structure, but probably had greater informal connections than the free officers. As in the case of the free officers, the willingness of the civilian auxiliaries to be counted on during a time of need and uncertainty established a personal link between them and Qadafi and assured their position as at least secondary members of the new republican elite. For better or for worse, they were the closest thing to revolutionary cadres that Qadafi had. In terms of size, the free officers were a much larger group than the civilian auxiliaries.

The coup was met with spontaneous and, by most accounts, sincere demonstrations of support throughout most areas of Libya. Opposition was minimal and dissipated rapidly. The king's time had clearly passed, and the coup, if nothing else, relieved the tension of its anticipation.

Spontaneous support for the coup, it must be stressed, was general support for change and not necessarily support for the Qadafi group. Indeed, upon the advice of Nasser, Qadafi and his group did not reveal their identity for some thirteen days, as a tactic to keep potential opponents at bay until they had adequate time to collect their thoughts and consolidate their position. To further obfuscate the situation, urgent appeals were broadcast for General Saad Ed-din Abu Shuareb, a highly respected officer living in self-imposed exile, to return to the country immediately, thereby giving the impression that General Abu Shuareb had masterminded the operation.

To the uncertainties surrounding the coup and its improbable and almost fairy-tale nature must be added the Revolutionary Command Council's own concern for their youth and relatively humble backgrounds. In a society that venerated age and tribal lineage, members of the RCC were likely to be perceived in most quarters as ungrateful and ambitious "kids" who were still "green behind the ears"; individuals not be taken seriously or likely to survive the rigors of the "real world." This point is of particular importance, for unlike the king, Qadafi entered the political arena without personal *baraka* or charisma. He was not a religious saint, nor were the institutions he inherited particularly legitimate in the eyes of the population. Indeed, in the following chapters, considerable attention will be devoted to Qadafi's efforts to build an aura of charisma around his person as a means of generating symbolic support for the revolution and legitimizing the political institutions of the revolution.

### The Elite Structure of Libya

From a methodological perspective, elite structure may be defined in a variety of ways.[6] One might, for example, define dominant elites as those individuals occupying the major formal positions of political authority. Or, elites might be defined as those individuals who actually make decisions. Or, lacking clear information regarding just who does make decisions, one might define elites as those individuals possessing a reputation for making decisions.

Our delineation of Libya's revolutionary elite produced consistent results regardless of the approach employed. The top of the elite pyramid in 1969 consisted of the original membership of the Revolutionary Command Council, a listing of which appears in table 3-1. Much further down on the hierarchy scale were the free officers, civilian auxiliaries, and members of the cabinet.

Two aspects of the elite structure in revolutionary Libya are particularly salient. First, the dominant position of Qadafi in many ways is analogous to Nasser's position in Egypt. Discussions within the RCC have been open and vigorous, yet there is little question that Qadafi exercises the final choice. This process has been strengthened over time with the ascendance of Qadafi as a charismatic leader. Elite status in terms of decision making, then, is directly correlated to one's confidence-access link to Qadafi. Since confidence tends to come from long experience and personal contact, it is perhaps only natural to assume that, in most instance, those individuals who have served Qadafi the longest would now occupy the dominant positions of authority.

To test this hypothesis, stratification patterns within the RCC, established on the basis of our interviews of prominent officials, were compared with the date and place that the RCC members joined the Qadafi group. In this regard, table 3-1 reflects the stratification of the revolutionary elite after two years in power, the earliest date after the revolution that clear stratification patterns began to become visible. Table 3-2, in turn, examines the hierarchy of the Qadafi elite in 1978, or eight years after the revolution and approximately two years after the RCC had been formally abolished by the meeting of the General People's Congress, a subject to be discussed in later chapters. Although the hypothesis was not totally supported in the sense that all members of the Sebha cell were more important than members of the other cells, the fact remains that all dominant members of the revolutionary elite in 1971 were closely tied to Qadafi through membership in one of the first cells.

In general terms, then, our hypothesis was sustained. Those individuals judged by our interviewers to exercise the greatest decision-making authority over the broadest range of issues were those people with the greatest personal contact with Qadafi. He clearly is the fount of authority. Even membership in the fourth and fifth levels of elite status was marked by attachment to Qadafi through the free officer's movement or through early participation in the civilian auxiliaries. Membership in the lower levels of elite status, it should be noted, also tends to depend on linkage with mem-

**Table 3-1**
**Hierarchy of Libyan Revolutionary Elites: 1971**

| Level | Name | Most Important Position Held | Elite Credentials | Revolutionary or Technocrat |
|---|---|---|---|---|
| 1 | Qadafi | Chairman, Revolutionary Command Council | First cell, Sebha | R |
| 2 | Jalloud | Prime minister | First cell, Military academy | R |
| 3 | Magareif | Military commander of Benghazi minister of housing | First cell, Military academy | R |
| 3 | Hawadi | Chairman of the Arab Socialist Union | First cell, Military academy | R |
| 3 | Yunis | Chief of staff | First cell, Military academy | R |
| 3 | Humaydi | Minister of interior Commander of the militia | First cell, Military academy | R R |
| 3 | Kharoubi | Director of military intelligence | First cell, Military academy | R |
| 3 | Mahashi | Minister of planning Assistant to Hawadi | First cell, Musrata | R |
| 4 | Gerui | Revolutionary Command Council member | First cell, Military academy | R |
| 4 | Huni | Minister of foreign affairs | First cell, Military academy | R |
| 4 | Najim | Minister of municipality later, education and housing | First cell, Military academy | R |
| 4 | Hamza | Revolutionary Command Council member | First cell, Military academy | R |
| 5 | Free officers[a] (majority) | | | R/T |
| 6 | Cabinet members and others[a] (majority) | | | |

[a]Some members are at both levels 5 and 6.

**Table 3-2**
**Hierarchy of Libyan Revolutionary Elites: 1978**

| Level | Name | Position | Elite Credentials | Revolutionary or Technocrat |
|---|---|---|---|---|
| 1 | Qadafi | Chairman of the General People's Congress | | |
| 2 | Jalloud | Executive secretary of General People's Congress | First cell, Sebha | R |
| 3 | Yunis | Chief of staff | First cell, Military academy | R |
| 3 | Humaydi | Former minister of interior, currently head of militia | First cell, Military academy | R |
| 3 | Kharoubi | Director of military intelligence | First cell, Military academy | R |
| 4 | Some members of the free officers corp | Leadership position in the army | Affiliated with the revolution | R |
| 5 | Secretaries of the General People's Congress and some former members of the civilian auxiliaries | Leadership position in the political institutions | Affiliated with the revolution | R/T |
| 6 | Cabinet ministers | Leadership in the government bureaucracy | Trusted by the revolutionary leadership | T/R |

bers in the upper elite strata as opposed to independent technical competence.

A comparison of tables 3-1 and 3-2 also indicates rather vividly that the requirement of Qadafi's confidence for elite status intensified markedly over the eight years of the revolution. It should be stressed that the distance between elite levels indicated in these tables represents significant differences in the ability of members of the elite to act independently. Finally, it should be noted that a comparison of tables 3-1 and 3-2 reflects a clear elevation in the position of some free officers during the first eight years of the revolution.

The relevance of this stratification pattern to the process of economic and social development in Libya becomes clear upon examining the "revolutionary or technocrat" column of tables 3-1 and 3-2. Individuals valued primarily for their technological skills do not enter the elite structure until approximately level five in both 1971 and 1978. This situation, of course, poses the danger that those individuals with the greatest specific expertise in economic and social issues will find it difficult to interact on a regular basis with Libya's primary decision makers, resulting in either decision-making bottlenecks in the modernization process or, conversely, in the making of modernizing decisions with inadequate technical input.

The second salient feature of the revolutionary elite structure was its almost total isolation from prerevolutionary elites. Only two members of the original RCC, in fact, were in any way related to what might be termed the Libyan aristocracy (See table 3-3). Both had left the elite structure by 1978.

The isolation of the revolutionary elite is relevant to Libya's progress toward political modernization in several ways. First, the isolation meant that the revolutionary leadership would have to start from scratch in building an apparatus to consolidate its position and to mobilize the Libyan population behind its modernization goals. Given existing institutional structures, this was probably a blessing rather than a liability. However, it also meant that the leadership would probably encounter the full opposition of former elites, all of whom found themselves threatened by the revolution. The isolation of the revolutionary elite as well as the presumed opposition of the former elites also presented the revolutionary leadership with the dilemma of finding well-trained and competent cadres for its programs. Most of the educated and experienced members of Libyan society who were capable of assisting the revolution in the application of its programs were tainted by their connection with the old regime. Finally, the isolation and newness of the revolutionary elite, by definition, meant it was inexperienced. The early years of the revolution would clearly be a period of on-the-job training for all concerned.

**Table 3-3**
**Social Background of Libyan Revolutionary Elites: 1971**

| Name | Military | Level and Type of Education | Foreign Education | Region | Demographic Origin | Socioeconomic Family Status | Age | Religious Intensity (by reputation)[c] | Prerevolution Philosophical Orientation |
|---|---|---|---|---|---|---|---|---|---|
| Qadafi | Yes | B.A. in military service | Yes | Cirtica | Bedouin | Poor | 31 | vr | Nasserism |
| Jalloud | Yes | B.A. in military service | Yes | Fezzan | Rural[a] Urban | Poor | 30 | r | Nasserism |
| Magareif | Yes | B.A. in military service | No | Benghazi | Urban[a] Bedouin | Middle class[b] | 31 | vr | Nasserism |
| Hawadi | Yes | B.A. in military service | No | Jufra | Rural[a] Bedouin | Poor | 30 | r | Nasserism |
| Yunis | Yes | B.A. in military service | No | Jedabia | Bedouin | Poor | 31 | vr | Nasserism |
| Gerui | Yes | B.A. in military service | No | Tripoli | Urban[a] Rural | Middle class[b] | 28 | vr | Nasserism |
| Humaydi | Yes | B.A. in military service | No | Sorman | Rural | Poor | 28 | vr | Nasserism |
| Kharoubi | Yes | B.A. in military service | Yes | Zavia | Rural | Poor | 30 | vr | Nasserism |
| Mahashi | Yes | B.A. in military service | No | Musrata | Urban[a] Rural | Upper middle class[b] | 30 | r | Nasserism |
| Huni | Yes | B.A. in military service | Yes | Tripoli | Rural[a] Urban | Middle class[b] | 30 | r | Nasserism |
| Najim | Yes | B.A. in military service | No | Benghazi | Urban[a] Bedouin | Middle class[b] | 29 | r | Nasserism |
| Hamza | Yes | B.A. in military service | No | Benghazi | Bedouin[a] Urban | Poor | 28 | r | Nasserism |

[a] Combined origins reflect recent urbanization resulting from the rapid urbanization patterns that occurred after the discovery of oil.
[b] Approximate economic position within the context of Libyan society.
[c] r = religious, vr = very religious.

## Elite Cohesion and Value Consensus

The more cohesive an elite structure, the more congruent its values are likely to be and the less intragroup conflict is likely to impair the execution of elite goals. The data presented in table 3-1 leave little doubt that the revolutionary elite began as a cohesive unit centering on the personal confidence of Qadafi. It would be a mistake, however, to suggest that the early years of RCC rule were without internal conflict. As early as December, 1969, two free officers serving in the positions of minister of defense and minister of interior initiated a plot to change the course of the revolution. Among their sources of discontent was the fear that Qadafi's elevation to the position of charismatic leader would relegate all other members of the elite to secondary status.

Intense policy conflicts also occurred in 1975 between Qadafi and a coalition of RCC members centering around Hawadi (chairman of the Arab Socialist Union) and Mahashi (minister of planning) as well as RCC members Huni and Hamza. The issues in conflict involved a full slate of local and international policies. The conflict was resolved by the voluntary exile or house arrest of the dissident faction. Najim and Gerui also withdrew from the RCC as a result of the incident. It is fair to say, then, that the 1975 confrontation greatly enhanced the ability of the RCC to formulate and execute its modernization plans and that henceforth, elite cohesion was not unduly impaired by group conflict. Qadafi clearly exercised the final choice in all decisions in a manner similar to democratic centralism. Open discussion of plans occurred prior to the making of important decisions, but active opposition ceased once a decision acquired Qadafi's stamp.

Ironically, the intense level of overt cohesion among the revolutionary elite after 1975 makes it difficult to test the hypothesis that cohesion leads to value consensus, because the only member of the revolutionary elite to initiate major value statements after 1975 was Colonel Qadafi. Public statements by other members of the elite tended to be elaborations of those value themes initiated by Qadafi. Accordingly, in attempting to delineate elite values for purposes of establishing the relative priority of modernization values, we have relied primarily upon the analysis of Colonel Qadafi's speeches and the analysis of explicit policies initiated by the regime. Some basis for assuming a general consensus of elite values, however, is provided by the relative congruence of the social background patterns summarized in tables 3-3 and 3-4. All members of the upper elite levels, for example, were professional military officers, a fact perhaps explaining the elite's pervasive skepticism of the motives and sincerity of civilians. All members of the upper elite levels described in the 1978 table emerged from very humble social origins, a fact underlying the strong equalitarian propensity of the elite and perhaps their pervasive popularist suspicion of wealthy urbanites

**Table 3-4**
**Social Background of Libyan Revolutionary Elites: 1978**

| Level | Name | Military | Level of Education | Foreign Education | Region | Demographic Origin | Relative Family Status | Age | Religious Intensity (by reputation)[c] | Prerevolutionary Philosophical Orientation |
|---|---|---|---|---|---|---|---|---|---|---|
| 1 | Qadafi | Yes | B.A. | Yes | Cirtica | Bedouin | Poor | 38 | vr | Nasserism |
| 2 | Jalloud | Yes | B.A. | Yes | Fezzan | Rural[a] Urban | Poor | 37 | r | Nasserism |
| 3 | Yunis | Yes | B.A. | No | Jedabia | Bedouin | Poor | 38 | vr | Nasserism |
| 3 | Humaydi | Yes | B.A. | No | Sorman | Rural | Poor | 35 | vr | Nasserism |
| 3 | Kharoubi | Yes | B.A. | Yes | Zavia | Rural | Poor | 37 | vr | Nasserism |
| 4 | Free officers (by majority) | Yes | B.A. | No | Scattered | Bedouin | Middle class[b] | 37 (average) | r | Nasserism |
| 5 | Secretaries of General People's Congress (by majority) | No | B.A. | No | Scattered | Bedouin[a] Rural | Middle class[b] | 37 (average) | r | Nasserism |
| 6 | Cabinet ministers Heads of unions Secretaries of General People's Congress (by majority) | No | M.A. (average) | Yes | Scattered | Urban[a] Rural | Middle class[b] | 38 (average) | r | Nasserism |

[a]Combined origins reflect recent urbanization resulting from rapid urbanization patterns that occurred after the discovery of oil.
[b]Approximate economic position within the context of Libyan society.
[c]r = religious, vr = very religious.

and their equally pervasive faith in the inherent virtue of the masses. The few RCC members who did not fit this pattern were eliminated from the RCC by the 1975 confrontation.

Colonel Qadafi, it should be noted, is of bedouin origin and often finds solitude in weekend visits to bedouin communities. Virtually all of the upper-level members of the 1978 elite structure also came from either rural or bedouin backgrounds. Tables 3-3 and 3-4 also reflect the fact that most members of the upper elite levels were educated primarily in Libya with only limited periods of foreign military training. They are thus similar to Colonel Qadafi in both the type of training they have received and in the limits of that training. Most were early converts to Nasserism as evidenced by their participation in Qadafi's Nasserite cells. At the very least, their most consistent exposure to revolutionary philosophies was provided by Nasser's *Voice of the Arabs*. Their schools were staffed primarily by Egyptian teachers, most of whom perceived their Libyan charges as slightly inferior and clearly in need of revolutionary indoctrination.

## Regime Values

A delineation of elite values based upon the content of Qadafi's speeches and upon his actual policy programs proved to be a relatively easy task. Qadafi is quite explicit in voicing value preferences and, given the fact that Qadafi's value statements carried the weight of law during the revolution's first decade, considerable congruence exists between his speeches and the initiation of policy programs. The hierarchical structuring of value preferences, however, proved to be considerably more difficult, a circumstance to be explained shortly.

A content analysis of Qadafi's speeches and policies and our interviews with prominent government officials lead us to suggest that elite values as they had crystallized by the second year of the revolution fell roughly into seven clusters: preservation of the revolution, anti-imperialism, Arab leadership, modernization, populism, religiosity, and militarism.

### Regime Maintenance: Preservation of the Revolution

Of the values listed, the maintenance of the revolution clearly occupied the position of premier importance. Unless the revolution could be maintained, all other revolutionary goals, by definition, could not be attained. The manner in which the RCC perceived the requirements of regime maintenance and the methods they used in achieving that goal are central to understanding the course of the revolution and have been made the topic of chapter 4.

We will only note at this point that the youth, isolation, and relatively humble backgrounds of the RCC members created an atmosphere of deep insecurity during the first years of the revolution; an atmosphere that was translated into a compelling urgency to consolidate the revolution and to build a base of mass support as rapidly as possible. The time frame in which the regime operated during its first decade was clearly "sudden service right now." This pervasive sense of urgency is crucial to understanding the rapid shift in policies that occurred during the revolution's first decade.

*Modernization*

Another explicit goal of the revolution, and one we would place second in the hierarchy of elite values, was the economic, social, and political modernization of Libyan society. The revolutionary elite's initial conceptualization of modernization centered on a general desire to make Libya as modern as the United States or Western Europe. This meant the establishment of goals such as industrialization, agrarian self-sufficiency, universal education, universal medical care, and universal housing. In political terms, modernization meant greater mass participation in the development of the state.

Aside from its general statement of objectives, the RCC had few specific plans for the achievement of its programs other than to keep an open mind and to pragmatically carry out whatever was necessary to transform Libya into a society in which the quality of life would be equivalent to that of the world's most technologically advanced societies. Indeed, Libya tended to view itself as a grand social experiment, many features of which might serve as a guide to the economic, social, and political modernization of other developing areas. Feature articles, for example, often appear in Libyan newspapers under the caption "Libya Experiments."

This experimental motif has been quite healthy, because an unsuccessful experiment is more readily discarded than a policy announced as being the panacea for all society ills. At the same time, Libya can take justifiable pride in the developmental experiments that have gone well.

*Arab Nationalism, Anti-Imperialism, and Arab Leadership*

Since the revolutionary leaders were reared in Nasserism and exposed to the *Voice of the Arabs,* it was only to be expected that one of their most pervasive values would be a strong belief in a Nasserite version of Arab nationalism. The four essential components of the Nasserite creed, all of which pervade the speeches of Colonel Qadafi, are: Arab unity, social and economic justice centering on the doctrine of Islamic socialism, anti-imperialism, and antireactionism.[7] Expressed in less esoteric terms, the ultimate goal of the Nasserite version of Arab nationalism adopted by Libya's revolutionary elite is a unified and modernized Arab nation, that is, an Arab nation on par with the United States and Western Europe. Imperialists, primarily the United States and Europe, are perceived as opposing a unified Arab state on the grounds that it would pose a threat to both their exploitation of Arab resources and to the continued presence of Israel. Imperialism is seen as a pervasive force and must be resisted anywhere in the world, not merely in the Middle East. Similarly, monarchies such as Saudi Arabia and Kuwait are viewed as reactionary in the sense that they are not working for the modernization of their states. They are also viewed as aiding imperialism, and obstructing Arab unity. They must be opposed at all costs.

In this regard, Libya has been a tireless advocate of revolution in what Qadafi considers to be the reactionary Arab states, a posture that has brought him into almost continuous conflict with Morocco and Saudi Arabia, not to mention the Sadat regime in Egypt, the Sudan, and to a lesser extent, Tunisia. Libya's aggressive antireactionary policies, including its support of the Chad Liberation Front, have thus created a situation in which Libya is virtually surrounded by hostile neighbors. This fact, in turn, has heightened the revolution's sense of urgency.

Libya's unswerving support for the principles of Arab nationalism reflects Qadafi's deeply felt belief that he is the legitimate heir to the mantle of Arab leadership vacated by the passing away of Gamal Abdul Nasser just a short time after the Libyan revolution. The desire for Arab leadership has become a central feature in virtually all Qadafi's speeches and has become increasingly manifest in recent years. It has also become manifest in Libya's growing conflict with what it terms reactionary Arab states and its deep involvement in such regional issues as Palestine, the Lebanese civil war, and the Polissairos.

In his role of leader of the Arabs, Qadafi has also attempted to transcend the image of Nasser and to place his own intellectual stamp beside that of Nasser. Qadafi's *Green Book,* in which he elaborates the third universal theory, is often seen as a step in that direction. The *Green Book* is examined at length in chapters 8 and 9.

## *Militarism, Populism, and Religiosity*

The value clusters relating to regime maintenance, modernization, and Arab leadership have resulted in specific policies either outlined previously or to be elaborated on throughout later chapters. Three additional elite values—militarism, populism, and religiosity—have found expression less in the formation of specific policy targets than in the means used by the regime to consolidate its position and to modernize Libya. In later chapters, for example, one will observe a clear tendency by Colonel Qadafi to rely heavily on various forms of mass military training as a means of integrating and mobilizing Libyan society. Also, Colonel Qadafi consistently tends to have greater trust and confidence in military than in nonmilitary colleagues.

The value cluster we have chosen to call populism, in turn, refers to an almost mystical faith in the common man. If the inherent virtues of the common man which were repressed by years of colonialism and reactionary rule could somehow be unleashed and harnessed to the goals of revolution, then the modernization of Libya, in Qadafi's view, would become merely a matter of time, and the revolution would be secured.[8] Qadafi's faith in the masses has provided the underpinning of the regime's two most interesting and innovative experiments in the area of political modernization and mass mobilization: the popular committees and the people's congresses, which currently form the fundamentally political structure of revolutionary Libya. They are discussed in detail in later chapters.

Finally, as indicated from the religiosity columns of tables 3-3 and 3-4, virtually all members of the upper elite strata are reputed to be intensely religious. The influence of religion is pervasive in revolutionary Libya, with the Koran serving as the constitution of the state and the sole point of reference in personal matters. Alcoholic beverages are not served in revolutionary Libya and Koranic strictures are rigorously observed.

Qadafi's manifest religiosity would appear to be an integral part of his populism and is an important facet of his charismatic appeal to the masses. In many parts of Libya, as noted in chapter 2, religious symbols remain more salient than nationalistic ones.

Some development theorists argue that religiosity is antithetical to the goals of economic modernization in as much as it tends to reinforce the ascriptive claims of traditional leaders and to justify the perpetuation of tribal social structures. As we will discuss at a later point, however, Qadafi finds little conflict between religion and modernity, stressing the socialistic concepts of Islam as the basis of economic development. Moreover, Colonel Qadafi's applications of Islam have left little scope for Libya's traditional religious leaders, a topic also to be discussed in later chapters.

**The Hierarchy, Congruence, and Stability of Elite Values**

In terms of analyzing the influence of regime values on modernization policy, it would clearly be desirable to establish a value hierarchy. This would enable one to ascertain just how important modernization was in the overall scheme of things and, perhaps, to predict which competing values would be most likely to take priority over modernizing values and thereby impair the modernization process. For the same reasons, it would also be interesting to trace trends in the hierarchy and congruence of elite values over time.

We had hoped that our content analysis of Qadafi's statements and regime policies would provide us with a clear picture of the hierarchy of regime values and their stability.

This effort was soon aborted, however, because aside from the preservation of the revolution, a clear hierarchy of elite values failed to emerge from our analysis. Rather than having a clear ordinal ranking of values or objectives, Colonel Qadafi and the revolutionary elite appear to pursue all of the values simultaneously, and with more or less equal vigor. Moreover, the diverse value clusters appear to be perceived by the regime as fully congruent. Modernization, in addition to being valued for its own sake, is viewed as providing the ultimate basis for maintaining the revolution and as a key ingredient in Qadafi's quest for Arab leadership. The quest for Arab leadership, conversely, enhances his charismatic stature immensely, thereby providing the regime with symbolic appeals for mobilizing the masses that might otherwise be lacking. The greater the regime's ability to symbolically mobilize the masses in support of its programs, at least in theory, the greater its ability to both preserve the revolution and modernize Libya. Religiosity, in addition to being important in its own right, also builds symbolic resources for the state and provides a means of creating a common bond between the elite and the masses. Populism (and the intense politicization of the masses described in later chapters) is perceived as perhaps the only way to build a strong legitimate base for preserving the revolution and for drawing the masses into the development process. The military, correspondingly, is perceived as the most cohesive, disciplined, and nationalistic element in Libyan society. A strong military, in Qadafi's view, is the best guarantee of maintaining the regime until the revolution's modernization programs establish a strong mass base of legitimacy and institutionalization. The military is also viewed as serving as a behavior model for the masses, particularly for the youth. Through development of the militia and the institution of universal military training for Libyan youth, a means has been provided for both protecting the revolution and socializing the masses with nationalistic values.

The fact that Libya's revolutionary leaders appear to view their values as congruent, of course, does not mean that the potential for value incongruence is absent or that potential value conflicts will not impair goals of political, economic, and social modernization. We will reiterate the compelling sense of urgency that surrounds the regime's modernization efforts, a sense of urgency heightened by Libya's hostile foreign environment. Haste often leads to a lack of sound planning, to the absence of quality control, and to the equating of monies spent with results achieved. It also leads to corruption and waste. One might also argue that giving the masses direct responsibility for the conception, execution, and supervision of development projects may be giving them more than they are ready to handle. Some might also suggest that the atmosphere of permanent crisis generated by foreign policy conflicts may divert scarce human and financial resources away from economic development projects. This might also be the outcome of the militarization of Libyan society.

The extent to which these and related value conflicts have impaired the development process will be explained in the chapters that follow. The next step, however, will be to examine the consolidation of the revolution.

# 4 Consolidation of the Revolution

The most urgent goal confronting Libya's revolutionary leaders on September 1, 1969, was the consolidation of their revolution. Without such consolidation, the years of planning and sacrifice would be for naught. So, too, would the lives of the revolutionary leaders and their aspirations for a modern Libya.

In its efforts at consolidation, the RCC was hampered both by the total absence of contact with established groups and elites and by its own youth and humble backgrounds. There were no internal political organizations upon which the leaders could rely, nor was their own stature sufficient to command a broad mass following. The RCC had literally pitted itself against all of the established political, social, and economic groups in Libya. Among other things, this fact helps to explain the immediate rise to minor elite status of those military and civilian groups that supported the RCC during the crucial first days of the revolution regardless of their lack of prior contact with the group. No one else existed to fill the vacuum.

In attempting to consolidate the revolution, the RCC moved with force in four areas:

1. Dismantling the old elite structure.
2. Forging the army into a reliable coercive weapon.
3. Generating popular acceptance for the revolution via accelerated disbursement of oil revenues.
4. Legitimizing the regime by transforming Colonel Qadafi into a charismatic figure.

**Dismantling the Old Regime**

The dismantling of the ancient regime began on the eve of the revolution with the arrest of most officers holding the rank of major or above, with the exception of five or six senior officers who joined the ranks of the free officers by proclaiming their support for the revolution at the time of its inception and another small group of technically oriented senior officers generally considered to be politically neutral.[1] The hard-core supporters of the monarchy, such as the leadership of the Cyrenaica Defense Force and the senior officers of the Libyan army, remained under internment for several years. Less threatening figures received lighter sentences, followed by appointment in the diplomatic corps. Others were placed in the bureaucracy. Virtually all were tried by televised sessions of the newly created people's court, an institution consisting of RCC members and representatives of the Libyan judiciary, the latter having been largely untouched by the revolution. RCC member Hawadi presided over the court, and RCC member Mahashi served as prosecutor.

The CDF was totally dismantled, with its senior officers arrested and its junior officers merged with the army. The national police, an object of great fear and hostility under the monarchy, was placed under military command and its members were publicly humiliated as being "the enemies of the people." Virtually all senior police officers were arrested and held up to public ridicule by the people's court. Remaining officers and rank and file policemen were disarmed and reissued nightsticks. In the words of one respondent, the police, in one fell swoop, went from being the most feared to the least feared individuals in Libya.

Their morale broken and their influence gone, the ranks of the police were further thinned by resignations. This condition continued until the ministry of interior, which houses the police, was reorganized under the leadership of RCC member El Hamaydi in early 1973. The present functions of the police involve little more than traffic control and routine security. The new slogan for the police forces became: "in the service of the people."

Senior bureaucrats were also paraded before the people's court, with the king's closest supporters receiving light prison sentences or being placed under house arrest for varying periods of time. For the most part, however, senior bureaucrats suffered little more than public scorn and were removed from government service with a severance settlement sufficient to enable them to either purchase sizeable land holdings or to enter private business. Several generals received similar treatment and were further mollified by the receipt of generous government contracts. Thus, a policy emerged in which members of the military and bureaucracy of questionable loyalty were removed from sensitive positions, yet were given the opportunity to profit by good behavior. Fanatical opposition to the regime was thus precluded by providing potential opponents of the regime with the prospect of a materially prosperous and secure existence, albeit one that disallowed any form of political activity.

Members of the royal family, Diwan, cabinet, and parliament were also arrested during the early hours of the revolution and tried before the people's court. By and large, the sentences of individuals not directly linked with the king were minimal, often involving little more than house arrest. Intimate aids to the king, such as the Shelhi family, received substantial sentences, but most were released from prison within a five-year period. There were no executions. The king and several prominent officers were out of the country at the time of the revolution and were tried as absentees. They were offered amnesty by the revolutionary government toward the end of 1975, but declined the offer and remained abroad.

The army, CDF, police, royal family, senior bureaucrats, cabinet members, Diwan members, and parliamentarians were, by virtue of their formal positions, the most visible opponents of the revolution. As such, they were the easiest to deal with. Also easy to deal with were the several thousand Italian settlers whose ownership of prime agricultural and business properties had long been an object of intense resentment among the Libyans. By removing the prerogative of Libyan citizenship from the Italian community and forcing their repatriation to the Italian peninsula, the RCC was able to both remove a perceived threat to the revolution and take an important step toward creating an aura of nationalistic charisma around the person of Colonel Qadafi. The sequestering of Italian properties also provided economic largess for distribution to large numbers of lower- and middle-class Libyans.

Far less easy for the RCC to deal with were those in opposition who had roots deeply engrained in the fabric of Libyan society. Particularly sensitive in this regard were the tribal chiefs. The tribal chiefs had prospered under the monarchy. Indeed, the local administrative boundaries of the dominant tribes were the de facto boundaries of local government, and tribal leaders dominated the local administrative positions. The RCC's opposition to the tribes tended to be threefold. Having prospered under the king and possessing a clear military capacity, the tribes, and particularly some of those in Cyrenaica and Fezzan, provided the logical avenue for a counterrevolution against the republic. Moreover, the members of the RCC were from Libya's least prestigious tribes. They had spent much of their lives being looked down upon by the prestigious tribes and felt that their ability to establish their own charisma or *baraka* demanded the blunting of traditional status lines. Finally, the RCC felt that the tribal chiefs would view the social and economic modernization of Libya as a threat to their own authority and that they would, accordingly, attempt to block it at every turn. This hypothesis is examined in light of our survey data in chapter 5. For a variety of reasons, then, the RCC was particularly wary of the tribal chiefs.

The initial attack upon Libya's tribal leadership was, by necessity, an integral part of the arrests and purges of the ancient regime outlined. Most senior officers, bureaucrats, parliamentarians, and members of the Diwan under the monarchy, were, in reality, the leaders or appointees of Libya's major tribes. Internment could only be a short-term tactic, however, because in reality, it was virtually impossible for the RCC to retain all of Libya's notables under arrest. Rather, a frontal attack was made on authority and social status of the rural Libyan elites by formally abolishing the tribe as a legal institution. Administrative boundaries based on de facto tribal lines were restructured to create administrative units consisting of segments of several tribes. This restructuring was followed, in turn, by the dismissal of all local officials, including governors, mayors, and deputy mayors, most of whom had been tribal shieks or their relatives; and replacement by a new class of local administrators whose values and social origins were compatible with those of the RCC, that is, educated members of less prestigious tribes with no ties to the old elite structure. The RCC thus attempted to tie the dismantling of the old elite to the creation of a new local elite whose loyalty and security were directly linked to the perpetuation of the revolution. The new local administrators also provided the core of the RCC's initial modernization efforts. The successes and failures of the modernizing administrators experiment will be examined in detail in chapter 5.

Equally tricky was the role of Libya's traditional religious elite. Religion, after all, had provided one of the two main pillars of the monarchy.[2] More importantly from the perspective of consolidating the revolution, both the Ulema and Libya's multitudinous local religious leaders continued to hold considerable influence over the Libyan population. It was entirely conceivable, for example, that religious appeals could provide the conduit for a Senussi resurgence. Indeed, the abortive coup in 1970 headed by the Prince Abdullah Abed El Senussi and including a coterie of business and military officers and ex-ministers, was designed to mobilize the substantial fervor of the Senussi movement that remained in Fezzan and Cyrenaica. In general, it was also felt that the religious leaders would aid and abet the tribal chiefs in their opposition to the new regime and that the religious leaders, like the tribal chiefs, would perceive the RCC's modernization programs as a threat to their own status and existence. It should also be noted that the Ulema served as major local opinion leaders. As such, they had to be brought under control.

The campaign against the local religious leaders was twofold. First and most directly, the RCC moved to establish its own religious credentials. Koranic strictures long dormant under the monarchy were enforced with a vengeance. Article 1 of the revolutionary constitution proclaimed Islam as the official religion of the state and the Koran as the ultimate source of Libyan law. All use of alcohol was abolished, with violators facing almost certain imprisonment. Alcohol, it should be noted, was allowed under the monarchy. Qadafi's own ascetic nature blended well with this campaign and he, himself, acquired some of the aura of the puritanical mystics so common to the area.[3] Also publicized were the strict codes of prayer and abstinence imposed upon members of the Qadafi cells during the arduous years of preparation for the revolution.

As his own religious image became engrained in the popular mind, Qadafi began to attack the established religious leaders as a class of superfluous priests. Islam, he preached, was a religion based upon the direct communication of the individual with God. It was a religion of equality and personal vigor that was available to all people regardless of how humble their personal origin. Libya must serve as a vanguard for the Islamic world by abolishing the obstructionist class of priests and returning to the fundamental link between God and man.

Also problematic for the RCC were those people in Libyan society who had the organizational or symbolic capacity to challenge the revolution, yet who, because of their opposition to the monarchy, were difficult to brand as enemies. Prominent in this regard were the nascent political parties, labor unions, and student organizations.[4] All had acted in opposition to the monarchy and all had proclaimed their support for the revolution. They could not be branded as enemies of the people. Nonetheless, the intense ideological positions of these groups and their demonstrated capacity to generate conflict, posed a clear threat to the new revolution. Moreover, the leaders of the various labor and political organizations were largely unknown to Qadafi and the RCC members. They lacked that element of personal contact which played such a crucial role in the formation of the new elite. Also, Qadafi, perhaps reflecting the influence of Nasser, manifested a deep personal distrust of political parties. Libya, Qadafi proclaimed, needed consensus and unity, not the exacerbation of its regional and tribal conflicts.

Following a brief honeymoon in which prominent opposition leaders were asked to form a cabinet, all political parties, labor unions, and student unions were disbanded. Qadafi proclaimed that there was no need to have such organizations mediate between the revolutionary authority and the masses. The masses, he said, should have direct contact with the leadership.

After a lapse of several months, the labor and student organizations were reconstructed under the auspices of the RCC, with leaders acceptable to the RCC. The ban on political parties, however, was not to be lifted. Ba'athism was anathema to Qadafi's Nasserite and religious views, and the movement was outlawed. Rumors also circulated that Qadafi had made contact with the Ba'athist organization prior to the coup and was rebuffed. The fact that Mahmoud Sulleman El Magrabi, a known Ba'athist, had become Libya's first prime minister after the revolution, was merely the result of early desperate attempts to press all known leaders of the opposition into service. Once the dust had settled, however, political organizations were rapidly abolished. Nasserites were informed that the revolution was indeed a Nasserite revolution. Members of the Muslim brotherhood were similarly informed that Libya had become a devoutly Muslim republic, and that the energies of their members could best be applied elsewhere. Former party members were given one month to drop their party affiliation. "He who belongs to a party is a traitor" became the slogan of the day. In place of the myriad political groupings formed under the monarchy, the RCC would eventually move toward the creation of a single political party, the Arab Socialist Union, a process to be discussed in the following chapter.

**Building Revolutionary Institutions: The Army**

Having launched a full-scale attack on all facets of the old elite structure, the RCC was under instense pressure to create a reliable coercive arm capable of sustaining the revolution during its early years. This vehicle was to be the army. The free officer movement, the origins of which were described in chapter 3, had wielded sufficient force at the time of the revolution to stem a viable counterattack. The free officers, their positions now elevated, continued to serve as the backbone of the RCC's revitalized army. Moreover, with the military in control of the government, most of the junior officers suddenly found themselves in positions of status and power. No one in Libya enjoyed more prestige or was treated with greater respect than military officers. Suddenly, obscure and extremely youthful men of humble backgrounds had become the toast of Libya. To further strengthen its position within the army, the RCC also elevated noncommissioned officers deemed loyal to junior officer rank, and RCC supporters in the military academy were given early graduation. Both were to play crucial roles in implementing the revolution. Within a few years of the revolution, the army had tripled in both size and equipment. Moreover, to further augment the strength of the military, the RCC offered Libya's superior secondary students special bonuses for entering the military academy and the almost certain guarantee of foreign study or training. When such inducements proved insufficient, the RCC began to debate the use of universal military service for all Libyans.

If the coercive measures employed seem extreme, it is important to recall the extreme vulnerability of the RCC's position stemming both from their obscure backgrounds and from their having chosen to attack virtually all of the established political and economic groups in Libya. Such feelings of insecurity were clearly justified, for the revolution had been the object of at least three coup attempts, each from a separate source. The first major attempt was organized in December, 1969, by the ministers of defense and interior. A second attempt on July 24, 1970, was organized and financed by former Prince Abdullah Abed El Senussi with the presumed support of Saudi Arabia. A third attempt was organized by RCC member Hawadi in 1975 and resulted in his arrest, the defection of Mahashi, and the withdrawal of several other RCC members.

**Legitimizing the Revolution: Qadafi as a Charismatic Leader**

During its first months, the consolidation of the revolution relied, by necessity, upon the military. For the revolution to endure, however, it ultimately had to develop a broad basis of mass support. Some means had to be found to legitimize the regime; to provide it with the ability to control and mobilize the Libyan population through symbolic gestures rather than ubiquitous displays of coercive force. The RCC was aware also that its support within the military was ultimately dependent upon popular acceptance of the revolution and its leaders. Qadafi's group, it will be recalled, was relatively small and necessarily an exclusive segment of the Libyan army. It was also only one of two and perhaps more groups plotting to overthrow the king. Strong mass support would discourage further plotting; mass unrest would surely encourage it.

The members of the RCC, however, were almost totally lacking in symbolic appeal. Young, rural, poor, and from humble origins, they possessed none of the ascriptive attributes generally associated with leadership in traditional Libya. Supposedly at the suggestion of Nasser, the method chosen by the RCC to legitimize the regime and develop a symbolic basis for controlling and mobilizing the Libyan population was to transform Qadafi into a charismatic leader.[5] Given the exigencies of the Libyan situation, there were few other options.

Charisma, as defined by Max Weber, is one of three types of legitimate authority.

1. Rational grounds—resting on a belief in the "legality" of patterns of normative rules and the right to those elevated to authority under such rules to issue commands (legal authority).

2. Traditional grounds—resting on an established belief in the sanctity of immemorial traditions and the legitimacy of the status of those exercising authority under them (traditional authority); . . .

3. Charismatic grounds—resting on devotion to the specific and exceptional sanctity, heroism or exemplary character of an individual person, and of the normative patterns or order revealed or ordained by him (charismatic authority).

The term "charisma" will be applied to a certain quality of an individual's personality by virtue of which he is set apart from ordinary men and treated as endowed with supernatural, superhuman, or at least specifically exceptional powers or qualities. These are such as are not accessible to the ordinary person, but are regarded as of divine origin or an exemplary, and on the basis of them the individual concerned is treated as a leader. In primitive circumstances this peculiar kind of deference is paid to prophets, to people with a reputation for therapeutic or legal wisdom, to leaders in the hunt, and heroes in war. It is very often thought of as resting on magical powers . . .

If proof of his charismatic qualification fails him for long, the leader endowed with charisma tends to think his god or his magical or heroic powers have deserted him. If he is long unsuccessful, above all if his leadership fails to benefit his followers, it is likely that his charismatic authority will disappear. This is the genuine charismatic meaning of the "gift of grace."[6]

Charismatic authority is thus specifically outside the realm of everyday routine and the profane sphere. In this respect, it is sharply opposed to rational, and particularly bureaucratic, authority, and to traditional authority, whether in its patriarchal, patrimonial, or any other form . . .[7]

Charisma, as we use the term in the anlaysis of Colonel Qadafi's emergence as a charismatic leader, is based on one individual's psychological identification with another individual.[8] Identification is defined as the emotional involvement of one individual with another individual or object whereby the identifyer perceives his own fate as being lilnked to that of the object.[9] One example of such identification is a mother's pleasure when her children do well in school and her corresponding remorse when they do poorly.[10] A similar manifestation of identification would be the tremendous exhilaration many individuals feel when their football team wins or becomes "Number 1." Somehow it makes them feel that they, too, are Number 1.

For individuals caught up in the breakdown of traditional societies, and Libya is certainly a classic example of this situation, identification with a charismatic leader provides a stable point of reference, the cues from which offer at least some means of coping with the pressures and ambiguities of change. David Apter, for instance, suggests that Nkrumah, the late deposed leader of Ghana, became the functional equivalent of the tribal chief in areas in which the traditional basis for the chief's authority had been undermined by colonialism.[11] Individuals began to look for cues from Nkrumah rather than from their weakened chiefs. Moreover, by identifying with a charismatic leader, one can share vicariously in his glories. Individuals humiliated by the condescension of colonial masters could find reaffirmation of their own worth and power in the exploits of the nationalist leaders with whom they identified.

At least in theory, Qadafi's emergence as the most powerful individual in Libya could trigger similar identification patterns among a preponderance of Libya's population, and particularly among the Libyan masses caught in the cataclysmic changes produced by Libya's rampant oil economy. Some scenarios of identification with Qadafi might be as follows: "Qadafi is strong and dynamic. He has *baraka*. I, consciously or unconsciously, identify with Qadafi; therefore, I share his strength and dynamism." "Qadafi knows where he is going; he possesses a sense of purpose. By identifying with Qadafi, I, too, acquire a sense of direction and purpose. At the very least, I can avoid uncertainty." "Qadafi has become a leader of world stature. He pushes around the major powers. By identifying with Qadafi, I, too, can share his pride. I am not the inferior toad the Italians said I was." "Qadafi is proud to be a Libyan. By identifying with Qadafi, I, too, have become aware of being a Libyan. I take pride in being a Libyan."

The more such scenarios could be established in reality, the more Qadafi could serve as a symbol of national unity and pride. Moreover, as the identification process is goal-fulfilling, the more intensely the Libyan masses identified with Qadafi, the greater personal stake they would have in his survival and in the success of his programs. His success would become their successes. His failures would threaten their own sense of security and throw their lives into confusion. Because they would have a personal stake in Qadafi and his programs, Qadafi would acquire an important tool for controlling and mobilizing the Libyan masses symbolically. He and his regime would acquire the legitimacy they so desperately lacked on the eve of the revolution.

As charismatic movements gain in stature, they also attract growing numbers of individuals who do not have strong psychological reasons for identifying with a charismatic leader but who "join up" for the sake of expediency. In periods of stress and uncertainty, there are ample reasons for being on the winning side. Although the commitment of such individuals may be questionable, the ends of expediency dictate that they act the part. As such, their behavior perpetuates the image of the movement's dynamism and weakens the resolve of others pondering the alternatives of fighting the movement of joining the bandwagon.

If a particular leader is to serve as an object of identification for a broad cross section of individuals and thereby exercise the ability to arouse mass emotions, he must be seen as offering a relevant solution to the problems of the identifying individuals. At least three factors are involved: image formation, image communication, and image reinforcement.[12]

First, the aspirant of charismatic status must be able to create an image of strength and generally epitomize whatever other virtues are perceived as relevant among the target audience. Without the image of strength, real or imagined, the leader is in a poor position to serve as a beacon of reference and security for those plagued by the confusion of social or psychic disorganization.

Second, if a charismatic leader is to attract a national following, he must communicate the image he has created and the programs he has proposed to individuals with differing problems, aspirations, and backgrounds. It is difficult to be all things to all people, but a charismatic leader must have at least something for everyone in the groups he seeks to mobilize.

A third "must" for charismatic leaders, one strongly emphasized by Weber, is that they continually reinforce their image; that they continue to provide a meaningful crutch for the faithful. If their power wanes, if competitive purveyors of charisma appear more relevant, or if concrete programs are in direct conflict with other mass values, the basis for their charisma is undermined and the quality or intensity of identification patterns decreases or becomes totally extinguished. A charismatic leader who fails to perpetually reinforce his image will more than likely cease to be goal-fulfilling for those who identify with him. To the extent that this occurs, he ceases to be a charismatic leader. He no longer enjoys the ability to mobilize the masses by means of symbolic assets based on their identification with him.

In addition, a fourth requirement for charismatic status would clearly be the need for exclusiveness or uniqueness.[13] If citizens were to be offered an array of potentially charismatic figures from which to choose, the chances are that they would identify with the individual closest to their own regional, tribal, or economic circumstances. Such a situation would hardly lead to national unity and would pose the very real danger of civil conflict if competing charismatic figures disagreed on crucial issues. Moreover, if competing objects of identification were readily available, it would be far too easy for citizens to shift loyalties from one leader to another during periods of stress or potential doubt, thereby lessening the need to remain firm in their commitments. Such potential shifting would be most likely among those who joined the bandwagon for opportunistic reasons. Any marked shifts in loyalty, of course, would lessen the image or *baraka* of the sole leader. For purposes of building solidarity and mobilizing the masses, then, uniqueness is essential. If Qadafi was to serve as a guide or the cue-giver for the Libyan masses by qualifying as Weber's superhero, then, he clearly had to perform feats of extraordinary prowess. In local parlance, he had to establish his personal *baraka*.

Once the dust of the revolution had settled, Qadafi moved quickly to create an image of strength and dynamism. Libya's sizeable Italian community was given very short notice to leave the country. Their sizeable property holdings, including much of the finest agricultural land in Libya, were confiscated. Italian churches were closed or turned into mosques. The grand cathedral in Tripoli was converted into a mosque and presented to non-Arab Muslims as their international headquarters. In the process, Qadafi claimed final victory over the Italians, the primary symbol of Libyan inferiority or humiliation. In much the same manner, leases for British and American military bases, also symbols of foreign domination, were ordered terminated. The British and the Americans evacuated from Libya almost immediately. Since these two groups were viewed by most Libyans as omnipotent, their expulsion was, indeed, a slightly miraculous act. Given Libya's proven oil resources, its meager army, and the potential complicity of the ancient regime, most Libyans had assumed that the expulsion of the West was either impossible or would result in the direct occupation of the country. The man was indeed blessed. In subsequent years, Qadafi has reinforced his image as international giant killer by repeatedly baiting the major powers of the West. Malta's conflict with Britain received strong support from the Libyans, as did Idi Amin's anti-imperialistic efforts in Uganda. The Irish Republican Army, too, has received Libyan support as has the Islamic Liberation Front in the Philippines. Of more recent vintage, Qadafi has reinforced his image of strength and dynamism by almost single-handedly forcing the revision of world oil prices, a move that clearly branded him as a major force in world politics.[14]

Particularly important in the early stages of Qadafi's efforts to acquire the aura of strength and sanctity was the blessing of Nasser, the unchallenged leader of the Middle East for more than fifteen years, and beyond question the preeminent national hero to a preponderance of Libyan youth.[15] By Qadafi's recounting, his own revolutionary activities were spawned by Nasser's speeches on the *Voice of the Arabs.* Egyptian teachers, textbooks, and cultural centers, the mainstays of the Libyan education system under the monarchy, all taught Nasserism to Libya's youth. Pictures of Nasser and Qadafi linked in an embrace of friendship became and remain ubiquitous.

After Nasser's unexpected death just months after the Libyan revolution, Qadafi further enhanced his charismatic credentials by staking his claim as Nasser's legitimate heir as the leader of the Arab revolution, a claim that gained momentum with Sadat's shift in policy.[16] No other leader could boast of Nasser's blessing or make a more legitimate claim to the leadership of the Arab revolution.

Qadafi's claims of Arab leadership, quite obviously, were rejected by the leaders of the Arab states, yet his unbridled pursuit of Nasserism did propel him into the limelight of Arab politics and provided him with international status far greater than that enjoyed by the king. Libya, under Qadafi, had become a force to be reckoned with, a fact that caused considerable exhilaration among young Libyans long accustomed to being the butt of Arab jokes.

Qadafi's first success in the field of Arab unity came with the proclamation of the still-born union among Libya, Egypt, and Syria, a union honored in the breach.[17] Though accomplishing little in concrete terms, the union elevated Qadafi to the level of the Egyptian president and made him a member of the inner circle of Arab leaders. Similarly, unity efforts with the Sudan, Syria, and Tunisia have also failed, yet have provided Qadafi with a pedestal from which to attack the lack of sincerity of colleagues and extend his own moral superiority.

As the champion of the Arab revolution, Qadafi launched vicious verbal attacks against the Arab world's remaining monarchs, labeling them reactionary tools of imperialism and offering to finance movements dedicated to their destruction. Counterattacks by the kings of Saudi Arabia, Jordan, Morocco, and later by Sadat of Egypt, were widely publicized, thereby further enhancing Qadafi's status as the main force in Arab politics, a position never before enjoyed by a Libyan.

In the realm of the Palestine issue, Qadafi soon established himself as perhaps the foremost advocate of the Palestinian cause. He has generously financed a variety of Palestinian movements and at one point established special training bases for a Palestine liberation force made up of international volunteers somewhat of the pattern of the French foreign legion. A law was also passed requiring that Palestinians residing in Libya receive preferential treatment over other non-Libyans in competition for government jobs. Most recently, Libya intervened actively on the side of the Palestinians during the early stages of the Lebanese civil war.

Image-building, of course, is also a matter of public relations. The Libyan press and mass media obviously have done their part to establish Qadafi as a leader of world stature and to generally build mass support for the regime. His exploits are widely publicized. Moreover, it is not uncommon for Libyan newspapers to devote a four-page pictorial section to Qadafi's activities at least once a week. The press, as Qadafi pointed out from the very beginning, is an instrument of the revolution. It must do everything possible to strengthen the revolution.

The impact of the Libyan media in transforming Qadafi into a charismatic leader, although formidable, paled in comparison to the impact of the foreign media. Praise from Nasser's *Voice of the Arabs* and damnation by Western media and their Arab supporters did far more to establish Qadafi as a leader of world stature in the eyes of most Libyans than the Libyan media could ever do. If so many major states were so upset with Qadafi, he must indeed be a man of extraordinary prowess.

The discussion of charisma as a theoretical concept also includes the need for a charismatic leader to be able to communicate with the masses on a one-to-one basis, and to fit in with the prevailing norms of their society. In this regard, Qadafi's intense piety was particularly well suited to his aspiring role as a charismatic leader, for the religious traditions of Muslim North Africa are replete with stories of pious ascetics of humble origins called by God to serve great purposes, not the least of whom was the grand Senussi.[18] His religious piety thus placed Qadafi's rise within the context of Libyan traditions and facilitated the development of emotional ties between Qadafi and Libya's intensely religious population. Establishing impeccable religious credentials further lessened his vulnerability to the attack of the Ulema and enhanced his ability to pursue his modernization values as the fulfillment of Islamic tenets, much in the precedent established by Nasser. As noted earlier, Qadafi's avowals of religiosity were reinforced by proclaiming the Koran as the constitution of Libya, and by the strict enforcement of Islamic civil codes.

Qadafi's ability to reach the masses was also enhanced by his personal life style. Except for official occasions, he has chosen to drive an unchauffeured car. His life style is simple and less pretentious than most known leaders of the Arab world. He has mingled freely with the masses during the early years of the revolution and extolled the virtues of rural society. Dropping all official titles, he has chosen to only answer to the address of "brother." He is, in short, very much a creature of the Libyan milieu. He is also a speaker of exceptional skill, quite adept at communicating with the masses in the local idiom.

If Qadafi seemingly had little trouble in establishing himself as a leader of extraordinary prowess and in communicating with the Libyan masses, he nevertheless faced the difficult problem of establishing himself as the sole leader of the revolution—the one leader, who above all, should serve as the object of mass loyalty. Although Qadafi had clearly served as the inspiration of the September revolution, the revolution was a group effort. To turn on his colleagues was unthinkable and would only serve to weaken the revolution. Thus, the strategy chosen by Qadafi was to place himself above the government, the daily operations of which would be left to the RCC and the cabinet.

The final theoretical requirement for a charismatic leader is the need to continually reinforce his image, or else he ceases to be goal-fulfilling to his flock. By and large, reinforcement of his image of strength has proved to be a relatively easy matter for Qadafi. His drive for Arab leadership, as noted above, has been pursued with vigor, much to the discomfort of Libya's neighbors. Libya, at least from the Libyan perspective, has become the vanguard of Arab unity.

Of equal if not greater significance has been Qadafi's success in almost single-handedly escalating the price of world oil in the face of stiff opposition from both the West and its Arab allies, a move that has enhanced Qadafi's image not only within Libya but throughout the entire Arab world. The Western press, needless to say, was a major factor in assuring that Qadafi receives his due for his oil exploits. Yet other examples of Qadafi's steps to extend his charismatic image will be examined in the following chapters.

## Consolidating the Revolution: Distribution

Strongly reinforcing attempts to legitimize the revolution by elevating Qadafi to the status of a charismatic leader were parallel to efforts to establish a broad base of mass support by dramatically opening the portals of Libya's oil revenues to all segments of Libyan society. The minimum wage for blue-collar workers and the salaries for all employees were increased by approximately 50 percent. Free housing was provided for those in need, with Qadafi himself designing what he felt would be ideal flats for urban workers. If housing was not readily available, applicants received interest-free loans from the government, the repayment of which was waived for lower classes in celebration of the revolution's first anniversary. In the second year of the revolution, workers were decreed part-owners in the corporations in which they worked and were declared eligible to receive from one-third to one-half of a company's profits, including the profits of the growing list of government businesses that exercised monopolies in such fields as insurance and banking and which turned large profits, indeed. In later stages, the workers became the owners of such enterprises. In many instances, an employee's annual share of the profits exceeded his annual salary. Libya's lower classes, including some 50,000 door watchers, coffee fetchers, and similar individuals, were suddenly well on their way to becoming comfortable members of the middle class.

For the farmer and agrarian workers, the revolution held similar benefits. All landless farmers became immediately eligible to purchase improved agricultural land, including machinery, housing, seeds, fertilizer, and livestock at approximately 10 percent of their estimated value. Purchases lands were interest-free and were to be amortized over twenty years. In many cases, farmers would receive approximately twenty-five acres of land and be paid a salary by the government until such time as the farm became capable of producing its own revenue, at which time its owner would assume a mortgage for 10 percent of its estimated value. The confiscated farms from the Italians were distributed to the farmers in the immediate locality or to those who used to work them on behalf of the Italian owners. Libyan farmers who already owned their own property were granted subsidies to build new houses, a procedure that required little more effort than applying for a housing plan from the architectural department, having it certified by local officials, and then taking it to the government bank to receive the money. As one might anticipate, certain abuses occurred in the program, strict supervision being a problem for Libya's severely overextended bureaucracy.

The revolution also became a boom for Libya's small business community, with the RCC moving rapidly to establish a policy requiring the distribution of government contracts to a large number of Libyan firms. Overnight, new businesses mushroomed, as clerks, bureaucrats, soldiers, and even workers rushed to government offices seeking government tenders for construction or supply, a procedure facilitated by new policies of the government bank allowing up to 95 percent financing for commercial business ventures. Thus a man could form a paper company, get a personal loan or use his savings to provide the necessary 5 percent capital, receive his loan from the government bank, complete 10 percent of the project by subleasing to a foreign firm, and start receiving a direct draw from the government which would be used to repay principle and interest and to reap a substantial profit. Procedures were even more generous for entrepreneurs wishing to initiate industrial ventures, with government banks offering 100 percent financing. All that was required were remotely plausible ideas. The magnitude of the redistribution of business wealth occasioned by the new economic policies is indicated by the fact that prior to the revolution, all government contracts in the city of Sabrata, the center of the province in which our survey was conducted, were controlled by three firms. Within two years of the revolution, no less than thirty firms in Sabrata were contracting with the Libyan government. In the western part of the country (Tripoli) alone, some forty thousand new grocery licenses were issued in the first seven years of the revolution.

The object of the RCC's economic initiatives was to provide the broadest possible cross section of the Libyan population with a direct economic stake in the revolution, and thereby increase the legitimization of the RCC and undercut the position of the old elite. They enjoyed success in this effort. The economic initiatives were also successful in drawing a formerly passive population into the economic life of the country and in stimulating declining agricultural production.

The success, however, was not without its costs. The new economic programs placed a multitude of burdens upon Libya's already overextended bureaucracy, thereby further diminishing the effectiveness of that agency of the Libyan government that would be called upon to both plan and execute Libya's social and economic modernization. The economic initiatives had also resulted in a fragmentation of Libya's business community into thousands of small, understaffed, inefficient, high-cost, high-profit operations. Later consolidation would be difficult. Further, the economic initiatives accelerated the slide of native Libyans into a leisure class, willingly dependent upon foreign labor and foreign expertise. It could also be argued that the original economic initiatives further extended an entrenched dependency on government subsidies. Concerted efforts to deal with these and related problems will be discussed in the next chapter.

# 5 Mobilization and Modernization

By and large, the policies pursued during the first years of the revolution were overwhelmingly concerned with the consolidation of the revolution. The mobilization of the Libyan population in support of the goals of social and economic modernization, though clearly important to the revolutionary leadership, necessarily remained secondary to the preservation of the revolution itself.

It is difficult to say when, if ever, a revolution is consolidated, particularly a revolution that has been the object of several attempted coups, and one that remains the object of intense regional and international hostility. By the end of the first year, however, it had become evident that the revolution, however improbable its origins, would not collapse of its own weight and that effective internal opposition to the regime had been neutralized. As Qadafi's and the RCC's confidence grew, they became increasingly preoccupied with the mobilization of Libya's human and material resources in support of the goals of economic, political, and social development. This shift of emphasis was also motivated by their belief that the ultimate security of the revolution lies in the total and radical restructuring of Libya's economic, political, and social institutions.

## The Goals of Mobilization

Consolidation is essentially a matter of control. It is essentially a negative concept. It requires that the population do little more than refrain from attempts to overthrow a regime. As illustrated in the preceding chapter, the RCC acquired minimal levels of control by a variety of coercive, economic, and symbolic means ranging from the dismantling of the CDF and the police through the lavish outlay of government revenues and the elevation of Colonel Qadafi to charismatic stature. Mobilization, on the other hand, is a positive concept. It requires that the population become actively engaged in the pursuit of regime goals. Passive acceptance is no longer enough. Individuals must become involved.

The specific mobilization goals of the revolutionary leadership were fairly well defined during the first two years of the revolution; they mirror the core values of the revolutionary elite outlined in chapter 3. In economic terms, the RCC felt strongly that Libya must cease to be a rentier economy.

The total collapse of the agrarian sector that had occurred in the final years
of the monarchy had to be reversed. Libya, Colonel Qadafi proclaimed,
would become self-sufficient in the agrarian sector. In much the same manner, dependence upon foreign imports and the over-reliance upon oil revenues for economic solvency could be eliminated only by Libya's industrialization. Such industrialization, it should be noted, required both the establishment of factories and markets where none had previously existed and
the transformation of Libya's traditionally oriented bedouin and peasant
population into a "modern" labor force. The latter was to be far more difficult than the former. Although Libya had ceased to be a rural state in the
strictly demographic sense of the word, its urban characteristics were largely
a result of recent oil revenues. As the data presented in chapter 2 indicated,
the behavior of Libya's population, urban and rural, remained very traditional.

In the social arena, government mobilization targets included universal
education for both youths and adults, guaranteed housing for all Libyans,
and total cradle-to-grave health and welfare programs.

Culturally, the RCC strove to create a Libyan identity. Nationalism
was to replace parochial lineage and regional attachments. Islam was reaffirmed as the official religion of the state, but the state, not the traditional
religious leaders, would become the primary source of religious guidance.

Politically, government mobilization targets called for the total involvement of Libya's citizens in the political and economic affairs of the
state. They were to become a resource of unlimited potential. The challenge
confronting the revolutionary regime was one of overcoming centuries of
inertia and somehow welding the Libyan masses into a constructive political
and social force.

Militarily, the RCC was vitally concerned that all Libyans be prepared
to take up arms against either an internal coup or a foreign invasion. Fear
of foreign intervention, as noted earlier, was generated by the limited size of
the Libyan armed forces in relation to its oil wealth, by the vigorous nature
of Libyan foreign policy, by Colonel Qadafi's dominant role in demanding
higher oil prices, and by his anti-Western political role in general.

Finally, in addition to these target areas, Colonel Qadafi also desired a
population totally loyal to the revolution and its goals. His ability to serve
Libya as a charismatic leader required no less.

These mobilization targets formed the main content of Qadafi's
speeches as the revolution moved beyond its first years. Their presentation
to the Libyan public was characterized by two features: their urgency, and
the uncertain means of their implementation. The revolutionary leadership
was clear in its delineation of goals, but vague in specifying the means for
achievement of those goals. Libyans, Qadafi urged, must be flexible and
pragmatic in achieving the goals of the revolution. The modernization of

Libya would be a grand social experiment. Libyans would not be afraid to try new ventures or to make mistakes. Thus, Libya would become a model for other developing nations and for the international community at large.

It should be noted that the RCC's mobilization targets involved the behavioral as well as structural transformation of Libyan society. A large part of the mobilization program lies in building new economic, political, and social structures. Equally important, however, was the task of reshaping the behavior of the Libyan population to make it congruent with the goals of the regime and the newly envisioned institutional structures. Institutions, whether factories or political systems, Libya's revolutionary leaders would find, are inanimate structures. Their performance depends ultimately upon the skills and values of the individuals responsible for their manipulation. Modern factories and bureaucracies filled with tradition-oriented individuals do not work the same as their Western (or Eastern) counterparts. In this regard, one can only recall Gamal Abdul Nasser's lament, "our factories are full of peasants."

The ability of the RCC to achieve its mobilization objectives in the context of the Libyan milieu delineated in chapter 2 required exceptional performance by a variety of agents and processes of mobilization. This list includes:

1. The ability of the revolutionary leaders to set and vigorously enforce a clear set of development priorities.
2. The ability of the leadership to design a development plan capable of matching Libya's human and financial resources with the regime's developmental objectives.
3. The ability of the national bureaucracy to successfully draft and execute the provisions of the economic plan.
4. The ability of local government officials to execute and gain popular support for the government's modernization programs.
5. The ability of the leadership to establish a mass-based political organization capable of serving as an effective link between the masses and the revolutionary elite; an organization capable of penetrating the wall of mass apathy and distrust vis-à-vis the government.
6. The ability of government financial and social assistance programs to generate positive enthusiasm toward the political system and its leaders.
7. The effectiveness of media and education programs in building regime support.
8. The ability of the army to maintain order and sustain the regime's coercive support.
9. The ability of Qadafi to continue his ascendancy as a charismatic leader and to thereby provide the regime and its mobilization efforts with a sense of legitimacy (identity assets) it would otherwise lack.

The objective of this chapter is to evaluate the operation and performance of each of these agents or processes of mobilization during Libya's initial stage of revolutionary mobilization, a stage lasting approximately from 1970 to 1973. Chapters 6 and 7 will continue the description of many of the same mobilization agents and processes through two additional stages of Libya's efforts at mass mobilization. This format clearly differs from a more typical and perhaps more logical analysis in which separate chapters are devoted to topics such as the executive structure and the bureaucracy. Our particular format was dictated by the cataclysmic changes that have occurred from one mobilization stage to the next as Libya's revolutionary leaders have attempted to grapple in pragmatic and flexible ways with their myriad problems of economic, political, and social development. Structuring the discussion on a topical basis would have proved more confusing than arranging it in a sequential format which, we believe, reflects the pattern of the RCC's thinking and, in some cases, better conveys its sense of frustration and despair.

## Revolutionary Institutions and Leadership

The formal structure of the Libyan political system during the initial period of mobilization consisted of two bodies: the RCC and the cabinet. Lines separating the two bodies were fluid, with the revolutionary leadership experimenting with various means of filling cabinet positions ranging from the technocratic model through a model in which most major cabinet positions were held by members of the RCC or the top strata of free officers. The cabinet did, however, continue to reflect a regional balance between Libya's three main geographic regions, an indication that undercurrents of the Tripoli-Cyrenaica-Fezzan rivalry remained very much alive during the revolution.

The relative cohesion of the formal decision-making apparatus and its ability to make firm, hard, and often spontaneous decisions were in large measure a result of the clear status hierarchy that had emerged within the RCC and, ipso facto, within the cabinet. Qadafi clearly dominated the decision-making hierarchy, followed in order by Jalloud and other members of the revolutionary hierarchy outlined in chapter 3.

Interviews with officials indicated that the pattern of decision making during this stage of Libyan history was one of vigorous discussion among members of the RCC, with Qadafi playing the role of "involved moderator," raising questions, shifting his weight from one faction to another, and eventually declaring his interpretation of the group consensus. Decisions, once declared, were overtly supported by all members of the RCC and cabinet. Qadafi's shifting of support from one group to another served to keep discussions open and precluded excessive rigidity among RCC ranks.

Politically aware Libyans soon sensed the dominance of Qadafi's position and began to seize upon his speeches and public statements as reference points to justify their own behavior. With the legal codes of the monarchy in doubt and the RCC and cabinet lacking sufficient time to totally revise and codify administrative regulations and procedures, Qadafi's statements soon carried the weight of law, often being cited as evidence in jurisdictional disputes among various government agencies. This trend increased dramatically as Qadafi gained stature as a charismatic leader.

In evaluating the revolutionary leadership vis-à-vis its role as an agent of mobilization during this period, one can easily applaud its sincerity and enthusiasm. Indeed, it might be suggested that the RCC was perhaps too enthusiastic. Its urgency in pursuing its mobilization programs placed tremendous pressure on the bureaucracy and local officials to show immediate results, regardless of how they were achieved or how superficial they might be.

Also, RCC members, in their enthusiasm to stimulate modernization, crisscrossed the countryside, visiting villages at will, discussing needed improvements with both the general public and local leaders, often pledging that such improvements would receive top priority. Such pledges were honored, and direct involvement of the RCC did provide clear impetus to their mobilization efforts. Such direct involvement, however, was not without its costs. Spontaneous on-site decisions by RCC members often conflicted with the budgetary priorities of local and provincial administrators, forcing them to deviate from established schedules. It also caused a certain amount of hesitancy on the part of local administrators who were fearful of their ability to anticipate RCC priorities.

In summation, however, the revolutionary leadership was a strong and direct force in behalf of Libya's modernization. Its enthusiasm for development, in fact, far outdistanced the enthusiasm and effectiveness of the other agents of mobilization to be discussed in this chapter.

## The Modernizing Administrators

From a theoretical perspective, clearly the most interesting and innovative program of the RCC's early attempts at mass mobilization was the restructuring of local government boundaries in a manner that fragmented tribal loyalties and replaced tribal-based administrators with a core of achievement-oriented modernizers selected more or less according to merit.

While tribal-based officials were in the process of being purged, a committee of twelve recent graduates from Libya's colleges, who held positions in the national civil service and were judged loyal to the regime, was convened to identify individuals they knew who met three general criteria: modernizing values, technical competence, and a socioeconomic background that precluded strong ties with the dominant tribal leadership. The individuals receiving the most nominations by the selection committee were then appointed to the governorships and mayoralties of Libya's newly established administrative districts. We will refer to this group as modernizing local elites or modernizing administrators.

The goal assigned to the modernizing local elites was to bring the revolution to the Libyan masses; to break the hold of the traditional tribal elites over the masses by demonstrating the importance of socioeconomic modernization to the very core of Libya's traditional population. As the RCC was pursuing the modernization of Libya from the top down, so the modernizers were to pursue the modernization of Libya from the bottom up.

The RCC's experimental substitution of modernizing administrators in roles generally reserved for tribal leaders raised several theoretical questions concerning the best means of mobilizing a large tradition-oriented mass. The RCC clearly assumed, for example, that the traditional tribal elites would oppose any political, social, or economic modernization programs that they saw as undermining the ascriptive basis for their authority, an assumption shared by most modernization theorists.[1] One question of clear theoretical importance thus concerns whether Libya's traditional local leaders were indeed opposed to change or whether they might have been co-opted into the change process.

The experiment also raised the question of whether outside modernizers lacking strong local credentials would be able to garner sufficient respect among the local populations to win support for the government's modernization programs. Would the local populations follow outsiders, or were they wedded to their traditional elites? To what extent could economic modernization be facilitated merely by changing the emphasis of local leadership?

*Traditional Local Elites versus Modernization*

The 1973 survey of Zawia province addressed these questions in some detail. When asked their views of the new modernizing administrations, for example, the ten tribal leaders minced few words.[2] The response patterns displayed in table 5-1 were frequently augmented by comments to the effect that the modernizing administrators were "young kids" and "green behind the ears" and that the Arab Socialist Union was a "kid's game."

A particularly interesting aspect of the attitudes of traditional tribal elites vis-à-vis modernization was provided when we contrasted their views of village needs with the views of an equal number of technical experts on community development, the results of which are provided in table 5-2. The results indicate a high level of congruence in the attitudes of the tribal lead-

**Table 5-1**

**Attitudes of Traditional Rural Elites toward Modernizing Administrators**
($n = 10$)

|  | Yes | No | Nonresponse |
|---|---|---|---|
| Would you consult with leaders of the local ASU in reference to community development? | 1 | 9 | — |
| Would you consult with national leaders of the ASU to promote community development? | 1 | 9 | — |
| Local government is staffed by competent people. | 1 | 8 | 1 |
| Public officials are concerned with bettering the community. | 0 | 10 | — |

**Table 5-2**

**Community Needs as Perceived by Traditional Leaders and Government Experts**

| Community Needs | Evaluation by Traditional Leaders | | Evaluation by Experts | |
|---|---|---|---|---|
|  | (n = 10) | | (n = 10) | |
|  | Inadequate | Adequate | Inadequate | Adequate |
| Worker productivity | 1 | 9 | 10 | 0 |
| Distribution of resources | 3 | 7 | 8 | 2 |
| Agricultural growth | 3 | 7 | 8 | 2 |
| Popular support for development | 2 | 8 | 10 | 0 |
| Commercial development | 0 | 10 | 5 | 5 |
| Housing problems | 2 | 8 | 8 | 2 |
| Transportation/communications | 4 | 6 | 8 | 2 |
| Utilities (water, sewage) | 6 | 4 | 10 | 0 |
| Education/culture | 3 | 7 | 7 | 3 |
| Health and medicine | 5 | 5 | 8 | 2 |
| Technical skills | 9 | 1 | 10 | 0 |
| Social welfare | 0 | 10 | 0 | 10 |
| Underemployment | 8 | 2 | 10 | 0 |

ers and experts toward specific problems such as the lack of technical skill or underemployment. But their responses to items relating to the need for increased productivity, however, were almost totally incongruent.

In sum, then, the traditional elites showed little inclination toward innovation or development either in terms of attitudinal predispositions or in perceiving innovative ways of improving the life in their villages. They were not, however, hostile to the abstract concept of change or to the desire to see the quality of life in their villages improved. They simply did not think in change-related or innovative terms. Their resistance to political change, however, was adamant, and they showed little inclination to cooperate or work within the structure of revolutionary institutions.

The data, then, suggested that the RCC was essentially correct in its contention that traditional local elites were not compatible with the scope and urgency of the regime's mobilization efforts. How successful, then, were its efforts to replace traditional local elites with young, educated modernizers? Can a radical change in local leadership, of itself, spur political and economic development?

*Modernizing Local Administrators: Mass Acceptance*

There are several viewpoints from which one could evaluate the success of the modernizing administrators program. From the perspective of political development, for example, one clear indicator of its success would be the extent to which it had succeeded in replacing the traditional ascriptive elites as the focal point of mass loyalty. Clearly, unless they won the loyalty of the masses, the modernizing administrators would find it difficult to either counter the opposition of the traditional elites or to mobilize the masses in support of regime goals.

The 1973 survey, conducted at the conclusion of the modernizing administrators experiment, addressed this question directly. Each of our 576 respondents, for example, was requested to identify the one or two individuals he felt was best suited to run the village. Each respondent was also requested to indicate the reasons for his choices. The data summarized in table 5-3, indicate that 68 percent of the respondents expressed a strong preference for the traditional tribal elites, while only 32 percent expressed a preference for the modernizing administrators.

Perhaps more illuminating in this regard were the attributes listed as the basis for leadership preference. As indicated in table 5-3, 40 percent of the sample listed purely ascriptive attributes, such as lineage and religiosity, as the basis for their preference. Only 25 percent, by contrast, listed purely achievement-oriented criteria, such as education and administrative experience, as the basis for their selections. The remaining 35 percent of the sample listed a mixture of achievement and ascriptive values.

Responses to these items were merged into a leadership preference scale: individuals who chose a purely traditional leader and purely ascriptive

**Table 5-3**
**Leadership Preference among Rural Libyans**
(*percentages*)

| | |
|---|---|
| Preferred elites | |
| Ascriptive | 67.8 |
| Achievement | 32.2 |
| | (n = 537) |
| Preferred leadership attributes | |
| Ascriptive | 40.2 |
| Mixed | 34.5 |
| Achievement | 25.2 |
| | (n = 527) |
| Leadership preference scale | |
| Ascriptive | 35.4 |
| Mixed | 49.4 |
| Modern | 15.2 |
| | (n = 527) |

attributes were in the most traditional category; individuals who listed non-traditional administrators and purely achievement attributes were in the most modern category. The marginal distributions for this scale (table 5-3) indicate that 35 percent of the respondents manifested strong ascriptive leadership preferences, whereas 15 percent showed a preference for leaders with achievement values. These figures offer strong support for the proposition that members of Libya's rural-oriented population did, indeed, provide a strong basis of popular support for the traditional elite structure, and that the modernizing administrators had failed to supplant the traditional local elites as the focal point of mass loyalties. This was particularly true among the more rural respondents.[3]

Given a clear predisposition on the part of the masses to retain their loyalty to Libya's traditional elites, the effectiveness of the modernizing administrators in mobilizing the local population in support of the RCC's developmental objectives depended to an even larger measure upon the level of trust or effective support they received from the Libyan population. If the modernizing administrators could gain the trust of their communities, they would serve as invaluable links in overcoming inertia, by persuading their subjects of the benefits of change and by inducing them to give revolutionary programs a chance to demonstrate their value. If, on the contrary, the modernizing administrators became the objects of doubt and hostility, their ability to promote social and economic reform would likely be nil.

To examine mass attitudes toward supporting the modernizing administrators and accepting reform programs, the questionnaire asked the re-

**Table 5-4**
**Evaluation of Modernizing Mayors**
(*percentages*)

|  | Public | Popular Committees | Traditional Local Elites |
|---|---|---|---|
| The mayor runs the town to suit himself. | | | |
| Very true | 16.0 | 13.3 | 0 |
| True | 29.0 | 33.3 | 10 |
| Untrue | 41.1 | 45.0 | 90 |
| very true | 13.0 | 8.3 | 0 |
|  | (n = 561) | (n = 60) | (n = 10) |
| The mayor gets very little done. | | | |
| Very true | 17.7 | 16.7 | 30 |
| True | 33.7 | 30.0 | 60 |
| Untrue | 25.5 | 41.7 | 10 |
| Very untrue | 13.1 | 11.7 | 0 |
|  | (n = 566) | (n = 60) | (n = 10) |
| The mayor does not represent the community at all. | | | |
| Very true | 12.3 | 15.3 | 0 |
| True | 29.0 | 23.7 | 0 |
| Untrue | 42.3 | 50.8 | 100 |
| Very untrue | 16.5 | 10.2 | 0 |
|  | (n = 563) | (n = 59) | (n = 10) |
| The mayor is not accepted by the majority of the community. | | | |
| Very true | 14.2 | 15.0 | 20 |
| True | 33.2 | 30.0 | 70 |
| Untrue | 39.8 | 41.7 | 10 |
| Very untrue | 12.9 | 13.3 | 0 |
|  | (n = 568) | (n = 60) | (n = 10) |
| Mayor performance scale | | | |
| Bad | 13.1 | 16.9 | 0 |
| Poor | 29.1 | 22.0 | 40 |
| Good | 38.9 | 44.1 | 60 |
| Excellent | 18.2 | 16.9 | 0 |
|  | (n = 561) | (n = 59) | (n = 10) |

spondents to evaluate the mayors of their villages and local officials in general. It should be noted that all of the mayors in question were "modernizers" appointed by the revolutionary government to stimulate the economic and social development of the area. This was also partially true of the public officials. In most instances, they, too, had replaced ascriptive tribal administrators and generally had few ties with the tribal rural elites. Tables 5-4 and 5-5 survey the respondents' evaluations of their mayors and local administrators. Table 5-6, in turn, evaluates local leadership in general. Combined scales were also constructed for each set of items and appear at the bottom of each table. Break points for the scales can be found in the notes section.[4]

The percentages presented in tables 5-5 and 5-6 indicate that approximately 50 percent of our respondents manifested at least minimal hostility toward the mayors and administrators appointed by the central government. Moreover, a reluctance on the part of many respondents to criticize the government may have disguised some latent hostility toward the local administrative structure.

Nevertheless, the percentages in tables 5-5 and 5-6 fail to reflect the pervasive opposition to the modernizing administrators that might well have been anticipated given the traditionalism of the Libyan population and the clear hostility of the traditional rural elites to the modernizing administrators program, further evidence of which is provided by the traditional elite column of tables 5-4, 5-5, and 5-6. The popular committee column in

**Table 5-5**
**Evaluation of Local and Provincial Administrators**
(*percentages*)

|  | Public | Popular Committees | Traditional Local Elites |
|---|---|---|---|
| They are popular and trusted by the public. |  |  |  |
| Yes | 52.6 | 22.8 | 10 |
| No | 47.4 | 77.2 | 90 |
|  | (n = 563) | (n = 56) | (n = 10) |
| They have the ability and quality of leadership. |  |  |  |
| Yes | 55.0 | 25.0 | 10 |
| No | 45.0 | 75.0 | 90 |
|  | (n = 562) | (n = 56) | (n = 10) |
| They are dedicated and decisive in their work. |  |  |  |
| Yes | 58.0 | 32.7 | 30 |
| No | 42.0 | 67.3 | 70 |
|  | (n = 564) | (n = 55) | (n = 10) |
| They represent the majority of the community. |  |  |  |
| Yes | 49.0 | 25.9 | 0 |
| No | 51.0 | 74.4 | 100 |
|  | (n = 563) | (n = 58) | (n = 10) |
| Administration performance scale |  |  |  |
| Bad | 32.4 | 56.9 | 70 |
| Poor | 9.9 | 11.8 | 20 |
| Good | 18.3 | 17.6 | 10 |
| Excellent | 39.4 | 13.7 | 0 |
|  | (n = 562) | (n = 55) | (n = 10) |

**Table 5-6**
**Evaluation of Local Leadership in General**
(*percentages*)

|  | Public | Popular Committees | Traditional Local Elites |
|---|---|---|---|
| Local leaders I know are very successful. | | | |
| Agree | 55.9 | 25.9 | 10 |
| Disagree | 44.1 | 74.1 | 90 |
|  | (n = 591) | (n = 58) | (n = 10) |
| They provide assistance to most citizens. | | | |
| Agree | 60.7 | 41.7 | 10 |
| Disagree | 39.3 | 58.3 | 90 |
|  | (n = 568) | (n = 60) | (n = 10) |
| Local government is successful in assisting agricultural development. | | | |
| Agree | 49.7 | 16.7 | 0 |
| Disagree | 50.3 | 83.3 | 100 |
|  | (n = 564) | (n = 60) | (n = 10) |
| Local government is successful in stimulating business. | | | |
| Agree | 55.4 | 23.7 | 20 |
| Disagree | 44.6 | 76.3 | 80 |
|  | (n = 570) | (n = 59) | (n = 10) |
| Local government is interested in citizen welfare. | | | |
| Agree | 52.3 | 18.6 | 60 |
| Disagree | 47.7 | 81.4 | 40 |
|  | (n = 568) | (n = 59) | (n = 10) |
| Local government has the ability to solve community problems. | | | |
| Agree | 47.3 | 25.9 | 10 |
| Disagree | 52.7 | 74.1 | 90 |
|  | (n = 567) | (n = 59) | (n = 10) |

the three tables also displays the hostility of the masses toward the modernizing administrators and will be explained shortly. What the figures do reflect, however, is that the local administration did lack sufficiently broad popular support to generate any real enthusiasm for the new and innovative programs. To be tolerated by the masses is not necessarily to lead.

Yet a third basis for evaluating the success of modernizing administrators was provided by the self-evaluations of the administrators themselves. In this regard, table 5-7 summarizes the self-evaluation of twenty modernizing mayors interviewed as part of the 1973 Zawia project. Although perceiving themselves as well regarded by the community, the majority of the ad-

**Table 5-7**
**Self-Evaluations by Modernizing Mayors**
($n = 20$)

|  | Excellent | Strong | Weak | Very Weak |
|---|---|---|---|---|
| How would your community evaluate your performance? | 25 | 65 | 5 | 5 |
| How would you evaluate your performance? | 5 | 20 | 70 | 5 |
| What would be your chances of being elected to your office by the community? | 15 | 30 | 40 | 15 |

ministrators clearly felt that their performance had been below par and that they had failed to gain sufficient support to be elected in their own right.

All three methods of evaluating the modernizing administrators program, then, suggest that it was not successful in providing a basis for the rapid mobilization of the Libyan population. The RCC had the same view, for the program was ended in 1973 and replaced by the popular revolution, which will be discussed in the next chapter.

*Modernizing Administrators: A Critique*

The importance of the modernizing administrator experiment as a potential vehicle for modernization both in Libya and other developing areas suggests that we take a closer look at just why the experiment failed and how it might have been improved.

The substantial opposition of the traditional elites to the modernizing administrators has already been documented and certainly contributed to their difficulties. Tables 5-4, 5-5, and 5-6 also indicate that the members of the popular committees who replaced the modernizing administrators as Libya's local officialdom also manifested considerable hostility toward the modernizing administrators. Thus, right from the start, the opposition of virtually all competing community leaders to the program was a clear strike against the modernizers. Nevertheless, tables 5-4, 5-5, and 5-6 also indicate that the public at large was far more supportive of the modernizing administrators than either the traditional elites or the popular committees. If other factors had not been present, the opposition of the traditional local elites might well have been overcome.

In an effort to gain a complete picture of the problems faced by the modernizing administrators, the 1973 survey approached the topic from two points of view: 1) responses by modernizing administrators to problems

**Table 5-8**

**Major Problems Limiting the Effectiveness of Modernizing Administrators**
(*n = 20*)

|  | Percentage |
| --- | --- |
| 1. Lack of skilled labor | 100 |
| 2. Lack of general labor | 95 |
| 3. Lack of adequate funds | 95 |
| 4. Lack of material resources | 95 |
| 5. Conflict among social groups | 85 |
| 6. Public ignorance and negativism | 85 |
| 7. Other public attitudes | 80 |
| 8. Conflict between political factions | 55 |
| 9. Lack of economic infrastructure | 55 |
| 10. Lack of bureaucratic support | 50 |
| 11. Lack of agrarian infrastructure | 35 |
| 12. Lack of public participation and involvement | 25 |
| 13. Low worker productivity | 15 |

**Table 5-9**

**Self-Evaluation by Modernizing Mayors: Major Reasons for Failure**
(*n = 12; 8 nonresponses*)

|  | Percentage |
| --- | --- |
| 1. Tribalism | 91.7 |
| 2. Low public regard for common interest (atomism) | 75.0 |
| 3. Lack of public cooperation | 66.7 |
| 4. Lack of civic responsibility | 33.0 |
| 5. Lack of authority | 25.0 |
| 6. Public negativism and apathy | 16.7 |

suggested by the interviewer, and 2) an identification of problems by the modernizing administrators themselves. Table 5-8 rank orders responses to items suggested by the interviewer as limiting the effectiveness of the modernizing administrators in the performance of their duties. Table 5-9, in turn, rank orders the modernizing administrators' evaluations of the areas of their greatest failure. Only 12 of the 20 mayors, it should be noted, availed themselves of the opportunity to discuss their failures.

Although approaching the problems of the modernizing administrators from slightly different positions, the two tables present a very consistent picture. The main trouble spots were clearly structural problems relating to a lack of skilled labor and inadequate resources, and behavioral problems relating to manifestations of tribalism and atomism (lack of public regard and a general lack of civic responsiveness). Two additional areas of difficulty, bureaucratic coordination and group conflict, were evident, but were of a lesser order.

In reference to the problems listed in table 5-8, one can only wonder why financial shortages should have almost universally been cited as a major problem of local leaders in an exceedingly wealthy country where the leadership had pledged its total support to local modernization. We suggest that the problem lies not in the shortage of money for local projects, but in the inordinately difficult bureaucratic red tape involved in channeling the money from the treasury to the local level.

In addition to the hostility of competing local elites, the apathy of the masses, and other problems discussed, it is also probable that many of the difficulties confronting the modernizing administrators were of their own making or resulted from the values and expectations they brought to their positions. With this thought in mind, the 1973 questionnaire contained a variety of questions designed to probe the values and behavior of the modernizing administrators. Table 5-10, for example, summarizes the leadership priorities of both modernizing administrators and traditional rural elites. Table 5-11, similarly, indicates the areas of greatest activity by the modernizing administrators as well as their own evaluations of their relative success in each area.

The picture that emerges from both tables is that the modernizing administrators did not appear to be overly concerned with modernization. Although 85 percent of the modernizers indicated that economic development was among their most important priorities, only 15 percent listed it as top priority. Perhaps more revealing is the fact that 70 percent of the administrators listed conflict avoidance as an important priority, and that 30 percent stated that it was their top priority. A similar picture emerges from table 5-11 with only half of the administrators listing economic development as a major area of concern (and an unsuccessful one), and almost all suggesting that their activities had been directed toward visible public improvements (buildings) and budgeting considerations. Both tables also indicate that the modernizing administrators made virtually no efforts toward political mobilization. In Table 5-10, for example, it is shown that only 20 percent of the modernizing administrators considered the development of citizen participation to be a priority concern. Table 5-11 similarly indicates that only 30 percent of the modernizing administrators were involved in the development of the political organization. Few felt their efforts were particularly successful. Both tables 5-10 and 5-11, then, suggest that the modern-

**Table 5-10**
**Priorities of Local Leadership**
(*percentages*)

| Which of the following do you consider to be your top priority? | Modernizing Administrators (n = 20) | Traditional Administrators (n = 10) |
|---|---|---|
| Economic development of society | | |
| Yes | 85 | 30 |
| No | 15 | 70 |
| Avoiding conflict and maintaining community harmony | | |
| Yes | 70 | 90 |
| No | 30 | 10 |
| National goals versus local goals | | |
| Yes | 10 | 10 |
| No | 90 | 90 |
| Providing citizen participation in local affairs | | |
| Yes | 20 | 40 |
| No | 80 | 60 |
| Finding new solutions for old problems | | |
| Yes | 75 | 90 |
| No | 25 | 10 |
| Education and motivation of youth | | |
| Yes | 65 | 80 |
| No | 35 | 20 |
| Which of the above is most important? | | |
| Economic development | 15 | 0 |
| Avoiding conflict | 30 | 20 |
| National versus local goals | 0 | 0 |
| Citizen participation | 5 | 0 |
| New solutions | 20 | 60 |
| Education/motivation | 30 | 20 |

izing administrator was not the proverbial ball of fire that the title might suggest. Indeed, when the priorities of the modernizers are compared with the priorities of the traditional leaders, very few differences are evident.

The modernizing administrators were also asked a variety of questions relating to their decision-making strategies, the results of which are summarized in tables 5-12 and 5-13. The items in table 5-12 were asked only of modernizing administrators; those in table 5-13 were directed to both the modernizing and the traditional leaders.

The data presented in both tables again provide a picture of administrators anxious to avoid community conflict and more than willing to sacrifice economic development priorities to the preservation of traditional values. Table 5-13 also provides a picture of the modernizing administrators as rather timid and as being unlikely to make waves whatever the cause in-

**Table 5-11**
**Areas of Emphasis by Modernizing Administrators**
(*percentages*)

|  |  | Level of Success | | |
| --- | --- | --- | --- | --- |
| *In which of the following areas have you been most active and successful?* | *Active (n = 20)* | *High* | *Medium* | *Low (n = 20)* |
| Economic development | 50 | 10 | 45 | 45 |
| Agriculture | 15 | 0 | 45 | 55 |
| Housing | 35 | 5 | 40 | 55 |
| Improving public buildings and facilities | 90 | 65 | 25 | 10 |
| Health services | 30 | 10 | 50 | 40 |
| Cultural services | 35 | 5 | 60 | 35 |
| Education | 15 | 0 | 20 | 80 |
| Social services | 70 | 35 | 50 | 15 |
| Building political organization | 30 | 10 | 30 | 60 |
| Budgetary activity | 80 | 70 | 15 | 15 |

**Table 5-12**
**Leadership Predispositions of Modernizing Administrators**
(*percentages*)

|  | *Strongly Agree* | *Agree* | *Disagree* | *Strongly Disagree* | *Sample Size* |
| --- | --- | --- | --- | --- | --- |
| It is best to cancel or change programs that could cause conflict. | 0.0 | 60.0 | 35.0 | 5.0 | 20 |
| Public decisions should have the unanimous consent of the (local current population). | 15.0 | 65.0 | 20.0 | 5.0 | 20 |
| In making a decision, it is best to reach as many interests as possible. | 5.0 | 95.0 | 0.0 | 0.0 | 20 |
| Local officials are overconcerned with resolving conflict. | 15.8 | 78.9 | 5.3 | 0.0 | 14 |
| Community harmony is more important than achieving the development plans. | 0.0 | 45.0 | 50.0 | 5.0 | 20 |
| A wise leader will promote harmony even at the expense of the community interest. | 0.0 | 68.4 | 26.3 | 5.3 | 20 |
| If a development project starts with the complete agreement of all factions and blocs, it soon becomes impossible to implement. | 10.5 | 73.7 | 15.8 | 0.0 | 19 |
| Social change should not be instituted at the expense of traditional values. | 31.6 | 68.4 | 0.0 | 0.0 | 11 |

**Table 5-13**

**Decision-Making Predispositions of Modernizing Administrators and Traditional Local Elites**

(*percentages*)

|  | Modernizing Administrators (n = 20) | Traditional Local Elites (n = 10) |
|---|---|---|
| I prefer to stop and think things over before making decisions, even on the smallest matters. | | |
| Strongly agree | 5 | 10 |
| Agree | 95 | 90 |
| Disagree | 0 | 0 |
| Strongly disagree | 0 | 0 |
| I generally consider matters at least twice to make sure I am not exceeding the bounds of my authority. | | |
| Strongly agree | 10 | 10 |
| Agree | 80 | 70 |
| Disagree | 10 | 20 |
| Strongly disagree | 0 | 0 |
| People should be more concerned with what they have than what they can get. | | |
| Strongly agree | 15 | 10 |
| Agree | 80 | 90 |
| Disagree | 5 | 0 |
| Strongly disagree | 0 | 0 |
| One should delay decisions until positive results are assured. | | |
| Strongly agree | 20 | 10 |
| Agree | 70 | 90 |
| Disagree | 10 | 0 |
| Strongly disagree | 0 | 0 |

volved. Indeed, the modernizers emerged every bit as cautious as their traditional predecessors.

Yet a third set of questions asked the modernizing administrators to indicate the different groups in the population and in other government agencies with whom they consulted on a regular basis. They were also asked to indicate which of the listed agencies they considered their most important source of support. The results are summarized in table 5-14, as are the results of similar items directed toward our sample of traditional local elites.

Perhaps the most important finding to emerge from table 5-14 is the fact that the modernizing administrators aligned themselves almost totally with the traditional bureaucratic apparatus of the state, an apparatus that had been publicly condemned as inefficient, noninnovative, and corrupt.

**Table 5-14**
**Comparative Reference Points for Traditional Local Elites and**
**Modernizing Administrators**
(*percentages*)

| Which of the following groups would you seek the active support of in implementing your programs? | Consultation Status | | Important Source of Support | |
|---|---|---|---|---|
| | Modernizing Administrators (*n = 20*) | Traditional Local Elites (*n = 10*) | Modernizing Administrators | Traditional Local Elites |
| Local Arab Socialist Union leaders | 15 | 10 | 5 | 10 |
| Higher Arab Socialist Union leaders | 5 | 0 | 0 | 0 |
| Higher administrative officials | 95 | 100 | 95 | 100 |
| Religious leaders | 15 | 20 | 0 | 0 |
| Influential community leaders | 55 | 100 | 45 | 80 |
| Upper socioeconomic class | 5 | 10 | 0 | 0 |
| Close friends and backers | 45 | 90 | 10 | 20 |
| Police authority | 55 | 80 | 15 | 30 |
| Central government | 85 | 90 | 90 | 70 |
| Public in general | 30 | 60 | 90 | 70 |
| Educated public (opinion brokers) | 20 | 70 | 5 | 0 |

By the same token, the modernizing administrators neither consulted nor were supported by the ASU at either the local or national level, a fact suggesting the existence of conflict between the two groups. Yet another clear trend in table 5-14, and one reminiscent of similar trends in earlier tables, is that the consultation and support patterns of the modernizing administrators reflected their marked reluctance to consult with either the general or the educated public, thereby isolating themselves from local opinion leaders and placing themselves in direct opposition to the RCC efforts to generate greater mass participation.

The isolation of the modernizing administrators from the general public was also stressed in our samples of the public, traditional administrators, and popular committee members. As the figures in table 5-15 indicate, more than half of the public respondents found the modernizing administrators to be isolated and remote; almost all of the popular committee members and traditional elites found them to be so.

In summary, then, the attitudes and behavioral predispositions of the modernizing administrators did not make them the hard-driving change agents that the RCC had hoped for. Rather than being revolutionary cadres, the modernizing administrators came perilously close to resembling

**Table 5-15**
**Evaluation of Interaction between Modernizing Administrators and the Public**
(*percentages*)

|  | Public | Popular Committee Members | Traditional Local Elites |
|---|---|---|---|
| Officials listen to community opinions on community affairs. | | | |
| Agree | 47.8 | 23.7 | 10 |
| Disagree | 52.2 | 76.3 | 90 |
|  | (n = 569) | (n = 59) | (n = 10) |
| Officials ask for citizen opinions frequently. | | | |
| Agree | 42.5 | 10.2 | 0 |
| Disagree | 57.5 | 89.8 | 100 |
|  | (n = 569) | (n = 59) | |
| Officials encourage the public to participate. | | | |
| Agree | 42.1 | 0.3 | 10 |
| Disagree | 57.7 | 89.7 | 90 |
|  | (n = 565) | (n = 58) | |
| Officials discuss community problems with the public. | | | |
| Agree | 42.5 | 20.3 | 0 |
| Disagree | 57.5 | 79.7 | 100 |
|  | (n = 570) | (n = 58) | |

the typical Libyan bureaucrats. Their preoccupation with conflict avoidance and their caution in decision making made them questionable modernizers at best. Confronted with a generally apathetic, if not hostile, local environment, their effectiveness as modernizing local leaders was minimal. In the eyes of the RCC, the modernizers had clearly failed the test as mobilizers. The program was scrapped.

From the perspective of evaluating the capacity of the revolutionary regime to execute its programs, the failure of the modernizing administrators program was particularly unfortunate, for with it passed the opportunity to develop a professional, merit-based cadre of local administrators. As we will see in the final chapter of the book, at least some efforts have been made to return to the concept of modernizing administrators by inducing university professors to share in the tasks of local and regional administration.

## Nationalism and Legitimacy via the Distribution of Wealth

Though less dramatic than the modernizing administrators program, the early mobilization goals of the RCC also involved strenuous efforts to initi-

**Table 5-16**
**General Economic Satisfaction**
(*percentages*)

|  | Public |
|---|---|
| People appreciate the government's efforts to improve their living. | |
| Strongly agree | 14.9 |
| Agree | 76.7 |
| Disagree | 7.9 |
| Strongly disagree | 1.4 |
|  | (n = 529) |
| Jobs are available to anyone who needs one. | |
| Strongly agree | 7.7 |
| Agree | 46.1 |
| Disagree | 40.6 |
| Strongly disagree | 6.0 |
|  | (n = 570) |
| Our economic system is fair and just. | |
| Strongly agree | 21.0 |
| Agree | 53.5 |
| Disagree | 23.2 |
| Strongly disagree | 2.3 |
|  | (n = 561) |
| How do you rate your income? | |
| Very satisfactory | 3.5 |
| Satisfactory | 35.7 |
| Adequate | 30.3 |
| Unsatisfactory | 23.5 |
|  | (n = 563) |

ate or accelerate a variety of reform programs designed to better the standard of living for the average Libyan and, it was hoped, to create among the Libyan population a sense of nationalism and a feeling of positive affectivity toward the central government. The development of a sense of national awareness and positive affectivity was crucial to the RCC's efforts to mobilize the masses and establish a sense of legitimacy for the revolution. The Libyan population, as noted in earlier chapters, had traditionally manifested hostility toward any central government and had viewed virtually all government initiatives with doubt and suspicion. Unless a sense of awareness and trust toward the government could be developed among the masses, mobilization behind the RCC's reform programs would go for naught. The drive to build mass awareness of and trust for the political system was also crucial to Qadafi's emergence as a charismatic leader. The two programs were to work together in building a mass base for support for the revolution and its goals. Because of the importance of the government's

**Table 5-17**

**Levels of Support for Government Reform and Welfare Measures**
(*percentages*)

| | Public | Popular Committees (n = 60) | Traditional Local Elites (n = 10) |
|---|---|---|---|
| **Agriculture** | | | |
| Farmers get all the assistance they need to increase and improve their production. | | | |
| Strongly agree | 24.9 | 20.0 | 10 |
| Agree | 60.6 | 63.3 | 20 |
| Disagree | 12.7 | 12.7 | 70 |
| Strongly disagree | 1.8 | 0.0 | 0 |
| | (n = 566) | | |
| The farmer's standard of living is going up as never before. | | | |
| Strongly agree | 25.9 | 16.7 | 0 |
| Agree | 58.6 | 68.3 | 100 |
| Disagree | 14.1 | 13.3 | 0 |
| Strongly disagree | 1.4 | 1.7 | 0 |
| | (n = 567) | | |
| Most agricultural problems are taken care of by our government. | | | |
| Strongly agree | 22.6 | 8.3 | 0 |
| Agree | 61.9 | 58.3 | 20 |
| Disagree | 14.7 | 20.0 | 80 |
| Strongly disagree | .7 | 3.3 | 0 |
| | (n = 570) | | |
| Agricultural satisfaction scale | | | |
| Excellent | 10.1 | 8.3 | 0 |
| Very good | 24.8 | 16.7 | 10 |
| Good/satisfactory | 52.5 | 61.7 | 20 |
| Poor/bad | 12.6 | 13.3 | 70 |
| | (n = 564) | | |
| **Health** | | | |
| Local government provides approaches to improving the health of the entire community. | | | |
| Strongly agree | 11.9 | 3.3 | 0 |
| Agree | 59.5 | 38.3 | 20 |
| Disagree | 24.2 | 50.0 | 70 |
| Strongly disagree | 4.4 | 8.3 | 10 |
| | (n = 570) | | |
| Medical care and hospitalization is readily available to the community. | | | |
| Strongly agree | 13.1 | 6.7 | 0 |
| Agree | 49.0 | 30.0 | 0 |
| Disagree | 32.9 | 55.0 | 80 |
| Strongly disagree | 4.9 | 8.3 | 20 |
| | (n = 571) | | |

*Table 5-17 continued*

|  | Public | Popular Committees (n = 60) | Traditional Local Elites (n = 10) |
|---|---|---|---|
| Health satisfaction scale |  |  |  |
| Excellent | 15.5 | 6.7 | 0 |
| Good | 41.7 | 21.7 | 0 |
| Poor | 20.2 | 20.0 | 20 |
| Bad | 22.7 | 51.7 | 80 |
|  | (n = 569) |  |  |
| Housing and Transportation |  |  |  |
| We have good housing and plans for improvement of residential areas. |  |  |  |
| Strongly agree | 6.6 | 1.7 | 0 |
| Agree | 39.6 | 26.7 | 0 |
| Disagree | 41.2 | 63.3 | 90 |
| Strongly disagree | 12.6 | 8.3 | 10 |
|  | (n = 573) |  |  |
| We have good recreational areas. |  |  |  |
| Strongly agree | 5.9 | .1 | 0 |
| Agree | 36.6 | 26.7 | 0 |
| Disagree | 41.4 | 61.7 | 90 |
| Strongly disagree | 16.1 | 10.0 | 10 |
|  | (n = 573) |  |  |
| We have good highways, traffic, transportation; and other facilities are under way in our community. |  |  |  |
| Strongly agree | 5.8 | 1.7 | 0 |
| Agree | 36.5 | 23.3 | 0 |
| Disagree | 40.8 | 66.7 | 90 |
| Strongly disagree | 16.9 | 8.3 | 10 |
|  | (n = 573) |  |  |
| Housing and transportation statisfaction scale |  |  |  |
| Excellent | 6.1 | 1.7 | 0 |
| Good | 37.2 | 20.0 | 0 |
| Poor | 38.7 | 66.7 | 90 |
| Bad | 18.0 | 11.7 | 10 |
|  | (n = 573) |  |  |
| Education |  |  |  |
| Our teachers are highly qualified and dedicated. |  |  |  |
| Strongly agree | 14.7 | 11.7 | 0 |
| Agree | 59.6 | 41.7 | 10 |
| Disagree | 22.5 | 43.3 | 90 |
| Strongly disagree | 3.2 | 3.3 | 0 |
|  | (n = 565) |  |  |
| Our schools have good facilities for modern education and are generally in good condition. |  |  |  |
| Strongly agree | 9.9 | 5.0 | 0 |
| Agree | 43.5 | 43.3 | 40 |
| Disagree | 40.5 | 45.0 | 60 |
| Strongly disagree | 6.2 | 6.7 | 0 |
|  | (n = 566) |  |  |

*Table 5-17 continued*

| | Public | Popular Committees (n = 60) | Traditional Local Elites (n = 10) |
|---|---|---|---|
| Education satisfaction scale (School): | | | |
| Excellent | 14.1 | 10.0 | 0 |
| Good | 34.6 | 28.3 | 10 |
| Poor | 28.4 | 28.3 | 30 |
| Bad | 22.9 | 33.3 | 60 |
| | (n = 560) | | |

popular reforms in building a sense of positive affectivity toward the central government, our questionnaire contained a variety of items designed to evaluate levels of national awareness and affectivity generated by the reform programs.

Table 5-16 contains several general economic indicators of popular demand-satisfaction levels, most of which do, indeed, reflect substantial awareness of and support for the government's efforts to improve the lot of the masses. Items suggesting that people appreciated government efforts to improve their standard of living, for example, registered more than 80 percent supportive responses. Only 25 percent of the population felt that the economic system was unjust.

Turning to more specific indicators of mass supports, table 5-17 reflects levels of support in four specific areas singled out by the RCC that emphasize their social and economic reform programs: agriculture, health, housing, and education. [5]

The percentages appearing in Table 5-17 reflect a very high level of public appreciation for government efforts in the agrarian area, with more than 85 percent of the population reflecting at least general satisfaction with the government's reform efforts. Approximately one-half of the sample, however, felt that government efforts in the other areas examined had been inadequate. It is very interesting to note, however, that on all scales, the general public was far more supportive of regime efforts to improve their lot than either the popular committee members or the traditional local elites. In the case of the latter, their attitude can only be described as clear hostility. The negativism on the part of the popular committee members might possibly be explained by an effort to debunk the modernizing administrators whom they replaced.

The generally high support for the government's agrarian efforts undoubtedly stems from the fact that Qadafi singled out the agrarian sector for special treatment. At the very least, the high level of agrarian satisfaction does indicate that, with effort, strong feelings of support can be generated in spite of apathy and traditional opposition.

In pursuing the above theme, respondents were also requested to indicate the extent of their participation in government assistance and reform programs. It was felt that this was a particularly important item, for without extensive mass involvement, the impact of reform programs in effecting radical social and economic transformation is likely to be minimal. Levels of involvement in government assistance programs are reflected in the items appearing in table 5-18. Quite clearly, Libyan masses have not been penetrated by the government's reform efforts.

### Mobilizing the Masses: Building a Political Organization

During the initial years of the revolution, the national government consisted of a small committee of junior officers who felt they spoke in the name of the people, yet who lacked any real contact with the masses. This absence was keenly felt, for Qadafi and the RCC members had an almost blind faith in the inherent virtue of the masses. If only the masses could be awakened, the revolution would be secure. If only mass energies could be harnessed behind the RCC's modernization programs, the modernization of Libya would be assured.

The most visible effort to bridge the gap between the RCC and the masses during the first years of the revolution had been the nascent efforts to transform Qadafi into a charismatic leader, a process that appeared to meet with considerable success. Qadafi was, indeed, becoming a figure of exceptional stature.

Despite Qadafi's growing popularity among the masses, the new regime had yet to develop a viable organizational link between the government and the masses. The mass support generated both by Qadafi's charisma and by the distributive economic policies of the regime remained diffuse, unstructured, and of little real value in supporting the regime and its goals. The harnessing and focusing of mass support toward specific ends could be achieved only by creating some form of mass-based political organization.

In his search for a mechanism capable of linking the Libyan masses to the revolution, Qadafi found few viable options. The linkage function under the monarchy and throughout Libyan history had been performed by tribal chiefs and religious leaders such as Senussi or by the fledgling political parties of Tripolitania. Both were anathema to the revolution's leaders. A second option was the cooperation of an existing mass party, such as the Ba'ath or the Communist party, each of which boasted of an elaborate ideological and organizational framework capable of integrating the Libyan

**Table 5-18**
**Participation in Government Assistance Programs**
(*percentages*)

| | Popular Committee Public (n = 60) | Popular Committee Members (n = 60) |
|---|---|---|
| How often have you received any assistance from the government? | | |
| Many times | 12.9 | 46.7 |
| Once or twice | 26.9 | 3.3 |
| Never | 60.9 | 50.0 |
| | (n = 573) | |
| In what areas have you received assistance? | | |
| Agriculture | | |
| Yes | 20.0 | 30.0 |
| No | 80.0 | 70.0 |
| | (n = 574) | |
| Education | | |
| Yes | 13.0 | 5.0 |
| No | 87.0 | 95.0 |
| | (n = 574) | |
| Housing | | |
| Yes | 5.4 | 16.7 |
| No | 94.6 | 83.3 |
| | (n = 574) | |
| Welfare | | |
| Yes | 3.8 | 0.0 |
| No | 96.2 | 100.0 |
| | (n = 574) | |

population and linking it to the central leadership. Neither the Communists nor the Ba'ath, however, had developed firm roots in Libya. Both posed an ideological or organizational challenge to the RCC. Therefore, all political parties were banned.

The situation being as it was, the only viable option available to Qadafi and the RCC was to create a national political organization patterned after Nasser's Arab Socialist Union. In contrast to the other alternatives, Nasser's ASU, the product of a long evolution that included the abortive liberation rally and national union, had several distinct advantages. Ideologically, the ASU stood for Arab unity, popular democracy, liberty, anti-imperialism, and Islamic socialism. It thereby embodied all of the core values of the RCC outlined in the preceding chapter. Organizationally, the ASU provided for the establishment of ASU branches in every village, urban neighborhood, school, and factory, thereby penetrating all strata of the population in a manner akin to the Communist and Ba'ath parties. Branch leaders would serve as agents of socialization and opinion brokers, explaining RCC's policies to the masses and assisting them in assuming their true role in Libyan society. Simultaneously, the branch leaders would serve as conduits for mass demands and provide the RCC with feedback relating to the effectiveness and acceptance of their policies. In terms of control, branch leaders would monitor the behavior of dissident elements. They would also participate in the forbidding task of keeping the bureaucracy on its toes. In terms of participation, the ASU would provide the general population with the opportunity to participate in the election of members to a general congress, the plenary and theoretically controlling organ of the ASU. Eventually, the general congress would serve as the revolutionary equivalent of the defunct Libyan parliament. Moreover, elections to the general congress would be supervised by local branch committees, committees that would screen out individuals lacking sincere concern for the revolution. The population would thus be provided with a mode of democracy that offered a choice of candidates, yet one that proscribed further exacerbation of Libya's regional and tribal conflicts. Finally, though not of least importance, the leadership of the ASU would not be beholden to political movements external to Libya, such as the Syrian-dominated Ba'ath or the far more insidious ties of the Communist party. At least in theory, then, the potential of the ASU as a mechanism for linking the masses to the revolutionary leadership was virtually limitless. The Arab Socialist Union was formally proclaimed on June 11, 1971, with its major objectives being outlined in Qadafi's speech of June 12, 1971.

*Structure of the Arab Socialist Union*

The institutional structure of the ASU consisted of three basic tiers, each of which provided for a mass assembly and an executive committee.[6] The executive committee of the general congress of the ASU, of course, was the RCC. The basic conference was the highest authority of the ASU at the mass level. It consisted of all the local members of the ASU, and met once every four months. Extra sessions could be called by the committee of the basic unit or by the petition of one-third of the conference membership.

The executive committee served as the executive of the local basic unit and consisted of ten members elected by the members of the basic conference. A secretary and two assistant secretaries of the executive committee were elected for a period of two years, the term for all members of the executive committee. The committee met at least once a month and directed all activities at the basic level. It also was responsible for implementing the directives of the executive committee at the *muhafaza* (province) level. It also sent monthly reports to the *muhafaza* committee. Finally, the executive committee of the basic conference elected two or more members, depending upon its size, to the *muhafaza* or province conference.

The *muhafaza* conference was the highest political authority at the *muhafaza* level and was composed of two or more representatives from each basic unit in the province, depending upon size. The term of the conference was four years, and it met once every six months unless called into extra sessions by one-third of its executive committee, one-third of its members, or one-third of the executive committees of the basic units within the province.

As at the basic level, the conference of the *muhafaza* elected a twenty-member executive committee from among its own membership, the members of which served a term of four years. The executive committee met at least once a month, elected a secretary and two assistant secretaries, established specialized subcommittees, and generally directed all political activities of the ASU at the *muhafaza* level. Also, the executive committee at the *muhafaza* level directed and supervised the work of conferences and committees at lower levels, and implemented all decisions and recommendations of the national conference of the ASU and the RCC. It also sent monthly reports to the RCC. Universities and colleges were considered the equivalent of a *muhafaza,* and were treated accordingly. Basic units existed among staff and faculty.

The highest level of the ASU was the general conference of the ASU, a body consisting of from ten to twenty members elected by each *muhafaza,* depending on its size. Representatives were also sent by the leadership of the army, police, youth, women's organizations, professional associations, and trade unions.

The term of the general conference was six years. It was to be convened once every two years, or in exceptional cases, upon the request of the RCC or one-third of its membership. The chairman of the RCC, Colonel Qadafi, served as the president of the general conference.

Membership in the ASU was open to all Libyan citizens eighteen or more years of age who were not exploiters and who, in good conscience, could say they believed in the revolution's principles of unity, freedom, and socialism. Criminals and perverts were barred from membership as were individuals specifically excluded by the RCC.

The charter of the ASU specified that workers and farmers would comprise 50 percent of all levels of the ASU memberships. Working people were defined as farmers, workers, soldiers, intellectuals, and owners of nonexploitive national capital. This requirement did not apply to universities and similar organizations.

Farmers were defined as individuals working essentially in agriculture whose families owned less than thirty hectares. Workers were individuals who received a daily wage, or who did not employ anyone outside their families in their business operations. A nonexploitive capitalist was defined as a person who was taxed on his earnings, used his capital in constructive ways, did not exploit others, and earned his living honestly. Intellectuals were defined as individuals engaged in writing or teaching, or who were otherwise constructively working to intellectually solve the problems of the nation.

*Duties of the Basic Units and Members of the Arab Socialist Union*

Of particular interest to our analysis of mass mobilization are the specified duties of the basic units and its members, for they represent a vivid picture of the aspirations the RCC held for its political organizations as well as their sense of foreboding about the problems the ASU would encounter in fulfilling its mission. The duties of the basic units, for example, included the following:

1. To awaken the masses politically and socially, to foster Islam and Arab nationalism, and to inform citizens of their rights and obligations in the political, economic, and social fields.
2. To assist the masses in their social, cultural, economic, and spiritual growth by cooperating with all relevant organizations and councils.
3. To understand the needs and problems of the masses at the basic level, assist local councils and organizations in meeting their needs, and refer all matters that could not be settled at the local level to higher levels of the ASU.
4. To increase production at the basic level.
5. To fight exploitation and all types of bureaucratic rigidity.
6. To explain the policy of the ASU to all citizens, and assist them in applying the ASU principles.
7. To apply all the resolutions and decisions of the *muhafaza* and national conference levels.
8. To ensure that all members of the ASU are performing their duties and that the ASU is working to promote socialism and democracy.
9. To encourage members of the ASU to participate in those institutes and councils in which political, economic, and social activities take place, and help those organizations implement ASU principles.
10. To give the opportunity to all members of the basic unit to exercise their rights as stated in the charter.

*Critique of the Arab Socialist Union*

If the potential of the ASU as a mechanism for linking the masses to the revolutionary leadership was unlimited, its performance was not. The ASU was ineffective in Egypt, and, as originally constituted, fared less well in Libya. One clear reason for the ineffectiveness of the ASU was its lack of cadres.

Cadres are the backbone of a political movement: They are the branch leaders, proselytizers, watchers, *stakhanovites* (workers who exceed their quotas).[7] The Libyan ASU, however, had few cadres. It had been born not of revolutionary struggle, but by government decree. Rather than serving as the political organ of mass-based revolutionary movement such as the FLN in Algeria or the Congress party in India or even the neo-Doustour in Tunisia, the function of the ASU was to create a politicized population where none had existed before. Its few initial cadres, as in the case of the restructured Libyan bureaucracy, were drawn from the ranks of Nasserite students known to Qadafi and the RCC through their contacts at the University of Libya at Benghazi or other institutes. One might, indeed, question whether the former students of Nasserite values who were pressed into service in the ASU really fit the description of cadres. The majority lacked dedication, discipline, and cohesiveness. Moreover, the term cadres refers not to the top leadership of a political organization, but to the existence of dedicated party workers at the middle and lower levels of political organization. The students pressed into leadership in the ASU formed part of a very small pool of semi-educated Libyans, a resource pool already strained by the reorganization of the bureaucracy. Students became the leaders of the ASU, not the followers. The ASU thus possessed few cadres at the middle and lower levels, a situation that led to having "insincere" people occupying positions of authority. Many citizens, Qadafi explained in a 1973 press conference, had accused the ASU of failure and neglect, particularly at the local level.

During the early years of the revolution, the cadre-leadership situation also suffered from considerable confusion concerning the role, authority, and modus operandi of the ASU. Grand statements existed concerning the mission of the ASU, but few guidelines existed as to precisely how this mission was to be accomplished. Thus, the limited manpower available was not used to full advantage. Egyptians provided some guidance, yet the differences in the Egyptian and Libyan situations were so stark that the Egyptian experience proved to be only minimally relevant.

If the ASU suffered from a lack of cadres, it also suffered from a lack of rank and file members. In spite of wide publicity and the opportunity to demonstrate one's support for the revolution, membership lagged. Although the 1972 general congress of the ASU accepted the membership applications of some 300,000 people, our 1971 survey of Zawia province indicated that less than 54 percent of the population belonged to the ASU or had friends or relatives who did.[8]

To some extent, the inability of the ASU to mobilize the masses and attract a broad following can be attributed to the magnitude of the task.

Political apathy in Libya, for example, became very apparent in the battery of participation predisposition questions presented to our survey respondents which appear in table 5-19. As late as 1973, two years after the initiation of the ASU, the general population was clearly willing to allow decisions to be made on their behalf by "experts" and showed little intense desire to become politically involved. Similarly, the overt participation items presented in table 5-20 indicate that Libyans had generally avoided all forms of political involvement, regardless of its nature.

**Table 5-19**
**Participatory Attitudes of the General Public and Selected Leadership Groups**
(*percentages*)

|  | Public | Popular Committee Members | Modernizing Administrators | Traditional Leaders |
|---|---|---|---|---|
| Only those who are competent on issues should speak |  |  |  |  |
| Strongly agree | 17.0 | 18.6 | 15.0 |  |
| Agree | 52.4 | 50.8 | 70.0 |  |
| Disagree | 25.6 | 27.1 | 15.0 |  |
| Strongly disagree | 5.0 | 3.4 | 0.0 |  |
|  | (n = 481) | (n = 59) | (n = 20) |  |
| Widespread participation in decision making often leads to undesirable conflicts |  |  |  |  |
| Strongly agree | 7.6 | 10.3 | 15.0 | 10.0 |
| Agree | 40.9 | 48.3 | 75.0 | 60.0 |
| Disagree | 43.0 | 32.8 | 10.0 | 30.0 |
| Strongly disagree | 8.4 | 8.6 | 0.0 | 0.0 |
|  | (n = 474) | (n = 58) | (n = 20) | (n = 10) |
| Participation of the people is not necessary if decision making is left in the hands of a few trusted and competent leaders |  |  |  |  |
| Strongly agree | 12.6 | 14.0 | 30.0 | 10.0 |
| Agree | 51.6 | 43.9 | 40.0 | 80.0 |
| Disagree | 28.6 | 33.5 | 30.0 | 10.0 |
| Strongly disagree | 7.2 | 8.8 | 0.0 | 0.0 |
|  | (n = 483) | (n = 57) | (n = 20) | (n = 10) |
| Political predisposition scale |  |  |  |  |
| Intense | 7.4 | 3.6 | 0.0 | 0.0 |
| Medium high | 27.9 | 30.4 | 15.0 | 20.0 |
| Low | 51.3 | 50.0 | 50.0 | 50.0 |
| Very low | 13.4 | 16.1 | 35.0 | 30.0 |
|  | (n = 476) | (n = 56) | (n = 20) | (n = 10) |

**Table 5-20**
**Political Participation of the General Public and Selected Leadership Groups**
(*percentages*)

|  | Public | Popular Committee Members | Modernizing Administrators |
|---|---|---|---|
| About how many of your relatives or good friends (check only one for each category) are active in the following areas? | | | |
| Arab Socialist Union | | | |
| Most | 6.3 | 10.0 | 10 |
| Some | 15.7 | 46.7 | 40 |
| Few | 23.2 | 26.7 | 45 |
| None | 54.9 | 16.7 | 5 |
|  | (n = 574) | (n = 60) | (n = 20) |
| Local government | | | |
| Most | 1.6 | 5.0 | 40 |
| Some | 14.3 | 35.0 | 50 |
| Few | 21.6 | 30.0 | 10 |
| None | 62.5 | 30.0 | 0 |
|  | (n = 574) | (n = 60) | (n = 20) |
| Community organizations | | | |
| Most | 2.6 | 1.7 | 0 |
| Some | 10.5 | 15.0 | 25 |
| Few | 18.8 | 49.7 | 55 |
| None | 68.1 | 41.7 | 20 |
|  | (n = 574) | (n = 60) | (n = 20) |
| Overt participation scale | | | |
| Very high | 6.1 | 13.3 | 40 |
| High | 7.7 | 25.0 | 35 |
| Moderate | 20.6 | 28.3 | 20 |
| Low | 21.3 | 23.3 | 5 |
| Nonexistent | 44.4 | 10.0 | 0 |
|  | (n = 574) | (n = 60) | (n = 20) |

Beyond apathy and the absence of a participatory tradition, the dismal membership record of the ASU may be directly attributable to the boy-cotting movement by the traditional tribal and religious elites. The revolution launched a full-scale offense on their authority, and they fought back as best they could, largely by ignoring the revolution and its institutions.

Also, our earlier discussion indicated that the modernizing administrators, too, had manifested hostility toward the ASU. Few of the modernizing administrators, it will be recalled, indicated a willingness to consult with the ASU at either the local or national levels. Only 30 percent indicated they worked to strengthen the ASU as a regular activity, and fewer yet felt they had been particularly successful in this regard.

The ASU, following sharp criticisms by Qadafi in 1973, had been the subject of almost ceaseless efforts by the RCC to improve the quality of its leadership, to somehow shape the ASU into a truly revolutionary movement. In part, such reforms involved the purging of undesirable elements and the improved training of ASU personnel. More importantly, the RCC moved to partially bypass total reliance on the ASU in its efforts to mobilize the masses through the establishment of popular committees, a process to be discussed at length in the following chapter.

## Mobilizing the Masses: Socialization and Resocialization

The survey of mass attitudes presented in chapter 2 indicated that Libya's citizens retained many attitudinal and behavioral vestiges of a traditional society, attitudes generally viewed as antithetical to programs of rapid modernization. Moreover, the mass behavior problems cited by the modernizing administrators indicated that a preponderance of Libya's citizens were particularistic, lacking in civic responsibility (atomistic), tribalistic, fatalistic, nonparticipatory, and engrained with the values of ascription and distrust.

If the masses were to live up to their potential as the backbone of the revolution, they clearly had to be liberated from the deeply engrained values of their reactionary past. The Turks, the Italians, and to a larger extent, the monarchy, had maintained their control through perpetuating tribalism, sowing distrust among diverse groups, socializing the masses to be passive and fatalistic, and discouraging any form of mass participation and political involvement.[9] If the masses were to become a true instrument of the revolution, the RCC would now have to embark upon a mammoth program of political socialization and resocialization.

In its efforts to shape the masses into a revolutionary force, the RCC would be forced to rely on four agents of socialization: local administrative officials, the ASU, schools, and mass media. Of these, the modernizing administrators, as noted earlier, seemed little concerned with their role as socializers, and probably had little impact on the reshaping of mass values. The ASU was too new and, as we have seen, too beset with its own problems to exert a substantial impact upon mass behavior during the first years of the revolution. The RCC's socialization efforts thus depended almost entirely upon the effectiveness of the education system and the mass media. Other crucial sources of political socialization, such as the family, tribal leadership, religious leadership, and peer group, could not be counted on to inculcate revolutionary values. In many instances, they served as conflicting sources of socialization because they instilled Libya's youth with traditional rather than revolutionary values. This seems to be particularly true of the tribal or religious elites. Thus, the burden placed upon the education system and the mass media in terms of political socialization was awesome.

The educational advances during the early years of the revolution were dramatic at all levels, a fact reflecting the revolution's deep commitment to education as the most direct means of modernizing Libya and revolutionizing its citizens. Increases in the number of classrooms and students during that time are summarized in table 5-21. Particularly worthy of note are the very concerted efforts of the RCC to draw females into the education system and to prepare them to become an effective element in the Libyan labor force. The educational system, of course, was restructured in order to bring it in line with the new revolutionary goals, ideology, and commitments.

Qadafi directed a great deal of attention to the students on all levels. He tried and is still trying to build a new generation with strong beliefs in the revolutionary goals and the new society. Although much of his emphasis has been on the precollege level, he has nevertheless attempted to create a strong base of revolutionary support at the university and college levels as well.

The RCC's early socialization efforts were largely dependent upon the media structure it had inherited from the monarchy, a structure that consisted mainly of a government-operated broadcasting service initiated in 1957, and five or six private newspapers operating under press censorship. Television did not make its debut until 1968, and extensive local programming was yet to be developed. Most Libyans had become accustomed to listening to foreign programs, such as the British Broadcasting Corporation or the Egyptian and Tunisian broadcasts. Thus, the Libyan media could not offer the RCC strong support in its early socialization efforts, nor has it been able to keep pace with the dramatic changes that have occurred in Libya since 1969. What popularity the Libyan mass media has enjoyed since the revolution has been a result of Qadafi's charismatic personality and his use of the media to discuss urgent events and to issue major policy statements.

The leadership's evaluation of the media has been intensely critical, a view generally shared by the public.[10] Time after time, Qadafi has criticized the media's ineffectiveness in transmitting revolutionary values. His typical comments include: "We should close down," or "it is not worth a penny," or "we should put it on auction."

**Socialization: A Critique**

The ultimate test of any political socialization program is the extent to which it succeeds in shaping mass attitudes and behavior in the direction specified by the dominant elite. Judged by this standard, the most educated Libyans and those with the greatest exposure to the mass media should have registered the highest level of regime support during our 1973 survey of Zawia province. Such a procedure is not entirely accurate, of course, for a

**Table 5-21**
**Educational Development: 1968-1981**

| Stages of Education | Number of Pupils | | | | Number of Schools | Number of Classrooms | | Number of Teachers | |
|---|---|---|---|---|---|---|---|---|---|
| | Boys | Girls | Total | Increase Percentage | | Number | Increase Percentage | Number | Increase Percentage |
| **Primary** | | | | | | | | | |
| 1968/1969 | 183,080 | 87,537 | 270,617 | — | 1,069 | 8,311 | — | 9,161 | — |
| 1972/1973 | 270,772 | 187,516 | 458,288 | 69.3 | 1,494 | 15,276 | 83.8 | 17,497 | 91 |
| 1975/1976 (projected) | 282,451 | 251,758 | 534,209 | 16.6 | 1,741 | 18,989 | 24.3 | 22,654 | 29.5 |
| 1980/1981 | 292,416 | 285,338 | 577,654 | 8.1 | — | 32,128 | 69.2 | 26,324 | 16.2 |
| **Preparatory** | | | | | | | | | |
| 1968/1969 | 25,637 | 3,544 | 29,181 | — | 144 | 818 | — | 2,076 | — |
| 1972/1973 | 43,653 | 13,026 | 56,679 | 94.2 | 216 | 1,757 | 114.7 | 3,771 | 81.6 |
| 1975/1976 (projected) | 78,186 | 38,444 | 116,630 | 105.8 | 444 | 3,839 | 118.5 | 7,024 | 86.3 |
| 1980/1981 | 102,156 | 88,749 | 190,905 | 63.7 | — | 9,464 | 146.5 | 11,284 | 60.6 |
| **Secondary** | | | | | | | | | |
| 1968/1969 | 6,237 | 944 | 7,181 | — | 25 | 250 | — | 608 | — |
| 1972/1973 | 8,926 | 1,976 | 10,902 | 51.8 | 43 | 385 | 54 | 974 | 60.2 |
| 1975/1976 (projected) | 12,276 | 3,563 | 16,839 | 54.5 | 66 | 633 | 64.4 | 1,720 | 76.6 |
| 1980/1981 | 36,373 | 29,336 | 65,709 | 290.2 | — | 2,189 | 245.8 | 5,394 | 213.6 |
| **Technical secondary** | | | | | | | | | |
| 1968/1969 | 517 | — | 517 | — | 6 | 31 | — | 87 | — |
| 1972/1973 | 2,348 | — | 2,348 | 311.2 | 9 | 90 | 190.3 | 379 | 235.6 |
| 1975/1976 (projected) | 3,600 | 100 | 3,700 | 57.6 | 12 | 155 | 72.2 | 455 | 20.1 |
| 1980/1981 | 7,920 | 230 | 8,150 | 120.3 | 15 | 300 | 93.5 | 1,002 | 120.2 |
| **Teacher's institutes** | | | | | | | | | |
| 1968/1969 | 2,956 | 2,203 | 5,159 | — | 23 | 180 | — | 466 | — |
| 1972/1973 | 6,738 | 4,088 | 10,826 | 109.8 | 56 | 382 | 112 | 713 | 56.9 |
| 1975/1976 (projected) | 9,156 | 12,090 | 21,246 | 96.2 | 110 | 769 | 101.3 | 1,629 | 122.8 |
| 1980/1981 | 6,451 | 5,703 | 12,154 | 42.8 | — | 887 | 15.3 | 919 | 43.6 |

Source: Socialist Popular Libyan Arab Jamahiriya, *Decision of the General Secretariat of the General People's Congress No. 1, for the Year 1979 Relating to General Popular Committees in the Municipalities*, p. 86.

large percentage of the educated members of the sample received their educations in whole or part prior to the revolution. Similarly, our media figures do not distinguish between Libyan and non-Libyan media. The figures presented do, however, test the proposition that educated and well-informed individuals should be more supportive of revolutionary modernization programs than less well-informed people.

Toward this end, the attitudes and behavior patterns of the uneducated, rural members of our sample were correlated with the behavior patterns manifested by their more educated, urban counterparts. These correlations are presented in table 5-22, and they suggest the following observations. In reference to the traditional attitudes and behavior patterns discussed at the beginning of the analysis, it is clear that "modern Libyans" are far less atomistic, fatalistic, and particularistic than their traditional brethern. "Modern" Libyans, however, were not significantly less religious than traditional rural Libyans, nor did they score much higher in terms of interpersonal trust.

Moreover, the more educated, urban Libyans were clearly more supportive of leaders selected on the basis of achievement and merit than the less educated, rural Libyans who, as noted earlier, continued to manifest a strong preference for ascriptive leaders. Educated Libyans were also far more likely to participate in the government agencies, such as the Arab Socialist Union, than their rural counterparts. To this degree, education appeared to be building some regime support.

On the negative side, the better educated Libyans and those with the greatest exposure to the press and television were less likely than their rural counterparts to display positive evaluations toward local or regional administrators. They were also less likely to be satisfied with government reform programs designed to build support for the regime and demonstrate its usefulness. If anything, education and the mass media have increased demands rather than supports. Although this trend is not strong, it does indicate that educating individuals and exposing them to greater information does not necessarily build support for the regime.

Explanations of why the revolution's education and media programs did not play a more dramatic role in the inculcation of revolutionary values are readily available. As noted earlier, the media and education systems inherited by the revolution were not well developed and clearly not geared to perform the socialization tasks envisioned by the revolutionary leadership. More problematic and certainly more difficult to overcome was the fact that many of the most crucial agents of socialization, including the family (particularly in the rural areas), local religious leaders, tribal elites, and peer groups, were beyond the reach of the revolutionary regime and were presumably inculcating values antithetical to the modernization values of the regime. Thus, the socialization of Libya's youth was inconsistent.

They received one message in the government's schools and another in the mass media; a contradictory message from traditional tribal, family, and religious institutions.

It should also be stressed that at the time of our Zawia survey, the revolution had only entered its fourth year. There had been little time for the revolution to design its socialization programs or to implement them on a comprehensive scale.

Whatever the reasons for their minimal effectiveness, Qadafi's 1973 assessment of the mass media and the Libyan education system called for sweeping revisions in both areas. Also, over the years of the revolution, Qadafi has developed a growing despair of ever revolutionizing Libya's older citizens and has focused his attention increasingly upon Libya's youth. One clear example of this new emphasis on youth was the initiation of political indoctrination camps, a subject to be discussed in the next chapter.

### Mobilizing the Masses: Bureaucratic Capacity

The primary function of a ruling elite is to make decisions. The primary function of the bureaucracy is to execute those decisions. Elite decisions that the bureaucracy cannot or will not execute remain unfilled. This unhappy piece of logic is particularly true of social and economic modernization programs in socialist countries or in countries lacking a strong entrepreneurial private sector, because the full burden of executing development decisions and programs then falls upon the bureaucracy. Libya is rapidly becoming a socialist state, and it lacks a strong entrepreneurial private sector. The success of Libya's revolutionary elite in executing its goals is thus linked directly to the performance of the Libyan bureaucracy. If Libya does not have a strong bureaucratic performance, its economic modernization will be reduced to random exercises, the major successes of which will be the accomplishment of foreign contractors. The Libyan masses, lacking a bureaucracy that is responsive to their needs, will become disgruntled and antagonized over the inability of the regime to keep its eloquent promises. And, the deeply engrained Libyan tradition of politcal alienation will be perpetuated. Without a strong base of mass support, of course, the revolution could possibly stagnate, and become totally dependent upon the army for its survival. Without a strong bureaucracy, Qadafi might find it increasingly difficult to extend his position as a charismatic leader.

This didactic sequence of deductions and their consequences is essential to understanding the tremendous pressure under which the Libyan bureaucracy operates and the perpetual state of conflict that has existed between the RCC and the bureaucracy throughout the revolution's first decade. It is

**Table 5-22**
**Information Exposure and Support for Political Modernization**
(*n* = 576)

| | Religio-sity | Particu-larism | Fatalism | Inter-Personal Distrust | Atomism | Leadership Preference | Mayor |
|---|---|---|---|---|---|---|---|
| Demographic scale[a] (education, urbanization, and television exposure) | G = [b] 0.175 | 0.460 | 0.400 | 0.257 | 0.643 | G = [c] 0.453 | 0.228 |
| Urbanization | 0.097 | 0.293 | 0.247 | 0.398 | 0.646 | 0.333 | 0.178 |
| Education | 0.211 | 0.501 | 0.473 | 0.156 | 0.629 | 0.451 | 0.164 |
| Television | 0.265 | 0.468 | 0.338 | 0.244 | 0.578 | 0.387 | 0.180 |
| Newspaper | 0.284 | 0.556 | 0.488 | 0.157 | 0.684 | 0.515 | 0.171 |
| Ability to recall recent political events | 0.060 | 0.313 | 0.296 | 0.074 | 0.246 | 0.468 | 0.026 |
| Ability to identify local and regional officials | 0.174 | 0.388 | 0.425 | 0.202 | 0.576 | 0.456 | 0.009 |
| Age | 0.429 | 0.384 | 0.249 | 0.081 | 0.329 | 0.224 | 0.035 |

Source: Omar I. El Fathaly, Monte Palmer, and Richard Chackerian, *Political Development and Bureaucracy in Libya* (Lexington, Mass.: Lexington Books, D.C. Heath) 1977.

[a]Questionaire items relating to television exposure, urbanization, and media exposure were combined into a demographic scale. All three items received equal weight. Possible scale scores ranged from 3 through 9, with 3 indicating rural status with no education or television exposure and 9 representing the highest of urbanization, education, and television exposure. Scores of 3 or 4 were considered traditional, scores of 5, 6, or 7, transitional; scores of 8 or 9, modern.

also essential to understanding the RCC's attempts to totally circumvent the bureaucracy under the provisions of the popular revolution, which will be described at length in a later chapter.

In analyzing the Libyan bureaucracy as a vehicle for economic and social modernization, we will concentrate on four problem areas:

1. the structure and physical apparatus of the bureaucracy,
2. the attitudinal and behavioral predispositions of the Libyan bureaucrats,
3. popular or client attitudes toward the bureaucracy, and
4. political inputs into the bureaucracy.

However, it is necessary to first survey briefly the historical origins of the Libyan bureaucracy.

| Adminis- trator | Agricul- ture | Edu- cation | Resident | Health | Accepted Govern- ment Assistance | Attitu- dinal Partici- pation | Overt Partici- pation |
|---|---|---|---|---|---|---|---|
| −0.151 | 0.091 | −0.365 | −0.111 | 0.218 | 0.245 | 0.245 | 0.466 |
| −0.075 | 0.157 | −0.187 | −0.129 | 0.168 | | 0.245 | 0.444 |
| −0.202 | 0.068 | −0.329 | −0.129 | 0.142 | 0.286 | 0.236 | 0.460 |
| −0.189 | 0.032 | −0.414 | −0.117 | 0.123 | 0.253 | 0.148 | 0.403 |
| −0.202 | 0.059 | −0.427 | −0.124 | 0.145 | 0.403 | 0.283 | 0.578 |
| −0.091 | 0.018 | −0.069 | −0.113 | 0.156 | 0.032 | 0.440 | 0.469 |
| −0.263 | −0.004 | −0.221 | −0.204 | 0.022 | 0.222 | 0.235 | 0.466 |
| −0.162 | 0.082 | −0.217 | −0.101 | 0.055 | 0.133 | 0.201 | 0.153 |

[b]Gamma coefficients. All coefficients over + .200 are significant at the .05 level or beyond. Coefficients were based upon a pairwise deletion of cases.

[c]Positive coefficients indicate a positive correlation between the independent variables relating to greater exposure to "modern" information and either a decrease in traditional attitudes or positive support for government modernization programs. Negative coefficients indicate that greater exposure to modern information either strengthened traditional attitudes or resulted in a negative reaction to governmental modernization programs.

## Libya's Bureaucratic Legacy

The origins of the Libyan bureaucracy go back as far as the Italian occupation and perhaps, to some extent, to the earlier Turkish period. The British added few structural changes to the Italian system, but did attempt to provide some rudimentary training in bureaucraic self-management.[11] With independence, the bureaucracy remained a fairly rudimentary structure performing few tasks other than administering the foreign aid upon which the monarchy depended for its survivial. Indeed, although somewhat difficult to visualize, the entire governmental apparatus rotated at regular seasonal intervals between Tripoli and Benghazi and later between Tripoli, Benghazi, and Beida, the king's choice for a new capital in the center of the Senussi-dominated Green mountains.[12]

The massive influx of oil revenues described in chapter 2 overwhelmed the existing bureaucratic structure. New units were added in a haphazard manner to meet immediate contingencies. The lack of trained Libyans precluded any quality control within the bureaucracy and resulted in an over-reliance upon foreigners. Opportunities for corruption and nepotism were manifest and seldom went unfulfilled. Public esteem for the bureaucracy collapsed.

Thus, the bureaucracy inherited by the revolution and upon which the revolutionary elite would rely to forge its dreams into reality was an organizational mess of uncoordinated and often overlapping units staffed by undertrained officials almost totally lacking in the technical support services generally taken for granted by modern bureaucratic organizations.

The bureaucratic situation was also complicated by measures the RCC was forced to take in its efforts to consolidate the revolution. The king's supporters within the bureaucracy obviously had to be removed, because otherwise they could use their positions to obstruct the revolution. For the most part, such purges were tactfully accomplished by offering lucrative cash inducements for early retirement. The inducements were readily accepted, with their recipients generally using the cash received to enter private business. Such purges, although necessary, depleted the pool of experienced bureaucrats even further, although some would argue that, given the problems of corruption, the losses involved were minimal. Several purged military officers were also put into the bureaucracy, often in high positions.

### The Structure of the Libyan Bureaucracy

Under the pragmatic format established by the revolution, the structure of the postrevolutionary bureaucracy has been the subject of almost constant change. It was hoped that structural changes would somehow make the bureaucracy more efficient in meeting the needs of the leadership and the people. The most persistent trend in this regard has been to maintain all established agencies, and to add more units as the need arises.

By 1972, the bureaucracy consisted of twenty-three departments headed by cabinet-level ministers. In addition, several public corporations had been created to either regulate or develop specialized functions. Areas of overlapping jurisdiction were numerous, particularly in the roles of public corporations and administrative departments. The most visible manifestations of such conflict were the existence of the department of agriculture and department of agrarian reform, both of which performed almost identical functions. The two ministries were united, but were again separated at a later point. So bad have the jurisdictional problems become, in fact, that the Libyans have coined a special word in its honor: *tabeka*.

Literally translated, it means "stew." Problems also arise because the bureaucratic offices of the same ministry are scattered helter-skelter and shift locations regularly.

Also falling under the rubric of organizational problems are the severe difficulties the Libyan bureaucracy has experienced in the area of manpower uilization. Although a high percentage of the Libyan labor force fills civil service positions, all bureaucratic departments reported severe shortages of Libyan personnel and were forced to rely extensively on foreigners, particularly Egyptians. Such dependence upon foreign civil servants has been partly a result of the underutilization of available Libyan talent. Approximately twenty thousand Libyans, for example, are employed as doorwatchers and errand runners, with another eighteen thousand serving as drivers.[13]

Staffing problems became more acute with the decision to "Libyanize" the civil service, a policy that called for all senior positions being filled by Libyan citizens. Such a policy was clearly essential in terms of assuring that the direction of Libya's government was in the hands of Libyan nationals. It was also necessary in terms of providing Libyan nationals with the expertise necessary to avoid dependency upon foreigners. The 1977 conflict between Libya and Egypt, for example, caused deep and abiding concern over just how dependent Libya was upon foreign personnel and what impact their potentially divided loyalties might have upon the security of the regime. Nevertheless, at least in the short run, the Libyanization program did result in the staffing of key bureaucratic positions with poorly trained personnel, a fact the government has attempted to compensate for by creating a very liberal program of foreign training for virtually all qualified officials who apply.

Yet a third structural problem impairing the effectiveness of the Libyan bureaucracy was the necessity of acquiring multiple authorizations and signatures to accomplish even the most routine acts. To enter school, for example, a student was required to have a birth certificate, a certificate specifying his or her permanent address, a certificate of nationality, a certificate of good behavior, and a medical certificate. All of these documents had to be resubmitted in each stage of schooling. At least on the local level, the main business of bureaucrats had become the issuing of certificates. Signatures of high officials were required for even the most petty and routine matters. Requests by a new professor to secure paper and pencil, for example, required the signature of the department chairman and the head of the university's finance department. If all bureaucracies suffer from red tape, the Libyan bureaucracy has perfected it to a science.

Red tape, it is important to note, does not always form of its own volition. In the Libyan case, prior excesses of corruption were countered by requiring multiple signatures, sometimes ten or more, on all vouchers in an effort to assure that government funds were being properly utilized. Also, the personal insecurity of many bureaucrats, one of several behavior patterns to be discussed shortly, could be allayed by requiring several individuals to participate in potentially questionable decisions, thereby reducing the vulnerability of any one official to reprimand. Whatever its origins, the phenomenal red tape in the Libyan bureaucracy has rendered it a slow and plodding instrument, at best.

*Administrative Behavior*

However severe the organizational problems of the Libyan bureaucracy might be, they pale in comparison to the attitudinal and behavioral problems endemic to Libyan bureaucrats. The most visible problems are attacked with great regularity in the press and in the public speeches of Qadafi and RCC members. They include demoralization, nonprofessionalism, corruption, haughtiness, insensitivity to the needs of the public, laziness, inefficiency, noninnovative rigidity, and wastefulness. Some flavor of public criticisms of the bureaucracy is provided by the following quotation from the July 9, 1976 issue of the Libyan daily newspaper, *El Jehad.*

> In spite of the fact that Colonel Qadafi frankly announced in his speech to the cabinet that he has lost patience with the bureaucrats and that the bureaucrats and opportunists must be revolutionized, and in spite of the fact that many of their faces have disappeared from the stage of bureaucratic work, other faces have replaced them. The same rusty minds follow the same behavior with the same speech, "The Director's out today, come back tomorrow." " . . . The Chairman of the committee is in a meeting." " . . . That's not our specialty."
>
> After hearing [Qadafi's] speech to the cabinet I assumed that supervisors, directors, institutions, organizations and companies would race to discuss fundamental changes in the behavior of their employees and compete among themselves for total and comprehensive improvement in their behavior . . . to innovate with all of the new methods of administrative organization which might succeed in improving public service as quickly as possible without excessive red tape and without excessive loss of time and frivolous delay and without insulting the intelligence of the citizens and ignoring them because of their circumstance such as the place from which they came, or the interests they pursue—but it did not happen. An administrative revolution did not spring forth. . . . While we recognize that a small core of people struggle day and night to serve the public, the bureaucrats, opportunists and exploiters are clearly apparent in our ranks. We will not put our affairs in order until we descend upon officials inadequate in the execcution of their obligations or who steal, or who accept bribes, or who bribe others, etc., and we hang them in the public squares of the Republic in front of the people so that they may serve as a lesson for all.[14]

The wastefulness of government employees is typified by the desire of almost every ministry to replace virtually all of its furniture, cars, and equipment on a yearly basis. The small municipality of Sabrata with a population of 30,000 spends approximately $100,000 annually for stationery alone. Virtually all bureaucrats of significance demand private cars and get them. Concerns with maintenance or budgetary constraint are nonexistent, an attitude summed up in the bureaucratic slogan *razeq Hakuma*, which literally means "government property, who cares."

The nonprofessionalism of Libya's bureaucrats is partially explained by a lack of training and experience. Similarly, their lack of innovation might well be explained by the fatalism that tends to characterize traditional Libyan culture. In addition to cultural predispositions, however, both the nonprofessionalism and lack of innovation characteristic of many Libyan bureaucrats result from the pervasive sense of insecurity that permeates the entire bureaucracy. Everyone tends to fear everyone else. Even new recruits are a source of fear, since recent university graduates tend to view themselves as suited for only executive positions and often accuse their supervisors of corruption and wrong-doing as a means of providing avenues for their personal advancement.

The atmosphere of insecurity, in turn, creates its own set of dysfunctional behaviors. Superiors will not delegate authority for fear that subordinates will use the perogatives to scheme against them. Innovative projects suggested by subordinates are stifled for fear that they might make waves or, if successful, give a competitive edge to the originator. This problem is particularly damaging to the small but hard core of the technocrats within the Libyan bureaucracy who have both the skills and the desire to embark upon creative and innovative programs. Precisely because the superiors lack or do not even understand technical skills, they are reluctant to allow their subordinates' projects see the light of day. According to the prevailing logic, what they cannot understand, they cannot control. Insecurity also places excessive emphasis upon the quantity of bureaucratic outputs (measured primarily in terms of money spent) rather than on the quality of bureaucratic performance. Also, somewhat ironically, bureaucratic insecurity born of covert backbiting has resulted in an overt norm of bureaucratic solidarity. No one will openly criticize the work of anyone else. Officially, everything is wonderful. Objective criteria for upgrading the bureaucracy and eliminating its weakest links are missing. The inevitable outcome of this situation is that both personal security and career advancement require an influential patron. The factionalization of the bureaucracy along patronage or clique lines, of course, merely serves to reinforce the prevailing sense of insecurity and to further perpetuate the behavior patterns in question.

If the behavioral problems surveyed were characteristic of all Libyan bureaucrats, the Libyan civil service would have totally collapsed. It has not. A minimal, though hardly revolutionary, level of performance is maintained. Much of the work that does get done, however, is the product of what administrative analysts sometimes refer to as a workhorse group: a small group of perhaps 10 percent of the bureaucracy who are technically competent, service-oriented, and dedicated to serving the people. This is very much the case in Libya. As the technical skills and the professionalism of the workhorse group increase, the gap between them and the rest of the bureaucracy also increases, often resulting in intensified conflict. The less-productive elements rely increasingly upon their connections and upon overt demonstrations of revolutionary loyalty to secure their positions. In many ways, this growing conflict has taken on many of the trappings of the red-versus-expert conflict so common in the People's Republic of China and the Soviet Union, a conflict that raises the very real question of whether the top positions in the bureaucracy should be allotted on the basis of technical competence or revolutionary loyalty. Although there is no doubt of the need for regime loyalty, the least-productive members of the bureaucracy have used overt dedication to revolutionary principles as a means of impugning the motives and dedication of the workhorse-expert group. This is particularly unfortunate, for there seems to be no better definition of revolutionary spirit than a desire to serve the people and expedite the execution of the regime's modernization goals. Impugning the motives of the workhorse group merely serves to lower the morale of that group and to raise their incentives for seeking employment outside of the bureaucracy. Desertion by the workhorse-expert groups from the Libyan bureaucracy, it should be stressed, is a particularly severe problem in Libya because competent and technically trained Libyans have had, until the socialist era, almost unlimited opportunities in the private sector. If anything, they remain with the government to their own detriment.

The insecurity of Libya's bureaucrats also resulted in the tendency of virtually all administrators in influential positions to surround themselves with foreign advisors, hoping that a seemingly endless procession of meetings would compensate for the lack of concrete programs. Such over-indulgence in experts, in addition to being of questionable usefulness, creates an incredibly costly budget item.

*The Bureaucracy and the Masses: Client Behavior*

The Libyan bureaucrats' disdain for the masses is returned in kind. The Libyan population has traditionally been hostile toward the bureaucracy and, with rare exceptions, responds to bureaucratic initiatives only when it is clearly beneficial to do so. Even though mass hostility toward the bureaucracy finds it origins in the traditional tribal family-centered behavior (surveyed in chapter 2), and in the abusive policies of the colonial era, the fact remains that the behavior of Libya's bureaucrats during the almost thirty years of independence has, if anything, widened the gap between the government and the people, a gap clearly evident in Qadafi's recent reference to the bureaucracy as "isolators."

### The Bureaucracy and the Revolutionary Command Council

Our survey of the woes besetting the Libyan bureaucracy would be inadequate if we neglected to discuss the political environment in which the bureaucracy must operate. The myriad problems that the bureaucracy faces are made greater by the intense pressure from the RCC to produce almost instant results. Planning and pretesting, particularly in a society virtually devoid of accurate statistics, is a slow process, yet one that will not brook compromise. The time constraints under which Libyan bureaucrats operate seldom permit adequate planning, at least the type of planning desired by the technocrats and workhorse groups. Those who want to take time and execute the proper planning techniques are criticized by their ambitious peers as being "obstructionist" and antirevolutionary.

Haste similarly impairs coordination among administrative units, coorination already in short supply because of structural and behavioral problems. The urgency to produce immediate results has resulted in several agencies performing parallel operations, and ordering similar equipment and teams of experts. Such administrative units were created without clear job specifications, authority lines, or institutionalized functions and have resulted in growing confusion and waste.

The urgency of the RCC's demands and the fact that the bureaucracy, for all of the reasons surveyed, lacks the capacity to execute those demands has resulted in bureaucratic success being measured in terms of dollars expended rather than in terms of the number of projects completed and working. Benefits go to the spender, not to the workhorse group. Thus, although Libya probably imports more machinery and technical equipment on a per capita basis than almost any other developing area, much of its equipment, a majority by some estimates, rusts in the desert before it can be used. The emphasis on spending as the ultimate indicator of progress has also resulted in a total disregard for maintenance. The normal life of buildings and equipment is a fraction of their life in the United States or Western Europe.

Just as the performance of the Libyan bureaucracy has suffered from the profound sense of urgency under which it operates, so it also suffers from the outpourings of invectives that have been heaped upon it by RCC members. Moreover, whatever tendencies toward innovation and creativity do exist tend to be stifled for fear of making a mistake and suffering further abuse. Indeed, some of our interviewers went so far as to suggest that the Libyan bureaucracy was approaching a state of civil disobedience. Rather than seeking innovative solutions to Libya's problems, many of its members appeared to seek personal security and survival by enveloping themselves in a cocoon of red tape and obfuscation.

The revolution's first effort at mass mobilization, then, could hardly have lived up to Colonel Qadafi's expectations. We will next turn to the changes that have been made to rectify this situation.

# 6 Mobilization Stage Two

As the Libyan revolution entered its fourth year, Colonel Qadafi's assessment of the regime's mobilization efforts were far from encouraging. The ASU had yet to mobilize the Libyan mass politically. The modernizing administrators program, although one of the most innovative programs of the early revolutionary period, had failed to penetrate the mass administratively. The bureaucracy was stagnant at best, and offered little promise of becoming a revolutionary instrument in the foreseeable future. Overt progress in terms of buildings and infrastructure construction had been substantial, yet had proceeded in a whimsical fashion without a coherent plan. Even the capacity of the revolutionary leaders to set and enforce a clear set of development priorities was called into question by the defection of the Hawadi group. Only drastic changes, Colonel Qadafi suggested, could get the revolution back on course to achieve its objectives.

Qadafi's proposals for revitalizing the revolution's mobilization efforts took four basic directions: (1) initiation of the popular revolution, (2) institution of politicization centers to augment the political socialization efforts of the education and media systems, (3) establishment of a people's militia to shore up an army over-extended by the vigor of Libya's foreign policy efforts, and (4) initiation of a three-year plan to chart the course of Libya's economic development. The objective of this chapter is to examine the four new revolutionary initiatives that gave shape to the second stage of the RCC's mobilization efforts, a stage lasting from approximately 1973 through 1975.

## The Popular Revolution

The mobilization efforts of the revolution's early years had been largely abortive. Moreover, the apathy of the Libyan masses and the stagnation of the bureaucracy were rooted deeply in Libya's historical evolution. Tested solutions to Libya's problems were not readily available.

The only rapid solution to the mobilization problems besetting the Libyan revolution, Qadafi determined, would be the initiation of a popular revolution patterned after Chairman Mao's Chinese cultural revolution. As viewed by our respondents, the Libyan leadership saw the Chinese cultural revolution as a mass uprising against the routinized elements in the state and party bureaucracies, and against the reactionary (traditional) and opportunistic elements in society at large. In one cataclysmic wave, the truly revolutionary elements of China were believed to have risen up and purged Chinese society of its detractors.

If the concept of a cultural revolution was borrowed from the Chinese, its application to the needs of a (then) intensely anticommunist, nationalistic state lacking a viable political party would be uniquely Libyan. Indeed, Libya's application of the cultural revolution would be its next grand experiment and would eventually form the basis of Qadafi's third universal theory, a topic to be discussed in length in later chapters. The popular revolution was proclaimed on April 16, 1973, in a speech delivered on the occasion of the prophet Mohammed's birthday.

The initial step in Libya's cultural revolution was the replacement of modernizing administrators by popularly elected administrative committees. Similar committees were also elected to manage government corporations and universities. Such committees, it was felt, would draw the masses directly into the political process and provide them with the opportunity to pursue and execute those projects they felt to be of the greatest urgency in their particular units and organizations. The process would thus bypass much of the obstructionism and red tape of the bureaucracy and forge the direct linkage between the masses and the elite that the RCC had been so desperately seeking. The popular committees would also provide the masses with the opportunity to purge the lower ranks of the bureaucracy, thereby eliminating its most recalcitrant elements and serving notice to officials at all levels that their careers were directly dependent upon their ability to serve the masses. Finally, in making Libya's citizens responsible for their own affairs, the popular committees were providing experience in citizenship training. Only through direct involvement could the masses be weaned from their traditional reluctance to participate politically. Also, only by direct participation could their awareness of themselves as citizens in a nation be developed.

Libya's popular revolution, it should be noted, shared little of the destructive anarchy that accompanied the red guard phase of the Chinese cultural revolution. Rather, in its Libyan application, the popular revolution became a careful first step toward popular involvement. Heads rolled only in the figurative sense that substantial numbers of managers and bureaucrats found their positions of status and authority considerably diminished. There was neither bloodshed nor mass arrests. In fact, the Libyan cultural revolution was far closer to Yugoslavian and Algerian experiments in worker self-management than to its Chinese namesake. More specifically, it was to become an experiment in popular self-administration.

In terms of structure, each of Libya's administrative zones created during the process of abolishing tribal boundaries was to elect a popular committee from among citizens of that zone. As a first step in this process, the ASU in each district selected a zone committee charged with the task of organizing and supervising the elections. Individuals selected to serve on the preparatory committees were generally teachers, principals, and local government employees; in other words, individuals of some stature, but not members of the traditional local elite structure. The preparatory committee, once constituted, accepted nominations for membership in the popular committee from citizens of its zone. Once nominations were closed, a list of candidates was made public and citizens of the zone received the oportunity to vote for as many candidates as there were seats on the popular committee. Elections took place at a general open meeting under the supervision of the preparatory committee which also counted the votes and sent the results to the ASU. The term of a popular committee was set at two years, following which the ASU would again call for nominations to an ad hoc preparatory committee, and the selection process would repeat itself.

Although the specified term of a popular committee was two years, provisions were made for the recall of ineffectual committees via a somewhat ill-defined process. Disgruntled citizens could denounce the existing popular committee and ask the ASU to select a preparatory committee to supervise the election of a new popular committee. The number of individuals required for the election of a new committee remained flexible, but instances exist in which thirty to fifty individuals were successful in overturning a sitting committee. The possibility of recall elections also received strong impetus from the speeches of Colonel Qadafi where he cited recall as a particularly effective means of assuring that committees retained their revolutionary vigor and were not infiltrated by undersirable elements.

It should be clarified that the ASU, although initiating preparatory nomination committees, remained independent of the popular committees. A direct link between the two institutions existed only in the sense that the chief of the local ASU aided in the selection of members of the preparatory nomination committee and would presumably favor ASU members.

Once constituted, the zone popular committee elected (1) a chairman, (2) one (or two) members to serve on the municipal popular committee, and (3) one member to serve on the provincial popular committee. In terms of functions, the zone committee would have absolute authority for managing the affairs of the zone, subject to the supervision of the higher committees.

In addition to the zone popular committees, each professional group within the municipality also elected a popular committee. In the case of teachers, for example, each school elected a popular committee, a representative of which would be sent to the municipal education committee. The functions of the municipal education committee were roughly equivalent to those of municipal school boards in the United States, albeit with a strong overtone of a teachers' organization. Labor, agriculture, and other professional groups followed roughly the same pattern, with larger municipalities having special occupational committees for teachers, farmers, lawyers, engineers, and other specialized groups. The occupational committees at the municipal level also sent delegates to the municipal popular committee and the provincial popular committee.

The municipal and provincial popular committees were independent bodies without direct connecting links. The municipal popular committee was responsible for municipal affairs; the provincial popular committee was responsible for provincial affairs. Once constituted, the municipal and provincial popular committees elected chairmen, who also served as the mayor of the municipality and governor of the province, respectively.

### Evaluation of the Popular Committees

As originally constituted, the popular committees got off to a rocky start. In part, a certain amount of confusion was inevitable inasmuch as the dramatic shift from the modernizing administrators to the popular committees allowed little time for advanced planning. It was anticipated that mistakes would be made and that both the popular committee members and the population as a whole would have to suffer through an arduous period of on-the-job training.

Also, as anticipated, the traditional leaders scorned the popular committees, a fact that clearly minimized mass participation. Participation was also reduced by the innovative nature of the popular committee movement and by a general tendency on the part of many people to assume a wait-and-see attitude. The reticence of the general population to become involved was particularly unfortunate, for it resulted in a majority of the popular committees being dominated by marginal elements.

The exodus of the modernizing administrators and the inexperience and marginal quality of many of the early members of the Popular committees left a clear void in terms of managerial skills. In many instances, the zeal of committee members combined with their inexperience led to an inordinately high level of error, placing in jeopardy public receptivity to the popular committee experiment. Tendencies also appeared on the part of many early committee members to use their positions to settle old scores and to pursue their particularistic interests. Also problematic, from the perspective of the regime, was the tendency of some popular committee members to compensate for their lack of experience by relying on the advice and council of the traditional local elites. Thus, although traditional leaders were banned from committee membership, their influence remained very much in evidence.

Indeed, the questionable quality of the popular committees as initially constituted was one of the underlying factors behind Qadafi's public speeches urging that ineffectual committees be recalled. There was also some concern that traditional elements had infiltrated the popular committee structure, a situation preparatory committees were anxious to avoid in future elections. The preparatory committees thus came to play a crucial "gatekeeper" function in maintaining the revolutionary purity of the popular committees. The ASU also shared in the gatekeeping function by serving as a source of information concerning the desirability of the individuals elected. Eventually, the RCC took charge of the electoral process, requiring that they approve the list of elected members prior to its public announcement. If the lists proved unsatisfactory, new elections were held, a process that was repeated as often as necessary.

In spite of the influence of the ASU in forming the popular committees, conflict soon developed between the two institutions. Qadafi's speeches had not clearly delineated their roles, and both the ASU and the popular committees claimed total authority for virtually all local decisions. Each claimed the authority to allocate the zone's budget. Both justified their claims by referring to Colonel Qadafi's speeches. Popular committee members claimed to be more professional, citing the fact that they enjoyed both offices and staff. The ASU generally had none. The ASU, in turn, claimed revolutionary orthodoxy, and clearly had the power to impugn the loyalty and effectiveness of a popular committee, a process that increased excessive conservatism and noninnovative behavior in popular committee members. In many ways, the jurisdictional conflicts that had existed between the ASU and the modernizing administrators reappeared as issues between the ASU and the popular committees.

## The Military and the Militia: Stage 2

As the revolution's foreign policy became increasingly vigorous, the RCC became ever more conscious of the need to strengthen its military position. It may be realled, for example, that during the 1973-75 period, the Libyan regime had come into conflict with Tunisia and Morocco to the west and with Chad in the south. Chad had presumably facilitated the abortive Royalist coup of 1970. Libya, in turn, was the prime supporter of the Chad Liberation Front, a Muslim independence movement operating in the Libyan-Chad border region. To round out the picture, Qadafi's relations with Egypt, the Sudan, Saudi Arabia, Great Britain, and the United States were beginning to show clear signs of deterioration. National security, then, was clearly a legitimate concern of the RCC. Efforts to strengthen the military during this period included:

1. The initiation of compulsory service for all Libyans born in or after 1944
2. The drafting of bureaucratic talent into the officers corps
3. The rapid augmenting of the prerogatives and benefits of the officer corps

In spite of these efforts, the RCC found it difficult to bring the military up to the desired strength.

To augment the military and, perhaps to provide a counterweight to its monopoly of coercive force (the police remained armed with light weapons), the popular revolution of 1973 also called for the creation of a people's militia. "Because of the awesome responsibilities facing the military and the smallness of their ranks," Qadafi stated, "the masses must learn to protect themselves." "It is the people's revolution, and it is the duty of every citizen to defend it." The militia was placed under the control of an RCC member and remained independent of the army and the police.

During its first year, the militia enlisted approximately forty thousand recruits, most of whom were provided at least rudimentary military training by the army. Subsequently, the militia developed its own training corps designed to both train new recruits and provide refresher courses for established militia units. The ultimate recruitment goal was at least one militia member from each family. The militia was open to both males and females, and the ages of members varied. They received uniforms and weapons; they did not receive wages. The functions of the militia include guarding major public buildings and manning remote border stations and checkpoints. The militia is also prepared for immediate mobilization and has been mobilized during times of crisis, such as the 1977 Libyan-Egyptian confrontation.

**The Three-Year Development Plan and**
**Related Distributive Measures**

The three-year development plan initiated in 1973 was Libya's first serious effort at centralized planning. Although vague references to one plan or another had been made during both the monarchy and the early years of the revolution, such plans were little more than general policy directives.[1]

The three-year plan had three fundamental objectives:

1. Improve the productive capacity of the Libyan economy
2. Reduce dependency on the oil sector
3. Build regime support by redistributing Libya's oil wealth as broadly as possible among Libya's populace

The production-oriented segments of the plan reflected the desire of the revolutionary leadership to both transform Libya into a modern industrial state and establish its agrarian self-sufficiency, objectives designed to prepare for the day when Libyan oil resources would be depleted. The distributive elements of the plan reflected both the RCC's egalitarian values and its strong desire to utilize distributive mechanisms as a measure for building regime support. General allocations for the three-year plan, 1973-1975, are provided in table 6-1.

The RCC hailed the three-year plan as a success, citing with considerable pride its massive expenditures and substantial growth rates achieved. Table 6-2, for example, summarizes overall growth rates during the three-year period. Figures 6-1, 6-2, and 6-3 reflect the magnitude of expenditures in industry and commodity subsidization, and the growth in health services, respectively, for the period ranging from 1969 through the end of the three-year plan. In reporting the results of the three-year plan, people tended to equate expenditures with implementation. In this regard, it should be recalled that Libya does not suffer from financing problems nor from problems relating to balance of payments, unemployment, or the erosion of economic gains by an exploding population. The problem is primarily one of absorbing capital in a skillful and productive manner.[2]

**Table 6-1**
**Allocations among Sectors in the 1973-1975 Plan**

| Sector | Allocations (in million U.S. dollars) | Percentage of Total |
|---|---|---|
| Housing | 1,213.968 | 18.4 |
| Agriculture | 1,101.408 | 16.6 |
| Electricity and water | 864.864 | 13.1 |
| Transport and communication | 853.768 | 12.9 |
| Industry | 778.176 | 11.8 |
| Education | 645.456 | 9.8 |
| Public services | 627.312 | 9.5 |
| Health | 238.560 | 3.6 |
| Petroleum | 164.304 | 2.5 |
| Construction | 20.832 | 0.3 |
| Other minerals | 9.744 | 0.2 |
| Bank and insurance | 1.344 | — |
| Reserves | 80.304 | 1.2 |
| Total | 6,602.400 | 100.0 |

Source: *The Three Year Plan* (1973-1975), Ministry of Planning, Libya, p. 90.

**Table 6-2**
**Main Trends of Growth Rate in the Libyan Arab Republic**

| | Unit | 1972 | 1975 | Growth Rate (percentage) Development Plan 1973-1975 | Growth Rate (percentage) Annual Compound |
|---|---|---|---|---|---|
| Fixed local gross investment | Million Dinars[a] | 375.0 | 850.0 | 126.7 | 31.5 |
| Gross saving | " | 605.0 | 900.0 | 48.8 | 14.2 |
| Rate of investment | Percentage | 27.6 | 46.6 | — | — |
| Rate of saving | " | 44.6 | 49.3 | — | — |
| Commodities exported | Million Dinars | 966.0 | 1,120.0 | 16.0 | 5.1 |
| Export of oil and natural gas | " | 960.5 | 111.0 | 15.8 | 5.0 |
| Exports of oil byproducts | " | 3.5 | 4.6 | 31.4 | 9.5 |
| Other exports | " | 2.0 | 4.4 | 120.0 | 30.0 |
| Commodities imported | " | 343.0 | 520.0 | 51.6 | 14.9 |
| Population | Thousands | 2,084.0 | 2,379.0 | 14.2 | 8.5 |
| Employees | " | 557.0 | 682.9 | 22.6 | 7.0 |
| National employees | " | 477.0 | 549.1 | 15.1 | 4.8 |
| Non-national employees | " | 80.0 | 133.8 | 67.3 | 18.7 |
| Number of workers in agriculture | " | 163.5 | 183.5 | 12.2 | 3.8 |
| Number of workers in industry | " | 38.8 | 48.3 | 24.4 | 7.5 |
| Total production | Million Dinars | 1,982.7 | 2,713.5 | 36.8 | 11.0 |
| Production in oil sector | " | 979.5 | 1,134.0 | 15.8 | 5.0 |
| Production in non-oil sector | " | 1,003.2 | 1,579.5 | 57.5 | 16.5 |
| Agricultural production | " | 57.9 | 87.0 | 50.0 | 14.5 |
| Industrial production | " | 84.4 | 163.0 | 93.0 | 24.5 |

| | | | | | |
|---|---|---|---|---|---|
| Gross local revenues | " | 1,573.8 | 212.0 | 35.0 | 10.5 |
| Gross revenues from oil sector | " | 909.3 | 1,053.0 | 15.8 | 5.0 |
| Gross revenues from non-oil sectors | " | 664.5 | 1,072.0 | 61.5 | 17.5 |
| Agricultural revenues | " | 40.6 | 63.3 | 56.0 | 16.0 |
| Industrial revenues | " | 1,356.3 | 1,824.0 | 34.5 | 10.4 |
| Gross national revenue | " | 1,330.8 | 1,784.0 | 33.0 | 10.2 |
| Gross national production | " | 1,356.3 | 1,824.0 | 34.5 | 10.4 |
| Per capital income in gross local | Libyan Dinars | 755.2 | 893.2 | 20.5 | 6.0 |
| Per capital income in gross national | " | 638.6 | 749.9 | 18.8 | 5.7 |
| Final consumption | " | 711.8 | 905.0 | 27.1 | 8.4 |
| Private consumption | " | 396.0 | 471.5 | 19.0 | 6.0 |
| Public consumption | " | 315.8 | 433.5 | 37.3 | 11.2 |
| Final consumption by the individuals | " | 341.5 | 380.4 | 12.9 | 3.9 |
| Private consumption by the individuals | " | 190.0 | 198.2 | 4.8 | 1.5 |
| Public consumption by the individuals | " | 151.5 | 182.2 | 23.1 | 6.7 |

Source: Libyan Arab Republic, Ministry of Information and Culture, *The Human March in Libya* (Tripoli) 1976, pp. 90-91.
a1 dinar equals approximately $3.30.

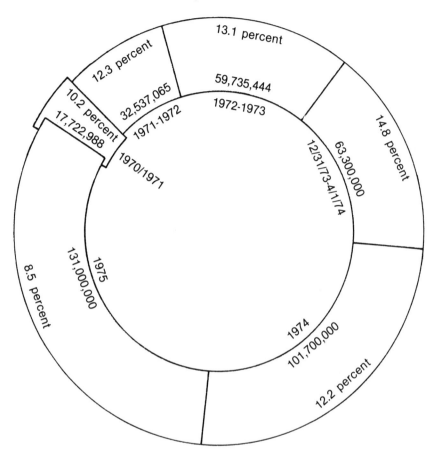

Source: Libyan Arab Republic, Ministry of Information and Culture, *The Human March in Libya,* 1976, p. 128.

[a]dinar equals approximately U.S. $3.30.

Note: For 1963 to 1969, (7 years), the figures are 5.2 percent and 32,498,956 million dinars.

**Figure 6-1.** Development of Expenditures in Industry: 1963-1975, in Million Dinars and as a Percentage of the Annual Budget.[a]


Housing was a particular source of pride for the RCC, with the government citing completion of 112,552 housing units during the course of the three-year plan, most of which were either distributed free to the poor (tent dwellers) or sold with subsidies up to 90 percent for citizens with yearly incomes of less than six thousand dollars. Under this program, 24,243 Libyan poor families had received a direct housing subsidy by 1974, a very substantial accomplishment in the area of resource distribution.[3] Sub-

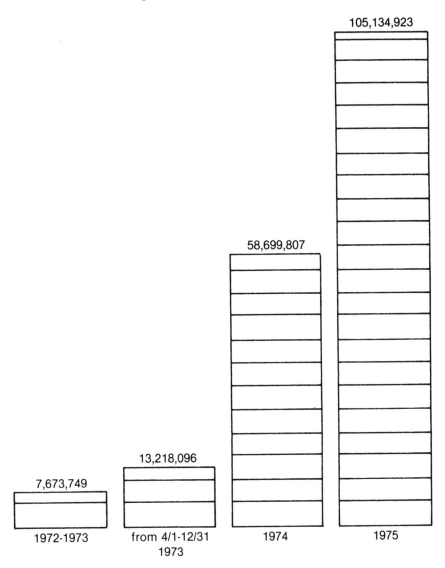

Source: Libyan Arab Republic, Ministry of Information and Culture, *The Human March in Libya,* 1976, p. 155.

**Figure 6-2.** Development of Expenditures in Commodity Subsidization of Essential Foodstuffs: 1972-1975, in million dinars

stantial progress was also made in public health, the figures for which are summarized in table 6-3.

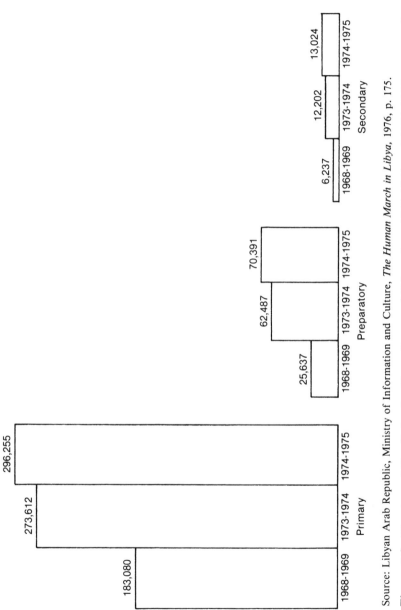

Source: Libyan Arab Republic, Ministry of Information and Culture, *The Human March in Libya*, 1976, p. 175.

**Figure 6-3.** Number of Pupils in the Three Stages of Education, 1973-1974 and 1974-1975 compared to 1968-1969

**Table 6-3**
**Health Care: 1969 and 1975**

|                                     | 1969  | 1975   |
|-------------------------------------|-------|--------|
| Hospitals                           | 42    | 61     |
| Beds                                | 6,421 | 14,695 |
| Dental clinics                      | 23    | 64     |
| Maternity and children's welfare    | 31    | 92     |
| Tuberculosis centers                | 5     | 19     |
| Trachoma centers                    | 5     | 14     |
| Health centers and central clinics  | 5     | 107    |
| Multidepartment clinics             | 1     | 22     |
| Public clinics                      | 414   | 594    |

Source: Libyan Arab Republic, Ministry of Information and Culture, *The Human March in Libya*, Tripoli 1976, p. 212.


### Critique of the Three-Year Plan

There is no question that the three-year plan involved massive outlays of capital for both productive and distributive projects, nor can one seriously question the fact that considerable growth did occur during the three years of the plan. This is not to suggest, however, that the revolution's first foray into centralized planning was without its drawbacks. Ruth First, for example, has argued that the three-year plan, following earlier patterns, was less a plan than a collection of budgetary requests by the various ministries. Among other things, she suggests, there was little statistical data existed upon which to base a three-year plan.[4] The following passage is representative of her analysis.

Pressure from the ministries caused the census due in 1974 to be brought forward a year. This census will at least enumerate all employment establishments and not only those listed as "large," for the vast majority are anything but large. Meanwhile the condition of the private economic sector is virtually unknown. Retail trade statistics have covered Benghazi and Tripoli only; the rest of the country has gone unassessed.

It is said, perhaps apocryphally, of the complaint by a Minister of Planning under the previous regime, that in the country's expectancy of miracles after oil wealth there was no time to plan. Ministries were under constant pressure to spend and had neither time nor strength to prepare properly.

Major Jalloud, then minister in charge of production, now Prime Minister, told a press conference of foreign correspondents the reason why. "It was natural," he said, "for any military group to produce economic and social plans for a radical change: so as to convince the people and the world at large that it was not a movement aiming only at a seizure of power. This was the way army leaders could prove that they had led not a military coup d'etat but a revolution."[5]

Certainly there was very little coordination among the requests of the various ministries. One might recall, in this regard, our earlier critique of the Libyan bureaucracy and judge accordingly the bureaucracy's ability to either effectively plan or execute a coherent development plan. Nevertheless, progress was made, but it was at what might seem to be an extraordinarily high cost.

### Distributive Mechanisms and the Rentier State

More problematic than the waste, duplication, and excessively high cost of the results achieved by the three-year plan, was the fact that the plan did not markedly alter Libya's status as a rentier state. The most tangible accomplishments lie in the construction of housing projects, roads, factories, and agrarian facilities. These accomplishments were important to Libya's development, but were achieved largely through the use of foreign contractors. The Libyans, in their role as a consuming class, watched from the sidelines. In a very fundamental sense, Libya's inability to break the rentier state pattern finds its roots in the distributive mechanisms employed by the monarchy and extended by the revolution in its efforts to build regime support.

Prior to the discovery of oil, Libya was destitute. Its population was largely illiterate, rural, and totally lacking in technical, entrepreneurial, or administrative skills. With the discovery of oil, a pervasive feeling existed throughout Libya that the new wealth was a blessing from Allah sent to compensate Libyans for years of poverty and suffering. Virtually any Libyan desiring a job found employment with the government. Being largely illiterate and devoid of production skills, supplicants here were given jobs as drivers, door-watchers, messengers, or coffee-fetchers. The pay was generous and the workload was minimal. Individuals with either connections or minimal literacy skills were fed into the bureaucracy. As the word of such glad tidings spread, what had been a trickle of urban migration prior to the discovery of oil suddenly became a flood. It seemed that everyone demanded, and, for the most part, received a government job.

During the early years of the revolution, this policy of distributive employment was extended as a direct means of building regime support. The minimum wage was almost doubled, thereby increasing the desirability of nonproductive welfare jobs.

Moreover, it was during the period of the three-year plan that the RCC implemented its programs to stimulate Libyan entrepreneurships and to build a middle class supportive of the revolution by decreeing a policy designed to (1) limit the size of private corporations doing business with the government, and (2) provide Libyan citizens with loans so they could begin their own small businesses. Such businesses, once initiated, were virtually assured of lucrative government contracts. Most, of course, relied upon foreign labor and foreign technicians. Many were merely fronts for foreign firms.

In much the same manner, a plethora of small shops mushroomed throughout the country, surviving largely on the low-volume, high-profit sales made possible by the abundance of the newly disseminated oil wealth. The same pattern was followed in the agrarian sector, with the revolutionary government offering farmers long-term loans for land and equipment on such generous terms that they might well be interpreted as bribes to return to the land. The standard joke of that era was that every Libyan farmer had livestock, a tractor, and two Egyptians.

The purpose of these programs, as noted previously, was to build regime support by means of distribution and to somehow force the involvement of the Libyan population in the economic process of the country. The economic programs were, in effect, structural cures for what the regime considered severe attitudinal deficiencies. The pattern that emerged, however, was one in which almost every enterprising Libyan acquired a bureaucratic position, a small business, and a farm. Foreigners were used to run the farm and the business, while the Libyan owner supervised both operations from the confines of a lucrative government job. In many instances, bureaucratic positions were used to promote contracts for the individual's business concerns, thereby exacerbating already severe levels of corruption.

In the final analysis, then, the distributive programs of the revolution's early years had the clear impact of reinforcing the rentier state pattern. Although the three-year plan sought to break this pattern, its modest efforts in this regard were overwhelmed by the conflicting distributive policies of the government. The structural reforms designed to create increased entrepreneurship did not solve the behavioral problem of the government dependency syndrome. Rather, they appeared to reinforce it. As we will see in the next chapter, the RCC was forced to take stringent measures to break the inherent contradictions in its programs.

**Political Socialization**

During its early years, the revolution's efforts at political socialization had focused upon the mass media and the education system. As suggested in the preceding chapter, the Libyan education system was not well designed to function as a political socialization unit, nor did Libya have the personnel to achieve a rapid transformation of the system. Indeed, a high percentage of the teachers were foreigners. Later chapters will also illustrate that teachers have been particularly resistant to many of Colonel Qadafi's reforms. The Libyan media also had failed to live up to Colonel Qadafi's expectations as a revolutionary instrument and had increasingly become the butt of his criticisms. The socializing impact of the family and the religious leaders was judged to be negative. Thus after five years of existence, the revolution remained without an effective agent of revolutionary socialization.

The primary responsibility for political socialization, it was determined, would fall to the Arab Socialist Union. The ASU, however, had yet to prove itself as an effective organization. In particular, it lacked a committed body of revolutionary cadres capable of administering a broad program of mass politicization.

To remedy this situation, the ten top leaders of the group earlier referred to as the civilian auxiliaries were subjected to an intensive training course during 1971 which included exhaustive discussions with Colonel Qadafi and other members of the RCC. The sessions also included long discussions with prominent Nasserites from Egypt and Beirut who played the role of educators in ideology, politics, and international affairs.

Their training completed, the ten graduates were to take their place among the top ASU leadership. All were reputed to be fanatically loyal to the revolution and to Colonel Qadafi. As in the case of all other members of the revolutionary leadership, their position and status were totally the products of the revolution. It was this group, then, that was assigned the task of socializing the masses and indoctrinating them into the revolutionary stream.

During the second stage of the revolution's mobilization efforts, the ASU leaders began conducting politicization camps for bureaucratic executives and other key officials. With time, and particularly as the revolution moved into its third stage, the politicization camps expanded to reach virtually all segments of the Libyan population. Specialized camps, for example, were eventually created for each of the following target groups: (1) ASU leaders in the various communities, (2) ASU staff in the communities, (3) all government executives, (4) college students, (5) high school students, (6) primary students, (7) members of the popular committees, (8) members of unions and professional associations; including farmers, teachers, and doctors, (9) zone leaders, and (10) sheikhs or Imams of the mosques.

By the second half of the 1970s, six to eight permanent politicization camps had been established in Tripoli and Benghazi, each with a permanent professional staff. The programs of the camps are tailored to the specific needs of each target group, and generally include lengthy speeches by Colonel Qadafi and at least one other RCC member, and lectures by prominent cabinet ministers and most or all members of the ASU leadership group.

There is probably no stronger indicator of the importance the RCC attached to the politicization camps than the fact that Colonel Qadafi has made at least one appearance at almost all of the camps during the first decade of the revolution. Qadafi's visits are considered the highlight of the session and are generally carried on Libyan television and radio. During the summer, the peak period for student politicization camps, one can observe Colonel Qadafi's presentations on television almost every night of the week. Some presentations run several hours.

Colonel Qadafi believes that the appearance of the top revolutionary leadership at the camps provides a means of building a strong personal link between the elite and the masses. It is an effort to make the elite tangible, and to make the camp members feel that the revolutionary leadership is personally interested in them. In this regard, Qadafi often uses his presentations before the politicization camps as a means of announcing new decisions or of "leaking" important decisions, thereby further conveying the psychological message that the people selected to attend the camps are, indeed, special.

Camps normally last from a week to ten days, with the exception of the student camps which may last four to five weeks and include trips to agricultural and industrial complexes. Youth camps also take on a boy scout flavor, with their participants becoming members of groups such as The Youth of *El Fateh*, The Arms of *El Fateh*, and The Children of *El Fateh*. *El Fateh* indicates the First of September Revolution.

In evaluating the success of the politicization camps, one sees that what began as an experiment in the early 1970s had mushroomed into the revolution's primary means of political socialization by 1979. The permanent camps appear to operate at full capacity and are augmented during the summers by the use of schools and public halls. People do report as scheduled; notices to appear for indoctrination are not lightly regarded.

The major popular complaint about the camps is that, with the exception of Colonel Qadafi's appearance, they tend to be dull. Members of the camps are expected to listen to intense speeches for six to eight hours a day. As such, the camps are not perceived as fun affairs. The student camps, of course, contain recreative components.

A second problem of significance, though not directly related to the camps, is the fact that in the process of political socialization, as in every other phase of the revolution, it is the top leadership that is doing all of the work. The revolution lacks competent middle management cadres. Thus, although the appearance of Colonel Qadafi and a full slate of cabinet and ASU officials provides camp members with a feeling of personal importance, it also serves to over-extend the scope and energies of the leadership group.

# 7 Mobilization Stage Three

In mid-1975, Colonel Qadafi again assessed the progress of the Libyan revolution. "It was too random," he said, "there was too much waste and confusion." The bureaucracy was still a burden upon society. The ASU had yet to effectively penetrate the Libyan masses politically, and the popular committees, whose formation was clearly a step in the direction of popular democracy, were not making as much progress as one might have hoped. Moreover, he continued, the country was sadly lacking an overall political framework that would integrate the revolutionary leadership, the bureaucracy, the ASU, and the unions into a cohesive and coherent political system through which the Libyan masses could express their revolutionary views democratically.

Turning his critical eye to other areas, Qadafi noted that neither the schools nor the mass media had become an effective revolutionary instrument. Frankly speaking, he said, the media made him nauseous. The economy, moreover, remained overly dependent upon oil revenues, and the three-year plan had failed to make adequate progress in the areas of agrarian self-sufficiency, industrial diversification, and per capita productivity. Libya had yet to become a truly productive society. Lines between the public and private sectors of the economy remained obscure. Too many merchants and contractors were grubbing for government contracts, yet they appeared to produce little for the monies received. Their services, Qadafi said, could best be employed elsewhere.

The popular revolution and the three-year plan outlined in chapter 6, then, had failed to provide the mobilization thrust that the RCC so urgently sought. Analyzed in terms of the agents or processes of mobilization surveyed earlier, the RCC appeared to express satisfaction only in the strengthening of the Libyan military and militia and in the development of its political socialization camps. Other areas remained critical. The ASU-popular committee system had been less than effective in penetrating the Libyan masses and in providing a suitable linkage mechanism between the masses and the elite. The bureaucracy, of course, remained intransigent. Moreover, there were no national political institutions for the masses to identify with. Indeed, the very fluidity of revolutionary political structures precluded the institutionalization of the revolution in the sense that mass loyalties were directed toward institutions rather than individuals. Further, the revolution could hardly boast of an ideology other than the pragmatic application of

Nasserist principles as interpreted by Colonel Qadafi. Lacking both a clear set of institutions upon which to focus their loyalties and a clear ideology to direct their behavior, the masses had little option but to turn to Colonel Qadafi as the sole source of effective political cues.

In the economic sphere, the three-year plan had stimulated extensive construction, yet had not provided a coherent and well-integrated pattern for growth. In particular, the plan had not addressed the rentier state problem discussed earlier. Libyans remained a consumer class heavily dependent upon foreign labor and foreign technology.

The problem of economic mobilization, he continued, would be addressed in a new five-year transformation plan that would build upon the successes of the three-year plan while benefiting from the lessons of its mistakes. In this regard, the policy of using Libya's oil wealth to provide the masses with lucrative opportunities for capitalist entrepreneurships would be drastically reversed. The government would now become a major partner in all economic ventures and would use its position to stimulate the productivity of the Libyan working class.

The cure for Libya's political ills, Colonel Qadafi announced, would require the total transformation of the Libyan political system into a system of direct popular democracy. Only in this manner, he said, could the problem of linking the Libyan masses to the political system be overcome. Also, the masses, by becoming fully involved in their political system, would learn to become revolutionary citizens. Also, he announced that the revolution would now have a formal ideology. Its tenets, including the philosophical basis for popular democracy, were to be outlined in the *Green Book*.

It is to the examination of these and related mobilization initiatives that occurred in a time frame running from 1975 through 1978 that the present chapter is devoted. First, the *Green Book: Part I* will be discussed, and then efforts to implement its main features will be described. The role of a charismatic leader in a popular democracy, and the economic reforms of this period and their relationship to the political system, will also be examined.

### The Philosophy of the Revolution

One of the main reasons for the lack of revolutionary progress during the early years of Libya's revolution, Colonel Qadafi suggested, was an over-reliance upon the philosophies of both the capitalist West and the socialist East. Both philosophies, in his view, led to the oppression of the masses. Neither was suited to the needs of the third world. Little progress could be made either in Libya or in the third world, he noted, until the third world developed its own revolutionary philosophy. This was as true for the economic sphere as for the political sphere. The two could not be separated.

Fortunately, Qadafi announced, the Libyan experiments over the last six years had provided the basis for a theory of political and economic development in the third world; a theory that provided true democracy without the pitfalls of representation, a theory that instituted socialism without dampening individual spirit and initiative. This theory, elaborated in detail in the *Green Book*, would provide the basis for the third stage of Libya's transformation, a transformation that would witness, upon its completion, the total self-management by the Libyan masses of all facets of their political, economic, and social life.

The depth of Qadafi's hostility toward Western democratic institutions as judged by their performance in the Middle East can be seen in throughout most of the *Green Book*.

Parliaments are the backbone of traditional democracy as it exists today. A parliament is a misrepresentation of the people and parlimentary governments are a misleading solution to the problem of democracy. A parliament is originally founded to represent the people, but this is in itself, is undemocratic as democracy means the authority of the people and not an authority acting on their behalf. The mere existence of a parliament means the absence of the people, but true democracy exists only through the participation of the people, not through the activity of their representatives. Parliaments have been a legal barrier between the peoples and the exercise of authority, excluding masses from power while usurping sovereignty in their place.

The prevailing traditional democracy endows the members of a parliament with a sacredness and immunity denied to other individual members of people. That means that parliaments have become a means of plundering and usurping the people's authority. Hence the people have the right to struggle through the popular revolution to destroy instruments which usurp democracy and sovereignty and take them away from the masses. They also, have the right to utter the new principle, NO REPRESENTATION IN LIEU OF THE PEOPLE.

Moreover, since the system of elected parliaments is based on propaganda to win votes, it is a demagogic system in the real sense of the word, and votes can be bought and falsified. Poor people fail to compete in the election campaign and it is always the rich—and only the rich—who come out victorious.[1]

Political parties, according to the *Green Book*, are also anathema to the true democratic expression of the masses.

The party is the contemporary dictatorship. It is the modern dictatorial instrument of governing. The party is the rule of a part over the whole. It is the latest dictatorial instrument. As the party is not individual, it exercises a sham democracy through establishing parliaments and committees and through the propaganda of its members.

The party is a dictatorial instrument of governing that enables those with one outlook and a common interest to rule the people as a whole. Compared with the people, the party is a minority.

The purpose of forming a party is to create an instrument to rule the people; namely to rule over non-members of the party. For the party is, fundamentally, based on an arbitrary authoritarian theory . . . i.e., the domination of the members of the party over the rest of individual members of the people.

The parties in their struggle resort, if not to arms, which rarely happens, then to denouncing and stultifying the actions of each other. This is a battle which is inevitably waged at the expense of the higher and vital interests of the society. Some, if not all, of those higher interests will be victims of the power struggle of instruments of governing. For the destruction of those interests supports the opposition party or parties in their argument against the ruling party. The opposition party, as an instrument of governing, has to oust the ruling body in order to have access to authority. To prove the unfitness of the instrument of governing, the opposition party has to destroy its achievements and to cast doubt on its plans, even if those plans are beneficial to society. Consequently the interests and programs of the society become victims of the parties' struggle for power. Such struggle is, therefore, politically, socially and economically destructive to the society, despite the fact that it creates political activity.

The party is only a part of the people, but the sovereignty of the people is indivisible.

The party system is the modern tribal and sectarian system. The society governed by one party is exactly like that which is governed by one tribe or sect. The party, as stated above, represents the outlook of a certain group of the society, or one belief or one locality. Such a party must be a minority compared to the whole people just as the tribe and the sect are.[2]

Nor, according to the *Green Book*, do plebiscites provide the key to popular democracy and the mobilization of the masses.

Plebiscites are a fraud against democracy. Those who say "yes" and those who say "no" do not in fact, express their will. They have been silenced through the conception of modern democracy. They have been allowed to utter only one word: either "yes" or "no". This is the most cruel and oppressive dictatorial system. He who says "no" should give reasons for his answer. He should explain why he did not say "yes". And he who says "Yes" should give reasons for approval and why he did not say "no". Everyone should make clear what he wants and the reasons for approval or rejection.[3]

The true principle of popular democracy and the unfailing criteria by which all democratic systems must be judged, according to Colonel Qadafi, is the principle of "no representation in lieu of the people." Representation in lieu of the people is fraud.

Until the issuance of the *Green Book*, according to Colonel Qadafi, the ideal of no representation in lieu of the people had been impossible to achieve on a national scale and had existed only in small bodies, such as local town meetings. The *Green Book*, he suggested, provides the answer to this dilemma.

THE GREEN BOOK announces to the people the happy discovery of the way to direct democracy, in a practical form. Since no two intelligent people can dispute the fact that direct democracy is the ideal—but its method has been impossible to apply—and since this Third Universal Theory provides us with a realistic experiment in direct democracy, the problem of democracy in the world is finally solved.

Democracy has but one method and one theory. The disparity and dissimilarity of the systems claiming to be democratic is evidence that they are not democratic in fact. The people's authority has only one face and it can be realized only by one method, namely popular congresses and people's committees. NO DEMOCRACY WITHOUT POPULAR CONGRESSES AND COMMITTEES EVERYWHERE.

First, the people are divided into basic popular congresses. Each basic popular congress chooses its working committee. The working committees together form popular congresses for each district, which are other than the basic one. Then the masses of those basic popular congresses choose administrative people's committees to replace government administration. Thus all public utilities are run by people's committees which will be responsible to the basic popular congresses and these dictate the policy to be followed by the people's committees and supervise its execution. Thus, both the administration and the supervision become popular and the outdated definition of democracy—Democracy is the supervision of the government by the people—comes to an end. It will be replaced by the right definition DEMOCRACY IS THE SUPERVISION OF THE PEOPLE BY THE PEOPLE.

All citizens who are members of those popular congresses belong, professionally and functionally to different categories and sectors, such as workers, peasants, students, merchants, craftsmen, officials and professionals. They have, therefore, to establish their own unions and syndicates in addition to being, as citizens, members of the basic popular congresses or the people's committees. Subjects discussed by basic popular congresses or the people's committees, syndicates and unions meet. What is dealt with by the General People's Congress, which meets annually, will, in turn, be submitted to popular congresses, people's committees, syndicates and unions. The people's committees, responsible to the basic people's congresses will, then, start executive action. The General People's Congress is not a gathering of members or ordinary persons as is the case with parliaments. It is a gathering of the basic people's congresses, the people's committees, the unions, the syndicates and all professional associations.

In this way, the problem of the instrument of governing is, as a matter of fact, solved and dictatorial instruments will disappear. The people are the instrument of governing and the problem of democracy in the world completely solved.[4]

In this way, the problem of the instrument of governing is, as a matter of fact, solved and dictatorial instruments will disappear. The people are the instrument of governing and the problem of democracy in the world is completely solved.[4]

## The Structure of Popular Democracy

The reorganized structure outlined in the *Green Book* recognized the redundancy between the ASU and the popular committees, as well as the jurisdictional disputes that had hampered the operation of both organizations. Under the revised system, this redundancy was ended through the abolition of the ASU. Any formal political organization, even the ASU, Colonel Qadafi reasoned, violated the precepts of total equality specified in the *Green Book*. The ASU posed the danger of creating an elite class and was therefore eliminated.

The new format of popular democracy specified in the *Green Book: Part I* organized Libya into three levels of popular self-management: the zone level, the municipality (and branch municipality) level, and the national level.

Under this three-tier system, the members of each zone meet and elect a zone popular committee to administer the affairs of the zone. By and large, the role of the zone committee is equivalent to the role of the justice of the peace in the United States, its main function being to settle minor disputes. The chairman of the zone popular committee, however, also serves as a member of the branch (municipal) popular committee for the branch in which his zone is located.

The zone level does not contain a zone congress or legislative assembly. All zones are components of municipalities, or in the case of Libya's larger urban areas, of branch municipalities. Tripoli, for example, consists of five branches.

Each municipality or branch municipality contains (1) a legislative assembly referred to as the basic people's congress, and (2) an administrative committee referred to as the branch popular committee (or municipal popular committee in the smaller cities where there are no branches). There are approximately 187 municipalities or branch municipalities. The exact number varies from time to time. The approximate number of municipalities is 46, a figure that also varies from time to time.

The basic people's congress is designed to serve as the legislative body at the branch-municipality level. Its membership consists of all residents of the branch meeting collectively. The basic people's congress meets quarterly. Its functions include electing a chairman and selecting five members to serve as the branch popular committee. The basic people's congress also makes recommendations and decisions relevant to the needs of the branch-municipality and debates the agenda of the General People's Congress which is provided in advance by Colonel Qadafi. In the latter regard, the members of the basic people's congress vote yea or nay on the agenda items and often add conditions or stipulations to their actions. Messengers then present the decisions of the basic people's congress at the meeting of the General People's Congress. (See chapter 10 and a lengthy transcript of the proceedings of the Fourth General People's Congress.) All voting is by a show of hands or by division into yea or nay camps. The messengers of the basic people's congress sent to the General People's Congress usually are the chairmen of the basic people's congress and the branch popular committee. Finally, the basic people's congress also serves as a watchdog of the activities of the branch popular committees and the administrative agencies working in its area of jurisdiction.

The branch popular committee is the administrative arm of the basic people's congress. It executes the decisions of the basic people's congress and the decisions of the General People's Congress as they relate to the branch or municipality. It also cooperates with the various specialized secretariats (national ministries) and generally runs the daily affairs of the branch.

In the case of municipalities having two or more branches, a municipal popular leadership committee coordinates the activities of the branch popular committees. The municipal popular leadership committee consists of the chairman and deputy chairman of the branch popular committees, who then elect a member to serve as chairman. He also serves as the mayor of the municipality. In the case of municipalities not large enough to have branches, the chairman of the branch-municipal popular committee serves as mayor of the municipality.

The system of basic people's congresses is capped by a General People's Congress which meets once a year. The General People's Congress is not a legislative body, for only the people collectively can legislate. This they do at the level of the basic people's congresses. Rather, the role of the General People's Congress is to coordinate and give uniform shape to the decisions and recommendations of the basic people's congresses. The meetings of the General People's Congress are broadcast and televised live and are attended by all high administrative officials, representatives of the unions, and a multitude of foreign dignitaries.

To manage its affairs during the months when it is not in plenary session and to administer the affairs of state, the General People's Congress has a variety of executive agencies. The most influential executive unit is the permanent general secretariat, the permanent general secretary of which during the period under discussion was Colonel Qadafi. The other members of the permanent secretariat were the remaining members of the recently abolished Revolutionary Command Council. The RCC, as in the case of the

ASU, was abolished in line with the *Green Book's* call for the total equality of all Libyan citizens.

Also selected by the General People's Congress (after nomination by Colonel Qadafi) was the general popular committee, a body that corresponds to the cabinet in the United States or Great Britain. Voting is by a show of hands. The general popular committee contains approximately twenty-two secretaries (ministers). It is the chief administrative agency of the state and supervises both the bureaucracy (which it heads) and the popular (administrative) committees at the municipal-branch level. Ministers are generally selected for three-year terms, but serve at the pleasure of the General People's Congress.

Finally, the General People's Congress also selects a general secretariat (as opposed to a permanent secretariat). The general secretariat with the help of special agencies in the administration, such as the ministry of finance, ministry of planning, and the committees' bureau, prepares the agenda of the General People's Congress sessions and solicits comments and opinions regarding the final decisions of the basic people's congress after they have been collected, tabulated, and reviewed. The general secretariat organizes the meetings of the General People's Congress, and a special committee appointed by the secretariat puts the decisions of the General People's Congress in their final form.

If one were to draw an analogy between the Libyan institutions and those of the Soviet Union, the general popular committee would correspond to the Soviet cabinet, and the general secretariat would correspond to parallel positions designed to maintain and strengthen the position of the party. The permanent secretariat would be the equivalent of the Politburo. This analogy is only approximate, however, for the Libyan system combines many features of the parliamentary and communist systems as well as making a variety of unique innovations.

## The Unions and Professional Associations

In addition to suggesting self-management at the zone and municipal levels, the *Green Book* also specified that all Libyan workers will be organized into unions or professional associations. Each union or professional association selects a leadership popular committee to run its affairs and to serve as a professional self-regulatory committee. The popular leadership committees, in turn, send delegates to participate in the federation of unions at the national level. The national federation of unions and professional associations then sends representatives to the General People's Congress to speak on issues of relevance to the unions. Unions, however, do not vote on major policy issues. As noted earlier, the General People's Congress merely records and adjusts the actions taken by the basic people's congress. Unions are not officially represented at the basic people's congress. The interaction between the unions and the people's congresses was outlined by Qadafi in a recent press conference.

> Q. What is the role of federations and professional unions in discussion of the agenda presented before the People's Congresses?

> A. The members of professional unions before they belonged to unions or achieved positions of prominence in the center of their professions were Libyan citizens avidly interested in the internal and external affairs of the state and it is essential that they participate, regardless of the means, in the fateful discussion of their state in their role as citizens.

> There are some issues, however, which are specific to the specialization of the unions and discussion of those issues should be completed within the union, after which members of the union within the Popular Congress act in their role as citizens to present the unions' view. Certainly the unions' view will undergo adjustments when the views of other citizens are applied to the case. It is clearly not the case that a member of the union stands up and announces that in our union we have decided this and that and we will not accept less than that. Not true! It is essential that members of the union not remain rigid in their positions once they are presented before the People's Congresses for they must listen to the opinions of individuals who are not members of that profession but who possess an interest in the case.

> [Suppose] you are a worker and say the union decided to increase wages, and I protest, and in the People's Congress we see people who are not workers and they mention that it is indeed possible to raise salaries except then the workers will have to bear the expense of their house and pay full market prices for flour, wheat, rice, milk, sugar, olive oil and electricity. Surely, when faced with this view from the people, and the people clearly have the right to express their views in this case in which you have a special interest as a member of the profession and in which the people have an interest from the perspective of the general will. The professional dimensions are discussed by the union because they are specialists in that area, but after that, the members of the union who are members of the People's Congress discuss the issue as members in the Popular Congress and as citizens. After any union member leaves the union meeting (and participates in the Popular Congresses) he becomes a citizen, not a worker, or student, or farmer, or official. He becomes a citizen and expresses his view as a citizen, not as as member of his profession.[5]

## University Students: A Special Case

In addition to the establishment of official unions for all occupational sectors in Libyan society (there are no unofficial unions), provision has also been made for the student self-management of the universities through the mechanism of the student union.

University students are of particular concern to Libya's revolutionary leaders, for in Libya, as in most developing areas, they represent a substantial portion of the nation's intellectual elite. As recently as 1952, there were virtually no university students in Libya, and they now enjoy a position of enormous respect in Libyan society. This position of respect, if not of awe, makes students potential opinion leaders of considerable importance. Their position of respect also provides them with at least some immunity against direct repression. To treat youths of such great promise with excessive force would be considered poor taste and perhaps a sign of weakness. At least some immunity, too, emerges from the fact that university students tended to come, at least until recently, from the more influential families. To injure a student indiscriminately would run the risk of alienating important segments of the political community. Finally, university students are clearly the most intensely politicized segment of Libyan society. Starting in the era of the monarchy, no group in Libyan society has been more vocal in expressing its opinions than the university students.

For all of these reasons, the political relevance of students in Libya is difficult to exaggerate. In the long-range perspective, the current generation of students must bear ultimate responsibility for the government's mobilization and development programs. The success or failure of the revolution's modernization programs, not to mention government efforts to reform the bureaucracy in general, will depend largely upon the training and political socialization of the current generation of students. Particularly problematic from the perspective of the RCC, was the cynicism that had crept into the universities under the monarchy. Such cynicism had to be eradicated. New programs had to be initiated that would produce high-level cadres dedicated to the revolution and its objectives. Also, some means had to be found to draw the university students into the revolutionary movement so as to utilize their persuasive powers to revolutionize the masses and to stop the political carping for which the universities had become famous since their creation by King Idriss. In the final years of the monarchy, to place the student situation in perspective, the Cyrenaica Defense Force was unleashed upon the students attending the university in Benghazi, killing several students and wounding many others. In the revolution, some students had used their special positions to manifest substantial opposition to the regime, thereby creating an unhealthy situation in which the universities were divided into roughly three factions: one supportive of the revolution, one critical of it, and one that was largely uninterested. The uninterested faction, though not a direct threat to the revolution, posed long-range problems in the sense that it clearly was not being revolutionized and could not be counted on to serve the revolution enthusiastically in cadre positions. The revolutionary faction, on the other hand, had to be reinforced and extended. It had to serve as a model of what Libyan universities should be and demonstrate the constructive role that students should play.

The system of popular democracy offered Libya's leaders the opportunity to solve the problem of the dissident and uninterested factions without direct government involvement in the academic affairs of the university. Henceforth, the universities would be run by student unions, each of which would eventually find representation in the General People's Congress.

Under this arrangement, each college or school within each of Libya's three universities (at Tripoli, Benghazi, and Beida) would elect a chairman and a cabinet which would be primarily responsible for the affairs of that college.

Each college now sends one or more representatives to the university student union central committee which, along with the president of the university, bears ultimate responsibility for running the university. The presidents of the universities serve at the pleasure of their respective student unions. In 1975, for example, the union changed the president of Fatah University (Tripoli) four times. Almost 90 percent of the Libyan professors (not foreigners) have held the position of dean at one time or another, usually for very brief terms.

## Critique

The system of popular congresses was designed to facilitate several of the mobilization functions that had eluded the revolution during the first two stages of its mobilization efforts. In particular, the system of people's congresses was designed to improve the supervision and performance of the administrative popular committees initiated during the second mobilization stage and to develop an effective link between the masses and the revolutionary elites.

Articles appearing in the Libyan press toward the end of the third stage of the revolution's mobilization program began to suggest that the popular congresses were failing on both counts. One particularly biting article (a brief excerpt of which follows) suggested that Libya might soon be forced to choose between either popular authority or progress. The references to deprivation in the article refer to the generations of severe hardship that preceded the discovery of oil.

> People's Congresses demand increased administrative services, more chairs, desks, electricity, cars, fuel, watchmen, errand runners, and messengers.
>
> And make recommendations and decisions without ceasing or limit.
>
> Yes . . . we certify the unhealthiness and non-legitimacy of the principle of today's generation sacrificing for the sake of future generations,
>
> Yes . . . we say that the years of deprivation were long and there must be

compensation . . . All of that is true and arriving . . . except that at the same time,

We must refuse to sacrifice future generations for the sake of today's generation . . .

And we must refuse to say yes to humanity today and no to humanity tomorrow.

We must refuse to exhaust our resources in the name of compensation . . . we must refuse to squander our gains with calls for erasing the legacy of deprivation,

We must refuse to sweep differences under the curtain of humanizing progress or of popularizing the revolution.

Were there not increases in greed (after the initiation of popular authority); increases in justifications and rumors; increases in laxity and laziness; increases in wasted time and effort; and the accumulation of satisfactions?

It is up to you. We must choose between the authority of the people or Progress.[6]

A more penetrating critique of the first three years of popular democracy appeared in the Libyan press and is paraphrased below.

The honeymoon has long been over and the revolution has now passed into its most historical stage; the stage of development and challenge. It is incumbent upon the basic people's congresses and the General People's Congress to make far sighted policies, and to select elements that are both competent and revolutionary to assume the responsibilities and leadership of the nation in this coming stage.

However, it has been observed that opportunistic and exploitive elements and elements of suspected ties with the defunct regime and elements possessing tribalistic loyalties have been able to infiltrate the public administration of our country and obstruct the path of the honorable elements. The disruptive elements have been able to veil themselves from the masses by assuming the mantle of the revolution. They use the microphone, and the camera and the public celebration to beguile the masses with revolutionary rhetoric, the same rhetoric they totally scorn in their private meetings and cabals. They contradict their revolutionary statements by their behavior in the municipalities and in their supervision of services and in their grubbing for commissions or lucrative contracts or in the trading of influence.

People are unable to complete their business in a department in which they do not have personal connections. The looseness in the administrative apparatus has reached the degree at which no one desires to assume responsibility or to take their decisions even in those areas revelent to the core of their assigned duties and specilization. Everyone appears to shift the decisions to legal advisors or to committees which never meet, absolutely. The result of this situation is that the interests of the citizens get lost somewhere between the offices.

The neglect and unwillingness to assume responsibility among some chosen members of the popular committees has attained the level at which they believe themselves to be the successors of God in his promised land. They believe that their three year terms of office make them inviolable, and that no human being can hold them accountable or remove them from their most comfortable positions. Accordingly, they renounce the interests of the citizens and concentrate on serving their personal interests and the interests of their relatives and supporters. Those seeking reelection do anything to curry the favor of their supporters; those who understand that they will not be reelected for an additional term, exploit their positions to the greatest extent possible.

The present administrative system is not on a true course. There are those in the system who believe in the essential changes in society, and there are those who believe that development means the frantic spending of huge sums of money on transformation projects far in excess of funds spent by other countries of similar circumstance. They simply have no comprehension of public finance. The administrative apparatus also contains individuals who obstruct fulfillment of mass demands as well as highly qualified technicians who have allowed their skills to become obsolete and who fail to show any inclination to maintain their professional competence. And finally, many of the leaders of this apparatus are not up to the standards demanded by the circumstances. We lose what they cannot give.

Some of the popular committees have also failed in applying the spirit of the popular revolution through their inability to put the right man in the right job. In particular, they have been unsuccessful in liberating the administrative apparatus from the emotional vestige of tribalism.

Given our rush into our experiment in popular democracy for the first time in our history, some errors are inescapable. Cancelling images of government and administration acquired over generations of foreign and reactionary domination and oppression is a difficult task. At present, many citizens do not sincerely believe that the masses have acquired the ability to select their administrative popular committees or that the popular administrative committees are directly responsible to the masses constituted as Basic Popular Congresses. Nor, do they fully believe that the masses set the policies and agenda of the popular administrative committees or that the masses, via the Basic People's Congresses, supervise the popular administrative committees and hold them accountable for the execution of Congresses' policies and programs. A large portion of the mass has not been mobilized to participate in the congresses, and remains passive. They are content to watch from a distance and carp (to themselves) inside their own quarters.

This passiveness on the part of the mass has opened the gate for the opportunists and the ignorant. For the sake of understanding of popular democracy and popular administration, it is essential that everyone participate in this, the people's work. It is crucial that *private* conversations whispered in private quarters be transformed into constructive thoughts publicized with a booming voice, that they be transformed into positive participation in the people's congresses, the bureaucracy, the press and in the programs of the mass media. The people must rush to the support of all causes of importance to the revolution.

It is requested that the People's Congresses reconsider their bureaucratic policies and behavior with a view toward abolishing or at least reducing the bureaucratic complexities which have grown in appearance. They must similarly end the negligence which has begun to blacken the concept of popular administration at the very time when the organizations of the public sector are being called upon to lead the way in assuring the success of Libya's modernization. The administrative excesses and fiscal contradictions which have occurred in some of the public organizations can not be allowed to continue without the accountability of the responsible parties lest they will create a hellish path leading to the distortion of the successes and gains of the revolution and to the killing of all thoughts of Socialist development in their cradle.[7]

### The Role of a Charismatic Leader in a Mass Democracy

The preceding discussion suggested that Libya had become a popular democracy in which the masses were both sovereign and self-regulatory. If such a situation exists, one might logically question the presence of a charismatic leader functioning as the de facto head of state.

The answer to this apparent contradiction lies in the fact that Libya is yet in the throes of its transition from tradition to modernity. As noted in our earlier discussion of charisma, Weber suggests that a charismatic leader must serve as the guide through the difficult transition from an unstable traditional society to the achievement of modernity. Only when modernity has been achieved, does his presence lose its urgency. Initially, the charismatic leader uses his symbolic or emotional authority over the masses to wean them from the ways of the past and to prepare them for the ways of the future. This might be referred to as the law-giver stage. As the masses begin to adopt the ways of modernization, the charismatic leader exercises less and less power, but uses his symbolic control over the masses to urge them to greater efforts and to keep the transformation of society on course until the ultimate state of modernization has been achieved. He also becomes a resource for democracy, assisting in the daily operation of government. Finally, he might also perform the Rousseauian function of assisting the masses in identifying the true "general" will of society, thereby helping them avoid the pursuit of individual or parochial interests.[8]

It is clear from Qadafi's speeches and press conferences that he very much sees himself as resembling Weber's charismatic model. Qadafi, for example has made no bones about the pitiful state of Libyan society prior to the revolution. Indeed, he speaks of the revolution leading to the creation of a state, implying, in effect, that Libya has yet to become a state in the true sense of the word.

The transformation from a condition of backwardness to one of civilization, from what we are to what we should be, the transition from the Revolution to the State will certainly not be easy.

The cost will be high, sweat will run and perhaps blood will be shed: it is the law of life, it is the cost of the progress, the liberation and the emancipation we want to attain.

Whoever tries to cross our path shall be eliminated.[9]

Qadafi's efforts to wean the Libyan masses from their traditional past has been outlined in detail in the two preceding chapters. The revolution, as Qadafi continually notes in his speeches, has begun. There is no turning back. One must be ever vigilant in defending against the forces of the past.

Brothers,

The transition of society from Revolution to State is something extremely dangerous, vital and important. Dubiousness, hesitation, indecision, fear or stopping half-way and looking backwards have deadly effects upon the vital interest of the people of Libya.

Being satisfied with the Revolution, without hurrying along the path leading from the Revolution to the State, is pure demagogy, confusion, a waste of precious time.

The only way that leads to a more advanced Society is the one passing through Revolution and through dozens of years of Revolutionary transformation.[10]

With the proclamation of the popular revolution in 1973, but more specifically with the issuance of the *Green Book* in 1975 and the launching of both the popular congresses and the five-year plan, Libya has been propelled into the final phase of its transformation into a modern state. The *Green Book* provides the masses with the philosophic map of the journey to be taken. It also reinforces Qadafi's charismatic status as a Platonic philosopher-king standing above the political foray and far above the remnants of the old RCC, the members of which have been left to find positions for themselves within the structure of the General People's Congress.

During this transitional stage, Qadafi has decreed, the people are totally sovereign. There is, in the purely theoretical sense, no government at all; only the people acting as a corporate body under the cardinal principle of the *Green Book*: there shall be no representation in lieu of the people. During this transition phase, unfortunately, this theoretical ideal will encounter certain practical difficulties. Thus, as Qadafi explained in a 1977 press conference, there are a variety of things that he and the former members of the RCC can do for the people.

First, it is difficult for the Libyan population, acting as a corporate body, to execute certain functions that have traditionally been reserved for the head of state.

The second part of your question was whether the RCC possessed sovereignty as the representative of the people and whether its decisions and laws were issued in the name of the people. We answer: There are no representatives of the people—no imposters. The people practice sovereignty totally and the powers of the RCC have terminated. But there are daily things which the RCC is able to do for the people (for the sake of convenience) for how could the people in its entirety perform daily tasks? We wish, for example, to appoint five ambassadors this month for countries in which we have opened new embassies. How do we proceed? Do we pass their names to the people and say to them, for example, that Ahmed and Omar, and Ali and Abu Bakr were appointed ambassadors? Do you agree or not? You would find those among whom you questioned who would say "who is Ahmed, I don't like his name, what is his family?"

And, in the past, ambassadors from foreign countries presented their papers before the RCC which accepted such credentials as the deputy of the people. Now this is an act of sovereignty which resides in the people and now we say to the people: How do you operate this matter? Do you want to allow the people (as a whole) to accept the credentials of foreign ambassadors and send word to foreign states via our ambassadors that we desire them to define directions for us because we have no one who is able to make decisions?[11]

Secondly, in the best Rousseauian tradition, Qadafi serves the people during the transitional stage as the interpreter of the general will. During this stage, the people are inexperienced and it is entirely possible that the specific interests of individuals and regions will come into conflict with the general will of the country. As permanent secretary of the General People's Congress, Qadafi interprets the general will of the congress and presents its views and decisions to the public in a concise and organized manner.

Moreover, just as Qadafi summarizes the general will, he also serves as a guide, suggesting areas of emphasis for the People's Congress to deliberate. Although the congresses have the power to introduce and discuss all subjects, Qadafi has remained, during the transitional stage, the major sources of new programs. Some feeling for this process can be gleaned from Qadafi's discussion of the need for greater productivity.

Verily, increasing our productive capacity requires a change in our administrative apparatus and the transformation of several classes or sectors from nonproductive to productive groups.

Our statistics now indicate that we currently possess 45,000 merchants. That means we have 45,000 non-productive Libyans. We make decisions as individuals, but in this case the General People's Congress made the decisions to transform the entire country into production. Merchants when they buy and sell merchandise make a gain but they do so without being productive. We recognize that merchants perform a service for the mass, but this service is performed for personal gain. Moreover, services aren't productive, and we are discussing production.

It is essential that the entire nation be transformed into production. When production is low and consumption is high, the end result is bankruptcy. We cannot permit this to happen. One of the cardinal principles of the revolution is the principle that when consumption exceeds production year after year because people eat, drink, and sleep at the cost of production rather than producing — a situation that was present and which posed a severe danger to the revolution — we had no choice but to apply the brakes and to transform it into a positive direction and away from the negative direction.

The 45,000 merchants recognized [by the government] during the past year were not productive. Now it is possible that the merchants will say that we are gainfully employed. They are free to say these words, but the fact remains that we have at least 45,000 non-productive [Libyans]. We must also inquire from where does this number eat and drink. They say we eat and drink from the profits of our commerce. No. The profits of your commerce are not what you eat and drink. What you eat and drink is the produce of farms. The clothes [you wear] are produced by the factories. You are served by the people who work in the electric plants, hospitals and roads . . . The food you eat is purchased at a reduced price because of public support. Your house was purchased at a cheap price and was taken from the productive people in society. You don't produce anything but commerce and when you say you eat and drink from the wealth of commerce you are really saying that you eat and drink from wealth gained without productivity, yet you consume what others have produced.

This does not mean the end of the merchants, but we request that they shift from work that is nonproductive and has no benefit to the state and its people into work that is of benefit to the people. Commerce is of specific benefit to the merchant, but not to the state. The state which does not produce — in which merchants benefit themselves but not the state — will come to harm. The merchants and their children, if they persist, will ultimately suffer from their work as well.

There are also in our midst some 50,000 door watchers and errand runners . . . who are particularly non-productive, a third of whom are under the age of forty, which means that 17 or 18 thousand sit on their hind end watching buildings, warehouses . . .

How is it possible for a country with so few people to allow these thousands to go underemployed? This is a crucial matter and it is essential that the people understand it and discuss the necessity of taking measures. This matter was discussed last year with the resulting decision that 45,000 merchants will be transferred to productive employment. Also, 50,000 door watchers and runners sitting virtually unemployed in front of schools and government buildings will be transferred into productive workers as well as most of some 17,000 drivers (chauffeurs) in the public sector the majority of whom chauffeur small cars which the bureaucrats are completely capable of driving. The General Popular Committee acting upon the recommendation of the General People's Congress in the past year has taken several decisions and recommendations in this regard to be published in order that the people's congress will be appraised of what the General Popular Committee intended in these recommendations. Executions of a series of these decisions which have been issued by the General Popular Committee will be completed shortly.[12]

Finally, there are specific areas that are beyond the jurisdiction of the popular committee in administrative terms (but not beyond the jurisdiction of the General People's Congress) whose execution remains in the hands of Qadafi and the RCC for the duration of the transitional period. These matters include national security and foreign policy.

Qadafi's pervasive role during the transitional stage from traditionalism to modernity quite logically poses the question of just how long the transitional stage will last.

The logical answer to this question, Qadafi has suggested, lies in the time it takes to achieve the normalization of the revolution. The normalization, in turn, is tied directly to the progress of the five-year plan, to be discussed shortly. In Qadafi's words:

> It must be clear to all of us that the period of transition from our Revolution to a State, inspired by the principles of the Revolution, will necessarily last for about ten years.
>
> This transformation process shall be conducted by more than one generation and not by an individual or by a Council, as some of you and some outsiders suppose.
>
> This will not be a period of dictatorship, as our enemy thinks it might be. Nobody shall govern the country in the name of the people; this shall be a period in which the moral and material reconstruction of the new society for which the Great First of September Revolution took place, will be finished.[13]

### Economic Mobilization Stage Three: The Five-Year Transformation Plan and a Hard Look at Revolutionary Distributive Policies

In reviewing economic activity during the second stage of the revolution's mobilization efforts, one is struck by the fact that the three-year plan operated independently and often in conflict with efforts to build regime support by means of distributing Libya's oil wealth to the broadest possible segment of the Libyan population. Indeed, if one looks at the entire mobilization efforts over the first six years of the revolution, one finds a series of innovative but almost totally uncoordinated mobilization efforts operating on parallel but unconnected tracks. By and large, such efforts were reactive attempts at crisis management.

The third stage of the RCC's efforts to mobilize the Libyan economy marks its first serious attempt to merge its political and economic initiatives. It also marks the ultimate transformation of Libya into a socialist state.

## The Five-Year Transformation Plan

The five-year transformation plan, the main features of which are outlined in tables 7-1 and 7-2, clearly falls within the reactive mode. The plan was conceived as the logical extension of the three-year plan and was designed to break Libya's dependence upon oil revenues through the diversification of its minimal industrial base and by extending efforts at agrarian self-sufficiency.

Aside from the specification of development priorities, three features of the five-year transformation plan are of particular interest. First, successful execution of the plan would require an even larger dependence upon foreign labor than had been required during the preceding years. Indeed, government figures indicate that by 1980, approximately 41 percent of the Libyan labor force will consist of non-Libyans (see table 7-3). Even though a high percentage of foreign labor is clearly necessary to augment Libya's small labor force, and particularly so in light of the massive expenditures envisioned for the five-year plan, the fact still remains that such large-scale importation does run the risk of perpetuating the rentier state pattern of remaining overly dependent upon foreigners and underutilizing the skills of trained Libyans.

Second, government sources indicate that Libya continues to have difficulty in absorbing all of the capital available for development projects. The main problem, then, continues to be one of attempting to proceed faster than labor, planning, and supervisory capacities permit. In particular, great care must be taken to resist previous tendencies of equating expenditures with the successful execution of development projects.

A third feature of note, and one not unrelated to the points just mentioned, is the fact that the five-year plan will be implemented almost totally by the public sector. The private sector was initially to have played a major role in the execution of the five-year plan, particularly in the areas of housing, general construction, and retailing, the three areas in which Libyan entrepreneurs had made considerable progress.[14]

As Colonel Qadafi's comments cited in the preceding section indicate, however, the political leadership had all but given up on the private sector even before the plan's formal announcement. Before the end of the plan in 1980, all vestiges of the private sector, including the merchant class, will be legislated out of existence by the popular congresses. Management of all economic enterprises in both the public and the private sector will eventually be assumed by self-management worker committees.

**Table 7-1**

**Five-Year Plan Targets of the Gross Domestic Product at Factor Costs, in 1974 Prices**

(*millions of libyan dinars*)

| | | | | Planned Growth Rate | | |
|---|---|---|---|---|---|---|
| *Economic Activities* | *1975* | *1976* | *1980* | *1976* | *1980* | *Annual Compound Growth Rates Percentage* |
| Agriculture, forestry and fisheries | 83.8 | 102.3 | 174.4 | 22.1 | 108.1 | 15.8 |
| Oil and natural gas | 2,276.6 | 2,735.7 | 3,306.9 | 20.2 | 45.3 | 7.8 |
| Mining and other quarrying | 19.0 | 21.0 | 31.0 | 10.5 | 63.2 | 10.3 |
| Processing industry | 84.7 | 113.6 | 323.4 | 34.1 | 281.8 | 30.7 |
| Electricity and water | 14.6 | 19.3 | 41.0 | 32.2 | 180.8 | 23.0 |
| Construction | 434.5 | 527.5 | 783.3 | 21.4 | 80.3 | 12.5 |
| Wholesale and retail trade | 204.4 | 226.9 | 344.4 | 11.0 | 68.5 | 11.0 |
| Transport, storage and communication | 231.3 | 269.9 | 544.8 | 16.7 | 135.5 | 18.7 |
| Finance, insurance and banking | 91.0 | 103.7 | 175.2 | 14.0 | 92.5 | 14.0 |
| House ownership | 126.2 | 143.0 | 211.6 | 13.3 | 67.7 | 10.9 |
| Public services, excluding health and education | 284.7 | 312.5 | 434.8 | 9.8 | 52.7 | 8.8 |
| Education services | 111.5 | 127.1 | 214.7 | 14.0 | 92.5 | 14.0 |
| Health services | 47.9 | 53.6 | 84.4 | 11.9 | 76.2 | 12.0 |
| Other services | 13.8 | 15.2 | 22.2 | 10.1 | 60.9 | 10.0 |
| **Total** | **4,024.0** | **4,771.4** | **6,692.1** | **18.6** | **66.3** | **10.7** |
| Made up of: Oil and natural gas extraction | 2,276.6 | 2,735.7 | 3,306.9 | 20.2 | 45.3 | 7.8 |
| Other activities | 1,747.4 | 2,035.7 | 3,385.2 | 16.5 | 93.7 | 14.1 |

Source: Socialist Popular Libyan Arab Jamahiriya, *Facts and Figures*, 1977, p. 147.

## The Demise of Capitalism

To understand disenchantment with the private sector, one must recall that the revolution's economic policies began with an almost totally unregulated period of laissez-faire capitalism, and then shifted rather dramatically to the creation of what we have chosen to call a new economic class. This class, it will be recalled from chapter 6, was created by allocating trade and con-

**Table 7-2**
**Major Targets of the Five-Year Development Plan: 1975 and 1980**

| Sector | Unit | End of 1975 | End of 1980 |
|---|---|---|---|
| **Agriculture** | | | |
| Agricultural lands | Thousand hectares | 719 | 076 |
| Irrigated lands | ,, | 168 | 268 |
| Dry lands | ,, | 551 | 808 |
| Wheat | Thousand tons | 107 | 336 |
| Barley | ,, | 216 | 245 |
| Vegetables | ,, | 620 | 825 |
| Fruits | ,, | 141 | 255 |
| Meat | ,, | 46 | 98 |
| Milks | ,, | 85 | 290 |
| Eggs | ,, | 9 | 28 |
| Improved cattle breeds | Thousand heads | 19 | 92 |
| Sheep and goats | ,, | 3 | 4.5 |
| Honey | Tons | 350 | 600 |
| Poultry (broilers) | Million birds | 11 | 26 |
| **Non-Oil Processing Industries**[a] | | | |
| Flour milling | Thousand tons | 258 | 600 |
| Fodder | ,, | 144 | 384 |
| Tuna and sardine canning | Tons | 2,000 | 4,500 |
| Mineral water bottling | Million liters | 23 | 40 |
| Textile | Million meters | — | 16.8 |
| Footwear | Pairs | 1,230,000 | 1,650,000 |
| Cement | Thousand tons | 726 | 4,025 |
| Lime | ,, | 14 | 125 |
| Bricks | ,, | — | 182 |
| Metal pipes | Tons | — | 40,000 |
| Pipes of spray irrigation | Million meters | — | 1 |
| Wet batteries | Thousand Units | — | 205 |
| Glass products | Thousand tons | — | 30 |
| **Oil Industry** | | | |
| Oil refining | Barrels/day | 69,000 | 349,000 |
| Urea fertilizer | Tons/year | — | 600,000 |
| Asphalt | ,, | — | 31,000 |
| Methanol | ,, | — | 297,000 |
| Synthetic fibers | ,, | — | 200,000 |
| Plastic materials | ,, | — | 250,000 |
| **Electricity** | | | |
| Energy generation | M.K.W.H. | 1,400 | 4,000 |
| **Education** | | | |
| Primary stage | Students | 534,209 | 552,654 |
| Preparatory stage | ,, | 116,630 | 190,905 |
| Secondary stage | ,, | 16,839 | 65,709 |
| Technical education | ,, | 3,700 | 8,150 |
| Teachers institute[b] | ,, | 21,246 | 12,154 |
| Universities | ,, | 13,517 | 25,470 |
| **Housing** | Housing units | 330,156 | 480,156 |

*Table 7-2 continued*

## Major Targets of the Five-Year Development Plan: 1975 and 1980

| Sector | Unit | End of 1975 | End of 1980 |
|---|---|---|---|
| **Transport and communications** | | | |
| Roads | Kilometers | 7,747 | 11,247 |
| Ports | Million metric tons | 10.2 | 21 |
| Telephones | Telephones | 2.1 per 100 persons | 6.8 per 100 persons |
| **Health** | | | |
| Physicians | Physicians | 1 per 1,125 persons | 1 per 1,000 persons |
| Hospitals beds | Beds | 5 per 1,000 persons | 7 per 1,000 persons |

Source: Socialist Popular Libyan Arab Jamahiriya, *Facts and Figures,* 1977, pp. 153-154.

aEstimated output.

bThe number decreased as a result of liquidating the teacher training institutes with five-year systems as of the scholastic year 1978-79, and limiting the enrollment at two-year system teacher training institutes.

struction contracts to the largest possible number of Libyan entrepreneurs in an effort to build a strong base of middle class support for the regime. The RCC was also utilizing its housing programs, price supports, and related distributive programs as a means of building support among the poorer segments of Libyan society. Simultaneously, however, the RCC felt it increasingly urgent to break the rentier state pattern of near total dependency upon foreign labor and the almost total dependency upon oil revenues to finance government expenditures.

During the period under discussion, however, a period corresponding roughly to the first half of the five-year plan, the revolutionary leadership was still groping for ways to fuse its distributive economic policies designed to build revolutionary support with its clear need to break the rentier state pattern by making the Libyan population productive members of the economy. The conflict between the RCC's distribution and productivity policies that emerged during the earlier period and Qadafi's growing frustration with the new economic class are clearly illustrated by the results of the RCC's project to provide Libyan entrepreneurs with low-interest loans to build rental housing. The program, as noted, was to serve a distribution function by providing mass housing and a productivity function by stimulating the acquisition of construction skills by Libyan entrepreneurs and their employees. According to this program, government employees who could not find adequate houses to purchase would receive subsidies to rent units constructed under the program to stimulate the domestic construction of rental units. Much of the construction of new units, however, was carried

**Table 7-3**
**Libyan and Non-Libyan Composition of the Labor Force: 1975 and 1980**

| Occupational Categories | 1975 | | | | 1980 | | | |
| --- | --- | --- | --- | --- | --- | --- | --- | --- |
| | Libyans and Non-Libyans | Libyans | Non-Libyans | | Libyans and Non-Libyans | Libyans | Non-Libyans | |
| | | | Number | Percentage of Total | | | Number | Percentage of Total |
| Managerial and professional | 27,670 | 11,620 | 16,050 | 58.0 | 44,900 | 19,940 | 24,960 | 55.6 |
| Technicians | 58,120 | 37,650 | 20,470 | 35.2 | 94,970 | 63,710 | 31,260 | 32.9 |
| Clericals | 37,560 | 31,410 | 6,150 | 16.4 | 51,590 | 44,650 | 6,940 | 13.4 |
| Skilled and semiskilled laborers | 346,590 | 251,365 | 95,225 | 27.5 | 475,180 | 307,160 | 168,020 | 35.4 |
| Unskilled workers | 207,160 | 122,055 | 85,105 | 42.2 | 262,169 | 109,740 | 152,420 | 41.3 |
| Total | 677,100 | 454,100 | 223,000 | 32.9 | 928,800 | 545,200 | 383,600 | 41.3 |

Source: Socialist Popular Libyan Arab Jamahiriya, *Facts and Figures* 1977, p. 156.

out by foreign companies using Libyan agents as fronts. The Libyan entrepreneurs, being assured of the success of their investments as a result of the government construction and rent subsidies, reaped huge profits, many of which were exported abroad. The poorer classes, receiving government subsidies, had little incentive to alter their pattern of government dependency. The risk-free investors merely reaped the rewards of foreign labor while adding little productive capacity of their own. The rentier state pattern of foreign dependency, thus, remained unbroken.

Similar patterns had occurred in virtually all areas of entrepreneurial activity generated by the RCC's entrepreneurial stimulus programs. Even more damning was the fact that members of the old bourgeoisie were in a far better position to profit from the RCC's entrepreneurial initiatives than were the poorer classes that the revolutionary leadership was so desperately trying to reach through its distribution programs. The old bourgeoisie were better educated, more familiar with economic activities, and above all else, better connected to the upper levels of the bureaucracy. The RCC thus ran the very real risk of creating a new economic aristocracy fully capable of challenging the equalitarian principles of the revolution.

In addition to massive investments designed to diversify the industrial and agrarian bases of the Libyan economy, the economic policies of the RCC during the third mobilization stage focused on three areas: (1) channeling the government's distribution efforts to the lower classes, (2) attempting to break the back of the new economic aristocracy created by its earlier entrepreneurial programs, and (3) increasing the productivity of Libyan labor.

Government efforts to breaks its newly created economic aristocracy began on September 3, 1975, when Colonel Qadafi announced a number of laws designed "to curb exploitation and end unlawful parasitical incomes." Under the terms of these laws, the government nationalized 3,000 housing units built by government loans under the program described. The loans totaled 64 million Libyan Dinars. In an even more fundamental move, the RCC abolished all foreign trading agencies. All foreign trade would henceforth be conducted by public corporations. Foreign trade, it should be noted, had provided one of the surest paths to rapid wealth for the new economic class. Huge commissions were paid to the new economic class for its ability to facilitate the granting of lucrative government contracts for their clients. Libya, it must be remembered, represented a boom economy in which virtually all consumer products and construction materials were purchased abroad. The budget figures presented for the three-year and five-year development plans represented, by and large, money to be spent for foreign goods and labor. With the enormity of the sums involved, millionaires could be and were created on the basis of one or two deals. The enormous sums involved also meant that the pressures on the bureaucracy to become corrupt were equally enormous. In a related move, the RCC also decreed that all Libyan contracting firms doing business with the government should be consolidated into large national firms. After the trading companies, the contracting business had offered the quickest avenues for rapid wealth to Libya's new capitalist class. These measures were to be drastically extended in 1978, a process to be considered in the next section.

While cutting back on their entrepreneurial programs, the government also moved rapidly to strengthen its distributive programs for the lower classes. The 3,000 rental housing units nationalized from the new economic class were redistributed to low-income families which had no homes of their own. Also, as the allocations listed in table 7-1 indicated, the provision of public housing continued to receive top billing. Price supports for vital goods were increased to keep pace with inflation. The minimum wage was increased fourfold. University enrollments were projected to double. It should also be noted that Qadafi's socialist economic measures during this period were only directed toward the new capitalist class which flourished during the early years of the revolution. Although the government complained bitterly about the number of Libyans wasted in nonproductive pursuits, such as driving, door-watching, and coffee fetching, no direct action was actually taken to change the situation.

In evaluating the impact of the attacks on the new economic class in terms of regime support, one must bear in mind that the Libyan society continues to be a fabric woven of extended families. Wealth achieved by one segment of the family tended to trickle in fairly generous proportions throughout the extended family network. Thus, the base of those benefiting from the new entrepreneurship of the early period of the revolution was quite broad, reaching perhaps 20 or 30 percent of the Libyan population. This 20 or 30 percent, it should again be reiterated, were among the most articulate, educated, and skilled members of Libyan society. Their prosperity gave them every reason to support the revolution and its programs. By attacking them directly, Colonel Qadafi sacrificed an important base of support and placed the hope of the revolution upon the lower strata of Libyan society in terms of education, skill, and general political experience. The attack on the new capitalist class, while limited in scope, set the course for eventual socialism.

Neither the attack on the new capitalist class nor the intensified distributive benefits for the poor, of course, directly affected the rentier state pattern. Many of the skills of the new capitalist class were removed from the productive sector of the economy. And, it must be noted that the new capitalist class did account for most of whatever productive capacity existed in Libya at that time. Sizeable amounts of domestic capital also began to leave the country at this time. The poorer classes remained in a subsidized state of nonproductivity. The greater expenditures of the five-year plan thus tended to produce an even greater reliance upon foreign labor, future projections for which were provided in table 7-3.

Libya's problems as a rentier state during this period, however, were deeper than its pervasive dependence upon the external provision of goods and services. Libyans also had an insidious psychological undercurrent that said they were inferior. While pouring millions of dinars into its education system, for example, the government was reluctant to take its own graduates seriously. Some feeling for the depth of this situation is provided by the following excerpt of an article published in the Libyan papers by the president of the popular committee of the college of engineering at Fatah University.

Beyond a doubt, the massive plans and development policies decreed by the People's General Congress demand that a crucial role be played by [Libyan] engineers in all phases of the various projects [envisioned by the Transformation Plan] beginning with design and field studies and continuing through supervision, execution, operation and maintenance.

Before I begin a detailed discussion of the role of engineers in these projects and the requisite changes needed in prevailing education policies to bring them in line with the directions of our projected development, I wish to ask two important questions to whoever is in a position to answer them. First, what are the details of the development plans for this country? Secondly, what is the purpose of the agrarian and industrial plan (in the overall scheme of things)?

The decisions of the state to consolidate its construction efforts by the formation of large national construction firms via the consolidation of the several small private companies does not mean that their demands for engineers will cease. Foreign firms are exploiting this delay (in the transformation from small private firms to consolidated national firms) to gather up as many projects as possible. They will then stretch out their completion of these projects over long periods of time, a process they will justify by a lack of equipment, and by planning delays. Libyan contractors, meanwhile, will sit with their materials and equipment in the warehouse waiting for a solution to the consolidation.

Also, if the state is concerned about the possible increased flow of money to foreign companies and organizations, why don't the Ministries of Industry, and Planning, Communication, and Agriculture begin to embrace Libyan universities and Libyan engineers for all stages of their development projects, thereby furthering the goal of self-sufficiency which has been established by the People's General Congress?

I implore and demand questions be put to the responsible parties concerning the actual number of Libyan engineers who have participated in the execution of the development plan. How many Libyan engineers have contributed to the design and supervision of projects in the Ministry of Industry? What industrialization projects have Libyan engineers planned in the Ministry of Industry? What projects have they designed or supervised in the technical division of the Petroleum organization? What technical and economic studies have been made by Libyan engineers in the technical offices of the Ministry of Agriculture?

In an even broader context, may I ask where is one project for which the field studies, the drafting, the execution and the supervision were all provided by Libyan engineers? I refer especially to the fields of industry and petroleum.

If we proceed in this way we shall kill the applied engineering professions in Libya as they relate to fields other than housing.

The current function of Libyan engineers is to receive foreign consulting engineers and provide them with a simple verbal picture of the projects under consideration.[15]

# 8 The Coming Decade

So far, we have examined the torturous path of the Libyan revolution during its first decade. The objective of this and subsequent chapters is to outline the blueprint for the revolution's next phase, the transformation of Libya into a "new socialist" state governed by the precepts of direct popular democracy. This chapter examines five variables drawn from the earlier discussion that we feel have played a predominant role in shaping the first decade of the revolution and which are also likely to play a major role in shaping the revolution's next decade. It also examines the *Green Book: Part II* and other documents designed to guide the transformation of Libya into a new socialist state.

**Evaluation of the Revolution's First Decade**

The first point of salience in charting both the past and future of the Libyan revolution is the social background of Colonel Qadafi and the other members of the Revolutionary Command Council. Being mainly poor members of minor tribes, neither their names nor backgrounds carried reputation or clout. They were almost totally without ties to either the rural or the urban economic bourgeoisie which emerged during the later years of the monarchy. They were even poorly known within the military.

The fact of the leaders' background meant, among other things, that they believed themselves to be under a state of siege by the supporters of the monarchy, foreign as well as domestic. The need to crush perceived opposition groups and to build a broad base of popular support became matters of the utmost urgency. Indeed, we suggest that it is virtually impossible to understand the course of revolutionary events without appreciating this pervasive sense of urgency. Revolutionary programs were expected to produce instant results. Those that did not were scrapped without further adieu, and the revolution moved on to new ventures. The sense of urgency also contributed to the transformation of Colonel Qadafi into a charismatic hero. The revolution needed *baraka*. The background characteristics of the revolutionary leadership also appealed to its egalitarian values, its general distrust of all segments of the old elite. Moreover, it was beholden to no one.

It is our observation that the sense of urgency that shaped the time perspective of the revolution during its first decade had diminished neither in pervasiveness nor intensity. The Libyan revolution, in spite of a decade of experience, continues to be in a hurry.

A second point of paramount importance in tracing the course of the Libyan revolution has been the clear dominance of Qadafi as its intellectual or psychological leader. His psychological dominance of the revolutionary elite was well established in the "cell" stage of the revolution and has increased with his subsequent emergence as a charismatic leader. By the end of the revolution's first decade, Qadafi's capacity to act in a singular, idiosyncratic manner was virtually limitless. Qadafi's goals and values increasingly became the goals and values of the revolution. Indeed, his televised discussion of the agenda for the Third General People's Congress of 1978, a process to be discussed shortly, approximated a stream-of-consciousness review of the major issues confronting his regime.

The goals of the revolution, as given expression by Colonel Qadafi's words and deeds during the revolution's first decade, can be delineated thus:

Security Goals
1. Elimination of internal opposition to the revolution
2. Deterrence of external opposition to the revolution via the creation of a viable Libyan military force

Economic Goals
1. Agrarian self-sufficiency
2. Industrialization and the substitution of industrial production for oil production as the foundation of the Libyan economy
3. Reduced dependence upon foreign labor
4. Involvement of Libyans in the production economy, that is, breaking the rentier state pattern
5. Development of a viable economic infrastructure

Social Goals
1. Universal education
2. Universal adequate housing
3. Universal health care
4. Freedom from want
5. Income equalization

Cultural Goals
1. Creation of a modernized Islamic ethic that would provide a fusion of Islamic ethical values, achievement-oriented production values, and civic-oriented political values

Political Goals: Mass mobilization
1. Creation of an effective political organization capable of linking the masses to the revolutionary leadership

2. Legitimization and institutionalization of the revolution
3. Mass participation
4. Creation of a Libyan political community
5. Building of a viable administrative capacity

Foreign Policy Goals
1. Arab unity
2. Anti-imperialism: (a) opposition to Western puppets; (b) opposition to Western influence in general
3. Full support for the Palestinians
4. Solidarity links with third world countries

The goals of the revolution thus changed little during the revolution's first decade. They did, however, become increasingly precise.

The third major point of importance in understanding the policies of the revolution's first decade is the fact that the leadership lacked the organizational capacity to implement its objectives. The established bureaucratic and military apparatus had been gutted by the revolution. There was no effective political organization upon which the revolution could build. The movement was virtually without cadres. Thus, the revolution was placed in the unfortunate position of having to pursue the urgent implementation of a multitude of complex goals without benefit of a tested organizational apparatus. The bureaucratic capacity of the regime has improved little over the first decade, a fact that will clearly contribute to its burdens during the second decade.

The fourth salient consideration in evaluating the first decade of the Libyan revolution is the fact that both the security of the revolutionary regime and the implementation of its objectives were threatened by the prevalence of what Colonel Qadafi has termed antirevolutionary behavioral predispositions among large segments of the Libyan population. Most rural and many urban Libyans were tradition-bound. They looked to the past rather than to the future. They tended to take their behavior cues from Libya's traditional tribal and religious elites rather than from its modernizing leaders. Among Libyans in the urban areas, a clear dependency syndrome had developed in the wake of the oil boom, with the government being expected to provide for everyone's basic needs via oil revenues. The Libyan population, to put matters as succinctly as possible, had neither the skills nor the incentive to become a productive labor force. They showed every sign of being increasingly content to serve as a leisure class living off the fruits of oil revenue and foreign labor. Under the best of circumstances, Libya was critically short of labor, and is likely to remain so during its second decade.

Also falling in the realm of antirevolutionary attitudes was the fact that Libyans provided little indication that they viewed themselves as members of an interdependent political community. Libyan nationalism and regime identification were low; group conflict and interpersonal distrust were high. Libyans clearly did not pull together as an economic or political unit. The state was not well integrated at the psychological, social, political, or even economic level. This, too, continues to be very much the case as the revolution prepares for its next decade.

Given the above parameters, a fifth point important to understanding the course of the Libyan revolution is the fact that the attainment of the revolution's myriad objectives required fundamental transformations in both the *structure* of Libyan society and in the *behavior* of the Libyan polity. Merely building new economic, social, and political infrastructures would be of minimal use in achieving the revolution's goals unless the attitudes and behavior of the individuals operating or interacting with the new structures also changed in kind.

From the perspective of the RCC, it was clearly easier to achieve the structural than the behavioral transformations of its revolutionary objectives. Contrary to many revolutionary situations, the RCC clearly had both the coercive and economic resources necessary to restructure the physical dimensions of Libyan society at will. Particularly perplexing for the revolutionary leadership—and for social scientists in general—was the question of whether or to what extent the structural changes initiated in Libyan society would, with time, produce the desired behavioral and attitudinal changes. Even more problematic was the fact that the urgent time frame in which the revolution operated left little scope for gradual, evolutionary behavioral transformation. Structures that could not produce immediate results had to give way to new structural arrangements that might produce the desired results. Also, as radical structural transformations were more likely to alter "antirevolutionary" behavior patterns than their more moderate measures, the structural experiments of the RCC became increasingly radical. In the political realm, for example, we have traced the evolution of the political structure through the modernizing administrators, ASU, popular committees, and people's congresses. We will shortly introduce the revolutionary committees. Similarly, in the economic realm the regime moved from a position of broadening the base of capitalist enterprise to a posture of mixed public and private enterprise, through a phase of joint ownership and finally, as we will see presently, into a pure socialist economy based upon self-management and the slogan "partners, not employees."

The need for the radical transformation of Libyan society, as Colonel Qadafi stressed in his periodic evaluations of the revolution's progress, was that the revolution's goals were not being fully achieved. Although the government was doing its best to provide the structural basis for a new society, the behavioral dimension was clearly lagging.

In citing the structural accomplishments of the revolution, Colonel Qadafi could point with considerable pride to the provision of public housing for virtually all Libyans residing in the urban areas, the institution of near universal education at the primary level, and a marked enhancement of health and welfare facilities. In the economic sphere, work was progressing rapidly toward the creation of a viable economic infrastructure of roads, ports, bridges, and airports. Industrial projects, including a steel mill, were being opened on almost a one-per-month basis. The decline in agricultural production that marked the final years of the monarchy was about to be reversed, and the Libyan government had sponsored plans for a lavish "green revolution." In the political realm, the people were, indeed, provided with the opportunity for direct participation in their political affairs.

Unfortunately, from Colonel Qadafi's perspective, many of the most visible structural accomplishments of the revolution's first decade were those construction projects which relied most heavily upon foreign contractors. This was clearly the case in terms of the regime's remarkable progress in the areas of industrial and agrarian development. Mass attitudes and behavior, however, had not kept pace with the revolution's structural changes and opportunities. Mass demands for government services and handouts increased over the period of the revolution. Productivity and skill levels remained low, a fact that could well be attributed to Libya's general inexperience with industrial technology. Entrepreneurship and economic innovation, never prominent themes in Libyan culture, appeared to decline in the face of increasing government involvement in what had been an almost totally laissez-faire economic system. By the end of the revolution's first decade, a high percentage of the Libyan work force remained in what Colonel Qadafi termed the "nonproductive sector of the economy," that is, merchants, contractors, drivers, and door-watchers. Blue-collar labor, regardless of wage incentives, remained anathema to most Libyans, regardless of skill levels. Conservation of scarce economic resources such as water and land was minimal, resulting in a dangerous lowering of the water table and threatened desert encroachment of cultivated areas.

In the political realm, participation levels in the popular committees and people's congresses did not reach anticipated levels, a fact evidenced by Qadafi's clear warning that individuals who failed to participate in the local people's congresses would have no recourse from the decisions taken in their absence. The structural innovations of the revolution thus remained poorly institutionalized. Civic responsibility remained low, and few manifestations of a political community or psychological national integration were apparent. Parochialism and cynicism remained prevalent. The bureaucracy remained ineffective, and reference to its growing corruption became the target of Qadafi's concern. Qadafi's own stature among the masses, however, appeared to increase daily. The power of the traditional religious and tribal elites had been weakened, but not broken. The religious elites, in particular, had moved closer to a confrontation as the regime moved to curtail the scope of their influence. Many members of the former economic elite, including those who had prospered during the revolution's early years, had withdrawn from active economic and political life. Some had fled to Western Europe. Well financed, they continued to be a distant but potential threat to the revolution.

In the foreign policy area, Qadafi had clearly succeeded in becoming the foremost spokesman of Arab unity, the Palestinian cause, and anti-imperialism. Perhaps the best testimony to his success was the fact that by the end of the revolution's first decade, Libya found itself surrounded by hostile neighbors. It was also embroiled in ideological conflict with Saudi Arabia and Morocco, not to mention the United States or Great Britain. Relations with the Eastern bloc, however, were improving dramatically.

As the Libyan revolution prepared to enter its second decade, then, Colonel Qadafi could look with pride to substantial structural accomplishments as well as to the fact that the revolution's programs had probably shaken the foundation of traditional Libyan society beyond the point of return. Libya could never again be quite as it was under the monarchy.

Nevertheless, the revolution's major goals remained unfulfilled. The revolution had provided the structural framework for the political, economic, and social modernization of Libya: the masses, beguiled by traditional tribal and religious leaders on one hand and the corruption of the urban bureaucracy on the other, had not been adequately responsive to the revolution's initiatives.

Direct democracy, as outlined in the *Green Book: Part I,* was to have provided the masses with the means to implement the goals of the revolution. The early results of direct democracy outlined in chapter 7, however, indicated that it could not operate effectively as long as vestiges of the old social, economic, and political systems remained intact. Thus, Qadafi decreed that the implementation of revolutionary reforms would no longer be approached in piecemeal fashion. The economic restraints on personal freedom had to be totally eliminated. The nonproductive sectors of the Libyan society would have to be mobilized toward the fulfillment of revolution goals. The state bureaucracy would have to either be made efficient or be replaced by a revolutionary bureaucracy; Islam would have to be "liberated" from the reactionary influence of a hostile class of priest and returned to the masses for whom it was intended. The masses would have to share in the protection of their revolution and not become dependent upon a professional military.

The economic basis for the total transformation of Libyan society was provided in the *Green Book: Part II,* excerpts from which will be examined shortly. Parallel measures relating to the bureaucracy and the military were outlined by Qadafi in the agenda of the Fourth General People's Congress of 1978 and are discussed at length in chapter 9, as are adjustments to the system of direct democracy. The effort to liberate Islam from the grasp of Libya's traditional religious leaders took the form of several speeches delivered by Colonel Qadafi during the course of various Islamic celebrations. His message, simply stated, was that the Koran was the gift of God as conveyed by the prophet Mohammed. As such, it was easily read, easily understood, and easily obeyed by the average individual without the intercession of a self-proclaimed class of priests.

In the remainder of the present chapter, we will examine the major themes of the *Green Book: Part II*. Chapter 9, in turn, will examine the transcript of the fourth session of the General People's Congress, a document which provides unusually vivid insights into the operation of direct popular democracy as well as Colonel Qadafi's withdrawal from the exercise of "administrative authority" and his concentration on the exercise of "revolutionary authority."

### The Green Book: Part II

Part I of the *Green Book,* "the Solution to the Problems of Democracy," was discussed at some length in chapter 7. It appeared in 1976 and outlined the rationale for the system of people's congresses which now constitutes the framework for the Libyan political system. After the Koran, the ultimate source of Libyan law, the *Green Book* is perhaps the best statement of Libya's political constitution.

The *Green Book: Part II* was issued in 1978 and provides the basis for total economic freedom. Its basic premise is that total political and spiritual freedom are impossible to achieve as long as the individual's basic material needs are controlled by others, regardless of whether those "others" are private capitalists or state bureaucrats. The heart of Qadafi's analysis is provided in the following excerpts from the *Green Book: Part II:*

> The industrial establishment is based on raw materials, machines and workers. Production is the outcome of the workers' use of the machines in the factory to manufacture raw materials. In this way, the finished goods pass through a process of production, which would have been impossible without the raw materials, the factory comes to a halt. The three factors are equally essential in the process of production. Without these three there will be no production. Any one factor can not carry out the process by itself. Even two of these factors can not carry it out. The natural rule in this case, requires that the shares of the three factors in the production be equal, i.e., the production of such a factory is divided into three shares, a share for each of the factors of production . . .

> The previous historical theories tackled the economic problem either from the angle of the ownership of one of the factors of production only or from

the angle of wages for production only. They have not solved the real problem, namely the problem of production itself. Thus the most important characteristic of the economic systems prevailing in the world today is the wage system which deprives the worker of any right in his production whether it is produced for society or for a private establishment.

The ultimate solution is to abolish the wage-system, emancipate man from its bondage and return to the natural law which defined relationships before the emergence of classes, forms of government and man-made laws.[1]

Moving from the problem of wages, the *Green Book* also specifies that an individual can be free only if he is not dependent upon others for his home and vehicle. These, too, must be guaranteed to the individual.

Continuing with his economic analysis, Colonel Qadafi stresses the fact that material resources are finite, and that a society's wealth must be distributed equally if there is to be enough to go around. Thus, although all individuals are entitled to the fulfillment of their basic material needs, no individual has the right to acquire wealth in excess of those needs.

If we assume that the wealth of society is ten units and its population is ten persons, the share of each in the wealth of society is 10/10 — only one of the units per person. But if some of the members of society possess more than one unit, then other members of the same society possess nothing. The reason is that their share of the units of wealth has been taken by others. Thus, there are poor and rich in the society where exploition prevails . . .

If an individual in that society needs only one of the units of the wealth of society to satisfy his needs then the individual possessing more than one unit is, in fact, expropriating the right of other members of the society. Since this share exceeds what is required to satisfy his needs, estimated at one of the units of wealth, then he has seized it to hoard it. Such hoarding is only achieved at the expense of others' needs, i.e. through taking others share in this wealth. That is why there are those who hoard and do not spend — that is they save what exceeds the satisfaction of their needs — and, there are those who beg and are deprived — that is those who ask for their rights in the wealth of their society and do not find anything to consume. It is an act of plunder and theft, but open and legitimate under the unjust and exploitative rules which govern that society.

Ultimately, all that is beyond the satisfaction of needs would remain the property of all the members of society. But individuals only have the right to save as much as they want from their own needs, because the hoarding of what exceeds their needs involves an encroachment of public wealth.

The skillful and industrious have no right to take hold of the share of others as a result of their skill and industry. But they can benefit from these advantages. Also, if a person is disabled or lunatic, it does not mean that he does not have the same share as the healthy in the wealth of the society.[2]

Taken collectively, the *Green Book: Part II* provides the basis for what Qadafi has called new socialism.

Thus the new socialist is no more than a dialectical consequence of the unjust relations prevailing in this world. It has produced the natural solution,
namely private ownership to satisfy the needs without using others, and
socialist ownership, in which the producers are partners in production. The
Socialist ownership replaced a private ownership based on the production
of wage-workers who had no right in what they produced.[3]

It is important to stress at this point that the *Green Book* is not merely
a random philosophic treatise. It is perhaps the most succinct statement of
Colonel Qadafi's basic values currently available. Moreover, as our earlier
analysis indicated, an almost complete congruence exists between the fundamental values of Colonel Qadafi and the values of the revolution in general. The *Green Book* thus provides the clearest indication of the direction
the Libyan revolution is likely to take during its next decade. Indeed, our
subsequent examination of the policies currently being debated by the people's congresses will indicate that the major tenets of new socialism are or
will shortly be enacted into law. Further, we will note that the *Green Book,*
both Part I and II, provides the fabric of the official ideology of the Libyan
revolution. The *Green Book* is taught in schools. Its passages decorate street
banners and punctuate Libyan radio and television on an almost hourly
basis. Passages similarly highlight the Libyan press and, in keeping with the
general spirit of the *Green Book,* the headlines of many Libyan newspapers
have been changed from red to green.

# Implementation of the New Socialist Transformation

The transformation of Libya into a new socialist state as outlined in the *Green Book,* and elaborated in Colonel Qadafi's speeches, proceeded at three levels: revolutionary authority, spontaneous mass action, and popular authority exercised by the people's congresses.

Revolutionary authority, in the Libyan context, is based upon the axiom that the principles of the revolution as embodied in the *Green Book* are inviolable. The revolution must be maintained and its principles must be implemented. Thus, revolutionary authority led to the establishment of the system of direct popular democracy in Libya, and it is the duty of the revolutionary authorities to assure that the direct authority of the masses is not subverted by the enemies of the revolution, be they remnants of the old regime or hostile foreign powers. It is also the responsibility of the revolutionary authorites to assure that the structure of direct popular democracy works well and that the masses avail themselves of the opportunities that popular democracy affords. It was in this vein that Colonel Qadafi called for the creation of revolutionary committees within the structure of the basic people's congresses as a means of stimulating revolutionary spirit and creativity among the masses. Revolutionary committees will be discussed at length in chapter 10.

Revolutionary authority, it should be noted, is distinct from administrative authority which has become the province of the people's congresses. Colonel Qadafi and the remaining members of the RCC, as the ensuing description of their interaction with the General People's Congress will illustrate, have decided to remove themselves from the day-to-day affairs of state and concentrate on their revolutionary activities. Although they presently serve as the secretariat general of the People's General Congress, this body, including Colonel Qadafi's position as secretary general, is scheduled to be filled at some point in the near future by members of the General People's Congress.

A second mode of implementing the *Green Book* has been the spontaneous or near spontaneous application of its tenets by the Libyan masses. One clear example of spontaneous mass action was the seizing of business concerns by their employees and the forming of self-management popular committees to operate them. Such seizures occurred during an intense media campaign stressing the slogan "partners, not wage earners" and were facilitated by revolutionary union groups. Virtually all business concerns are now self-managed by popular committees. The revolutionary committees mentioned in the last chapter were also created on a more or less spontaneous basis within the basic people's congresses, following Qadafi's call for the "creation of revolutionary committees in all places."

Aside from the area of revolutionary authority and the few instances of spontaneous mass action, the full responsibility for all decisions relating to the transformation of Libya into a new socialist state and for the regular administration of the state rests with the basic people's congresses. Indeed, as the basic people's congresses become fully acclimated to their role, the need for spontaneous mass action should disappear.

### Background of the Fourth General People's Congress

A remarkably frank portrayal of the authority of the people's congresses, their mode of operation, and their interaction with the revolutionary authority of Colonel Qadafi and the secretariat is clearly presented in the following description of the proceedings of the Fourth General People's Congress of 1978. The proceedings also provide rare insights into many of the difficulties and complications that have arisen in efforts to institute direct mass participation at the national level. The description of the proceedings was paraphrased from a general transcript of the fourth session of the General People's Congress provided in the Libyan press. In our view, the record provides a reasonably accurate picture of the events as they occurred and is congruent with the impression of the sessions provided by informal interviews conducted subsequent to the congress.

To set the stage briefly: Colonel Qadafi appeared on television in the weeks prior to the Fourth General People's Congress and set up a proposed agenda for discussion by the basic people's congress.[1] Copies of this agenda were then forwarded to the basic people's congresses, accompanied by special memoranda outlining the details of each item and often adding specific observations on how the item might be implemented. The basic people's congresses then designated messengers (not representatives) to convey their decisions to the general people's congress. The federations and associations also sent messengers, often the president of the group, to express their opinions on specific items of relevance to the association. Colonel Qadafi and the remaining members of the RCC served as the secretariat of the Fourth General People's Congress, with Qadafi serving as the secretary general. The popular committee of the general people's congress, composed of the secretaries (ministers) of the major administrative departments, was also present. It served to provide technical advice for proposals added to the regular agenda by the basic people's congresses and to answer questions concerning the progress or lack of progress of projects scheduled for the various localities represented by the basic people's congresses. A committee of form exists within the general people's congress for the purpose of (1) collating the recommendations and decisions of the basic people's congresses, and (2) working out uniform decisions and recommendations that accurately reflect the diverse responses of the basic people's congresses. For the sake of simplicity, we have used letters to designate individual federations, associations, and basic people's congresses.

## The Fourth General People's Congress: 1978

The purpose of the first session was to shape the decisions and recommendations communicated to it by the basic people's congresses.[2] The congress was inaugurated by Mohammed Abdul Aziz, secretary for the Popular Front for the Liberation of the Sahara, who praised Colonel Qadafi and the tremendous revolutionary accomplishments of the Libyan masses. The committee on organization and regulation of seats and the committee on form took a count of the number of basic people's congresses in attendance. There were 182. Qadafi congratulated the basic people's congresses for executing the decisions and recommendations of previous congresses and urged them to carry out those matters yet to be executed.

Qadafi then asked the secretaries of the basic congresses to make observations concerning the extent to which the decisions and recommendations of the preceding congresses had been implemented. The secretaries of twelve areas spoke, expressing satisfaction with their congresses regarding implementation efforts, and they pledged increased efforts to complete remaining projects. They also indicated that bureaucratic delays had occurred in the execution of development projects scheduled for their areas. Qadafi requested an explanation of these delays from the relevant secretaries of the general popular committee (ministers). They explained that the delays were a result of an increase in the cost of bids made by contractors and said that measures were being taken to broaden the base of foreign contractors. They said that this situation would be further improved by the new administrative procedures for local contractors. (This appeared to be a reference to the new self-management concept.)

Also, some of the basic people's congresses commented on the decision to increase productive capacity and requested a review of the steps underlying this action. Qadafi requested a clarification from the president of the general popular committee concerning the implementation of this decision. The president indicated that implementation involved forming a committee of secretaries and delegating to them the authority to prepare this decision for execution. Actually, he said, this committee compiled the number of door-watchers, fetchers, drivers, and others in similar nonproductive positions in the government and found the number to be 26,881 individuals. The committee then directed them toward productive work. Qadafi noted in this regard that it was the responsibility of the basic people's congresses to supervise the popular committees and to hold them accountable, and that it was the role of the revolutionary committees to guide and inspire the basic people's congresses to exercise their authority to its fullest extent.

Some of the secretaries of the people's congresses were upset about the need to rush into unfinished dwellings and to impose penalties upon those individuals who had occupied them prematurely. Qadafi reaffirmed that this responsibility fell on the shoulders of the basic congresses and that it was incumbent upon them to supervise the application of decisions in this and in other areas.

Some of the secretaries requested an increase in the basic level of allowances and pensions. Qadafi indicated that the subject of salaries and wage levels had been determined by the basic people's congresses and that the issue would be presented to them shortly.

Similarly, some of the basic congresses requested the provision of family allowances for individuals in the private sector. Qadafi explained that after the mobilization of the workers in realization of the saying "partners, not wage earners," the *jamahiriya* will no longer have public or private sectors. Everyone will be part of a single socialist organization.

Some of the basic people's congresses requested cancellation of policies relating to compulsory military conscription, militarization of citizens, and establishment of an armed population. In response, Qadafi observed that it was the basic people's congresses that had decreed compulsory conscription, following which the idea of militarizing the civilian population had appeared (to him) as a means of creating an armed population in the shortest time possible. A militarized population would end the need for compulsory conscription. It would also end the need for an organized army. Qadafi then noted that "it is not really relevant for you to decide to abolish compulsory conscription and you have not militarized your civilians as yet. Be assured that the subject of compulsory conscription and the existence of an organized army will end spontaneously with the militarization of civilians and the arming of the population. We shall see in the coming sessions if the basic people's congresses agree upon the militarization of civilians or not."

He stressed that compulsory conscription was in the interest of all Libyans, for it provided them with the means of defending themselves and their possessions, and he noted that "fleeing from conscription was the result of the dregs of an odious past which saw the Italians enslaving Libya's land and conscripting its men by force to fight for the sake of the imperialist Italian state. Now, however, compulsory conscription is in the interest of each citizen and provides him with the possibility of defending himself, his family, his home, his village, his farm and his factory, and most importantly, it provides him the opportunity to defend his freedom." He clarified that compulsory conscription was not in the interest of one person or another and that even those who fled from conscription (by remaining abroad) until they passed the specified age limit still retained a national obligation and were responsible for their behavior before all citizens.

At this point, Qadafi indicated that in his view, the Zionist enemy was now on the borders of Libya with an army of a million and a quarter men and that anyone who did not wish to train and prepare himself was obliged to raise the white flag of surrender and accept slavery.[3] He also stated that it was incumbent upon the basic congresses to institute militarization of the civilian population before they decided to cancel compulsory conscription.

*First Day: Evening Session*

On reconvening, Qadafi traced some of the organizational problems of the basic people's congress at A, particularly those related to the behavior of the secretary of that congress and his replacement by the assistant secretary.[4] This was followed by a discussion of the organizational problems of the basic people's congress in B, problems that had resulted in a failure to convene a meeting to discuss the agenda.

Qadafi announced that it was not possible for the general people's congress to discuss the needs of the basic congress in C because it had not met for its initial discussion. No one, it seems, would delegate authority (to a secretary) on the false interpretation of the saying (*Green Book: Part I*) "no representation in lieu of the people." Similarly, some of the problems that occurred in C returned in the final analysis to conflicts over the place to hold the meeting and the behavior of the secretariat of the basic people's congress.

The secretary of the basic people's congress at D expressed satisfaction with his congress for executing its decisions and recommendations regarding various procedures for protecting agricultural land. He mentioned that thirty hectares of forest had been cleared to establish fields for horsemanship. Qadafi later said that the people had decided to conserve the agricultural land and that this decision must be enforced throughout the country. He noted that there was an abundance of nonagricultural land that could be profitably exploited for other projects (such as horsemanship fields).

The secretary of the basic people's congress for E expressed his congress's satisfaction with its execution of the recommendations and decisions relating to the transformation (development) plan. He requested the construction of dams on the wadis of his region. At this point, the secretary of land reclamation and land reform indicated that E was, indeed, included in the area scheduled for work contingent upon a scientific analysis. He also noted that it had been established that the area was unsuited for a forest station or for fruit tree projects. Similarly, the secretary for dams and water resources indicated that studies had been made in regard to building dams in

E and that arrangements would be made with the secretary of land reclamation to assure the coordination of their work.

Also, the secretary of information and culture responded to the observation that visual broadcasts (television) did not reach F. He indicated that his secretariat was attempting to cover the entire country, but that until that was achieved, priorities would be allocated on the basis of population density.

The secretary of the basic people's congress in G observed that loans for the housing cooperatives in his region had been delayed. The secretary of the treasury responded by saying that the volume of loan applications had been exceptionally heavy, which had led to delays by the central bank in meeting the needs of some of the cooperative societies.

The discussion of the general people's congress turned to Article 2 of the agenda, specifically to a review of the implementation of administrative and transformation budgets for 1978. The president of the committee on form indicated that all basic people's congresses—187—had reviewed these budgets and that their opinions had been transferred to all secretariats of the general popular committees for information and execution.

The secretary of the basic congress for H indicated that a water line in his region had been 85 percent completed when work on the project stopped. Qadafi said that after observing the project, he personally had ordered work to stop, because the region was neither agricultural nor industrial and was blessed with neither water nor rain. It was, he said, a destitute area. He added that this and other regions were currently being studied in terms of resettling their inhabitants in a new city to be built by the sea. This would occur after adequate water was provided via the building of a desalinization station for seawater. Qadafi added that extending the water line to H was not a decision of the basic people's congress, nor was it being done on the basis of scientific studies. It was, he said, lost effort and wasted opportunity. He added that it represented irresponsible behavior.

The discussion turned to Article 4 of the agenda, relating to the establishment of general popular committees at the municipal level. The president of the committee on form said that all of the basic congresses agreed with the principle of forming such committees. Qadafi presented a draft plan for establishing specialized popular committees at the municipal level that would correspond to the specialized popular committees at the national level.

*The Second Day: Morning Session*

After brief remarks by Qadafi, the second session of the Fourth General Popular Committee moved to a discussion of Article 17 of the agenda.[5] This article related to the report on foreign policy, the Arab situation, and the transformation in the attitude toward the Arab world in reference to support for the struggle against racism and imperialism in Africa. Article 17 was considered at this point because of the presence of Yasir Arafat and the Palestinian delegation.

Qadafi requested that the president of the committee on form read the decision of the basic people's congresses relating to support for Syria and occupied Arab lands. A total of 187 committees voted to support the Palestinian resistance (100 percent); 186 voted to support Syria (99.46 percent); 183 voted to support Jordan (97.88 percent).

Twenty-six of the congresses decided to support the Palestinian resistance on the condition that the diverse factions of that resistance be unified and that they continue their struggle. Yasir Arafat spoke to clarify this and related issues raised by various basic congresses. He indicated that the unity of the Palestinian movement was difficult to achieve at the present time, but he assured them that the struggle would continue until victory. This was followed by long discussions by Arafat and Qadafi on the history of the Palestinian-Jordan conflict.

Qadafi reviewed Article 17 as it related to Jordan and Syria, indicating that the people's congresses resolved to give support to these countries provided that their borders be open to the Palestinian resistance in support of their guerrilla activities, and provided that they do not negotiate with the enemy.

Qadafi requested a clarification from the president of the committee on form regarding the number of basic groups supporting Article 5, which related to economic crimes. The president indicated that there was a variety of views and differences of opinion regarding the type of penalties to be imposed, and their duration. He announced, however, that all of the basic congresses recommended imposing some form of punishment for economic crimes. One basic congress presented an integrated proposal in complete legal form. He added that twenty-three congresses recommended the death penalty; six recommended penalties ranging from imprisonment to the death penalty. Others varied in their opinion on virtually every paragraph of the special memorandum accompanying the article. The secretary of the Musrata basic congress stated that his congress recommended imposing the Koranic penalty of the sword for economic crimes. After discussing the issue, Qadafi stated that the Koranic stricture to which the secretary referred was not applicable to this type of crime.

Qadafi observed that some of the decisions being made by the basic groups did not reflect their general view but were clearly the view of a single individual or group, such as the example of the one congress that held a special session to limit the size of the dowry. It is clear, he said, that the obligations of the congresses do not permit any one individual or group to decide the fate of all the people. He said that democracy must prevail, that the people must rise to the effective exercise of their authority, and that the job of the revolutionary committee is to inspire them in that role. He observed that the goal of the revolution was to intervene to assure that the masses would attain the authority to decide their own destiny, and that "we, as the leadership of the revolution, reject any tutelage over the people or domination of them. We will resist it by force of arms and we stand ready to intervene in the interests of the people and their freedom and their democracy until the threat of dictatorship is ended and the people are rescued from political oppression."

Qadafi also clarified that the penalties which appeared in the recommendations of the basic groups varied on the basis of the severity of the economic crimes. He also added that the examples of economic crimes included in the special memorandum sent to these congresses included (1) intentional destruction of public organizations, (2) the intentional malappropriation of public monies, (3) the purposeful making of errors which result in the loss of public monies, and (4) the smuggling of money outside of the country. Qadafi said that combating smuggling was the responsibility of all citizens in all regions of the *jumahuriah*, and that they should combat smuggling operations, expel smugglers, and seize their goods. This, he said, was in addition to the application of whatever penalties might be decreed by the basic congresses. The president of one of the popular committees indicated that the existing laws relating to smuggling and its penalties clearly had to be revolutionized and brought into line with the revolutionary life style. This view was supported by the secretary of the basic group in I. Qadafi then ended the discussion, and said that the recommendations and decisions regarding economic crimes would be forwarded to the secretariat of justice to be shaped into laws.

The general congress then moved to Article 6: the conditions of granting or withholding Libyan citizenship. A total of 183 basic groups recommended granting Libyan citizenship to Libyans only. These congresses also agreed to allow citizenship to Arabs married to Libyans and to foreign women married to Libyans. They recommended granting citizenship to Islamic Ulema. The president of the committee on form also indicated that the congresses had established three conditions for withdrawing Libyan citizenship: (1) individuals not of Libyan origin, (2) Libyans who marry non-Libyans, and (3) Libyans who possess dual citizenship.

The basic congresses specified eleven conditions under which Libyan citizenship could be severed: (1) committing treason, (2) failing to return from professional training abroad or to return home when summoned, (3) fleeing from military service, (4) being accepted as a political refugee by another state, (5) smuggling money abroad or refusing to return smuggled money, (6) embracing a religion other than Islam, (7) having the status of "missing," (8) fleeing the country after the revolution, (9) accepting dual citizenship, (10) living abroad for ten years without an official assignment, and (11) fleeing from the application of socialism.

The secretary of the basic group in Derna said that his congress felt that citizenship should be withdrawn from those who fled the country after the revolution for the simple reason that they failed to share in building the country or in supporting it. The basic group in J felt that the mission of withdrawing citizenship should fall to the secretary of interior in consultation with the secretary general of the basic groups (Qadafi). Other congresses felt that the general popular committee should administer withdrawal of citizenship after consultations with basic people's congresses and the municipality popular committees.

Qadafi asked the secretary of justice for a clarification regarding the temporary withdrawal of citizenship. The secretary answered that present statutes did not address the question adequately. Qadafi suggested that the spirit of the current recommendations of the basic congresses would be shaped into law by the committee on form.

*The Second Session: Evening Meeting*

In its evening session, the general congress turned to a discussion of Article 3, relating to the administrative and transformation (development) budgets for 1979. The president of the committee on form indicated that the basic groups presented draft budgets originating in the local popular committees, and that they had been forwarded to the secretariats of planning and treasury for their comments.

The president of the federation of sutdents then spoke, citing the necessity of imposing maximum penalties upon students in Egypt and abroad who do not execute the decisions of the general congresses regarding severing relations and withdrawing recognition from the Egyptian government following the shameful visit made by the President of Egypt. Such penalties would include the withdrawal of their citizenship and the nonrecognition of their diplomas. He also requested the central bank of Libya and the treasury to forbid the transfer of funds to students in Egypt. The president of the federation of students also talked about flight from military conscription and the practice by some bourgeois families of sending their children abroad for study in order to avoid the draft. This was followed by general discussion, including statements by Qadafi supporting the need for students studying abroad to meet their obligations to the state.

Qadafi added that the presidents of federations, associations, and unions had the right to participate in the discussions of the general congress by virtue of their membership in basic congresses. They also had the right to discuss and to relate to the general congress the decisions of their professional or union congresses.

Qadafi next asked the secretary of the treasury to present a clarification of the budget. The secretary explained that the basic congresses had passed an administrative budget for the 1978 fiscal year of 665 million dinars. Expenditures, however, totaled 741 million dinars. The budget deficit resulted from excessive costs in some secretariats. "The budget deficit might have been higher," he said, "had other secretariats not economized on parts of their budgets." "The secretariat of justice, for example," he said, "had released a large group of highly paid foreign consultants."

The secretary indicated that the excessive expenditures were explained to the basic groups in a report, including a statement that the administrative budget was not a permanent problem. He stressed that it was essential for those individuals entrusted with the economic transformation sector to develop new sources of revenue other than oil. He added that it was necessary to sacrifice any increases in the administrative budget for the sake of providing the huge sums necessary to meet increases in the transformation budget decreed by the basic congresses and by the need to build a strong and modern military force capable of defending the gains of the people.

The secretary of treasury also noted that the popular committees had presented budget suggestions to their basic congresses for the 1979 administrative budgets, and noted the figures suggested were realistic. He also stressed that this was a good sign of the success of Libya's experiment in direct democracy. He indicated that the requests for the 1979 administrative budget totaled 1,022,000,000 dinars.

Qadafi called for a report on the activities of the department of antiquities, which was provided by the secretary for education and training. The report indicated that the mission of the department was to discover and preserve antiquities and that the department had used their budget of 100 thousand dinars to conduct studies and create museums and related projects.[6]

This was followed by the secretary general's observation that the planning and execution of the museums had been done by foreign companies and that the works cited in the report had not been accomplished by the department of antiquities. He went on to indicate that some parts of the administrative apparatus were not doing anything except wasting money and that the department of antiquities was one of them. After calling for greater supervision of the department, Qadafi stated that its present activities, in spite of obvious historical importance, had little relevance to the present Libyan culture or national consciousness. He suggested that Islamic and Arab research in the Arabian peninsula might be more relevant, or that if people wished to be concerned with the Greek and Roman periods, they might wish to examine their agrarian policies. "That," he noted, "would be relevant to present problems."

Qadafi turned to the discussion of the Libyan press, indicating that it falls under the provisions of the *Green Book* which specifies that democracy is popular rule and not popular individual expression. "It is possible," he said, "for each sector such as the workers, the police, the students, the engineers, etc., to publish specialized newspapers inasmuch as any newspaper which is the expression of all [people] must be participated in by all people, and not merely a small group of people or editors who claim that they speak for public opinion or for the total public." "This individualistic view," he said, "is an error, for a newspaper under such circumstances expresses only the view of its owners." He indicated that it is the burden of all groups in society to form administrative committees for the purpose of publishing their own specialized papers. Qadafi explained that he considered the money spent on the secretariat of information to be lost, and he expressed the view that the officials employed in the secretariat of information could be more usefully employed elsewhere.

Qadafi also explained that "we have little need for broadcasting and we are not responsible for it." "Previously when a government wanted to spread propaganda," he said, "it would buy a broadcasting system and pay it money to support the regime. Inasmuch as we do not have a regime, we do not see any need to disseminate its voice." He added that "our system of direct popular democracy is, of itself, a sufficient broadcasting system."

The secretary of planning indicated that all of the information available relating to the transformation plan as of the end of September had been placed in two reports and forwarded to the basic congresses. One report listed all of the successes at the economic level by sector. The other, presented to the congresses at their last meeting, outlined the projects allocated for them and the stage of completion that had been achieved. This report, he said, was in line with the goal of providing true mass participation in the preparation of the budget and in the supervision of its execution.

He indicated that the provisions of the transformation budget for 1978 totaled 1,775,000,000 dinars distributed over its various sectors, noting that 938,000,000 dinars had been expended as of the end of September. The total projected expenditures for 1978, he said, would be 1,380,000,000 dinars, or 80 percent of the total appropriations.

The secretary of planning offered comparative figures for previous years, indicating that 1978 was the third year of the five-year transformation plan. In 1977, he said, expenditures totaled 1,294,000,000 dinars, whereas in 1976 expenditures totaled 1,187,000,000 dinars. The three-year total expenditures for the transformation plan thus equaled 3,852,000,000 dinars. "Moreover," he noted, "total expenditures for the three-year plan (1973 through 1975) was 2,200,000,000 dinars." "Thus," he continued, "the expenditures for the first three years of the five-year plan have almost doubled the expenditures under the three-year plan."

The secretary of planning clarified that this investment represented increased capital outlays which would lead in the end to increased agrarian and industrial production and improved services. He cited that the reclamation of more than 70,000 hectares of agricultural land had been completed as well as the opening of more than 56 factories. An additional 38 factories had entered the labor training and final execution stage, with another 34 factories under study or placed under bids. The total number of new factories was thus 127.

The secretary of planning added that this activity is helping to meet the planned growth rate of 10.89 percent annually, with the non-oil sector having a goal of 14 percent growth and the oil sector 7.8 percent. He indicated that the economy had grown 11 percent during the last three years. He added that during 1978, agricultural production increased an average of 20 percent. Electricity production, he noted, increased 22 percent. Turning to services, he announced roads had increased, as had the number of ships, planes, and telephones. A profusion of relevant figures was provided.

"In regard to education," the secretary of planning announced, "the number of students had increased from 680,000 in 1975 to approximately 910,000 by the end of October, 1978, figures including all educational divisions." He also cited, "impressive increases in health facilities including the increase in hospital beds from 10,800 in 1975 to 17,475 in 1978." "This rate of increase," he said, "far exceeds that of neighboring countries or other oil-producing countries." "Similarly, the number of doctors increased from 2,779 in 1975 to 3,637 in 1978, or approximately one doctor for every 900 inhabitants." "This average," he noted, "exceeds that of many European states." "Similarly," he continued, "the number of rehabilitation centers increased from 12 in 1975 to 28 in 1978, the number of clinics from 584 in 1975 to 750 in 1978.

He further said that per capita income in Libya was 1,379 dinars in 1975, and had increased to 1,910 dinars in 1978. "This," he said, "equates to a per capita income of approximately $6,000, a very high figure regardless of whether one is comparing advanced or developing countries." He noted that the per capita income in many African states was less than $500 and that the per capita income of many oil-producing states did not exceed $1,000 or $1,600 annually.

The secretary of planning surveyed recommendations received from the basic congresses for the 1979 transformation budget and noted that they had expressed satisfaction with the projects completed and had urged the rapid completion of those projects yet to be executed. "Many basic congresses recommendations," he noted, "also suggested new projects, with particular emphasis being given to the provision of increased services." "When we collated the requests we found that the recommendations totaled 3,500,000,000 dinars which, in turn, had to be added to the projects outlined in the five-year plan which totaled 7,500,000,000 dinars last year and which are projected to be 9,250,000,000 dinars [for 1979]."

The secretary of planning pointed out that the transformation plan alone would make an investment of enormous size and would demand extraordinary efforts. "In reality," he said, "the problems of execution would make it difficult to increase planned allocations over the next two or three years." "This," he added, "was unfortunate because when the requests of the basic people's congresses were added to planned investments, the total came to approximately 13,000,000,000 dinars, a figure that limits our ability to successfully execute those projects or to benefit from them, and that may prevent us from achieving the results specified at the outset of the plan." "Nevertheless," he said, "we have before us the decisions and recommendations of the basic people's congresses for spending in various sectors which totals 3,500,000,000 dinars, while in reality many projects recommended by the basic people's congresses during the previous year are [listed] as continuing or nonexecuted." He said that "possibilities thus existed for redistributing [funds] from those projects so that they may be reallocated with the cooperation and decision of the basic people's congresses without adding to the plan." He suggested that an absolute cap be placed upon new expenditures, and suggested allocating resources on the basis of priorities established in the five-year plan.

At this point, Jalloud offered some observations about the transformation and administrative budgets. He found the increase in the administrative budget frightening. He added that oil revenues must be utilized to build a strong economy, but that this goal was threatened by the alarming increase in the administrative budget. He said that he found it absolutely unthinkable that the administration of a Libyan population numbering 2 million exceeded 770 million dinars, and warned that the administrative budget must not be allowed to eat up oil revenues needed to develop agriculture, schools, industry, and so forth.

He also indicated that 186 thousand individuals were employed by the secretariats of the general popular committee and warned that the leadership's concern with consumers (as opposed to producers) was not limited to merchants. He stressed that this was a very important subject and that he believed (the state) was plagued with excessive duplication. He said he failed to understand the need for central government organizations to employ 22 thousand individuals, municipalities to employ 32 thousand, secretariats to employ 121 thousand and various other agencies to employ another 10 thousand. He said, "We believe that the entire bureaucratic apparatus should not exceed 30 thousand or 40 thousand employees, and the labor force for public administration should not exceed 30 thousand." He also said that he found it totally incomprehensible that approximately 40 percent of the labor force was tied up in consumer rather than productive positions, and observed that in the secretariats, a few individuals seem to do most of the work while the remainder get in the way. He clarified that 50 percent of the state revenues currently go to services and the remainder to productive projects.

Jalloud then commented on the transformation budget, expressing his astonishment over the demands for additional projects. He said that it was his observation over the past year that shortages of capital and technical capacity as well as the limited ordinary labor force made (centralized) planning a more urgent need than ever before. The people, he said, must not covet positions, but must work for the good of the revolution and general public. He drew attention to the fact that oil was a limited resource and that the life of Libya's reserves must be prolonged and not squandered.

He also said that, "we do not know how the secretaries of the basic people's congresses selected by the people operate or why they do not guide the basic people's congresses and help them understand their role." He stressed that the revolutionary committees were established to guide the congresses toward urgent projects that represent pressing needs and that have realistic expectations of achieving human or material benefits.

Qadafi then urged the revolutionary committees to play an active role in guiding the congresses, saying that "we are continuing to learn how to govern ourselves by ourselves and it is incumbent upon all of us to make sacrifices." "We will not," he said, "retreat from popular rule, and that is unique."

Qadafi then clarified that the preparation of the budget and the establishment of factories and new schools begin with the request for scientific studies and that such projects are evaluated in terms of cost and service and must fit defined programs. He reviewed all of the budgetary demands presented earlier, including the administrative budget, the transformation budget (five-year plan), and the projects proposed as a means of demonstrating their absurdity in light of available resources and the nation's concern for the preservation of oil reserves.

He mentioned that the allocations of the first administrative budget following the revolution (1971) totaled 183 million dinars, while its projected total for the present year (1978) was 700 million dinars and its projection for 1979 is approximately 775 million dinars. "This increase," he said, "is unbelievable." "Let us search for answers to this problem in the coming year," he said, noting, "that if this trend continues, the administrative budget will be transformed into the transformation budget and [our wealth] will be absorbed in wages, allowances, and related things." "The projects for factories, agrarian development, schools, health and such," he said, "will have to be cancelled." "You have two choices before you," he said, "our present consumer path or a path of laying a sound foundation for industrial and agrarian growth in preparation for the day when our oil resources are depleted." He said that for some congresses his warning would be of no avail.

He explained, for example, that almost every one requested a health institute for their region. In the case of K, it would have to be calculated where the students would come from if a medical institute opened there. He noted further that a medical institute required equipment, books and teachers. The region K, he continued, needed water more than anything else, and plans will soon be made to transplant K to a site where there is water.

He explained that spending millions to establish youth projects, such as playgrounds and swimming pools, was an example of traditional thinking, for such projects do not return income to the state. He cited the example of a request for a tomato-processing factory in L, asking the question, "where are the tomatoes in L?" He added that the requests for projects totalling 40 million dinars in M, N, and O were not scientific or logical. Similarly, the request for a wool factory in P made little sense, because the region already had abundant wool. This was followed in turn by wonderment over a request for 4 million dinars to build a plastic factory in Q. "Where," Qadafi asked, "does one find the materials for plastic in Q?"

Qadafi called upon the secretary in R to explain their request for the establishment of a paper mill. The secretary answered that the masses had recommended building the paper mill (dependent upon a feasibility study by the secretariat of planning) in order to provide employment for the citizens of the region. (However, labor shortage rather than unemployment is the problem in Libya.) The secretary of planning then clarified that earlier studies indicated that raw materials were not adequate for the projects requested by the basic congress in R.

*The Third Session: Morning Meeting*

The general congress resumed its meeting the next morning, December 18.[7] First, the president of the federation of producers pointed with pride to the workers' revolution and to their seizure of the means of production. He indicated that many of the companies seized were merely skeleton structures used primarily by agents of foreign firms as a means of exploiting Libya's wealth.

Qadafi returned to the subject of the requests for new projects. He said that after the proposed projects had been reviewed by the various secretariats, it was found that there were many duplications. He also explained that the congresses must realize that projects often require a long period of preparation before they can be executed. He cited the nuclear projects as an example, indicating that their preparation has consumed more than ten years. Jalloud divided the requests into two categories: those which increase productive capacity, and those which pose problems of duplication. The former, he said, must be implemented. The projects that pose problems of duplication have resulted from the fact that information concerning the requests of other basic congresses was not available at the time decisions were made. This, he said, "was a mistake, and we will put before the masses announcements relating to that."

Qadafi assailed the Secretaries of the congresses and the popular committees for failing to generate citizen consciousness vis-à-vis projects specified in the plan. He pointed out that the general congress was being obliged to discuss many proposed projects that had already been included in the plan. He added that such potential duplications consumed precious manpower and material resources in addition to wasting money.

The shortage of manpower, he pointed out, was particularly severe. He stressed that Libyans must learn to rely on themselves rather than foreign labor. In this regard, he noted that there had been requests to establish technical training centers, but suggested that it would be better to attain the maximum benefit from the existing centers. He underscored this point by indicating that present technical training facililties had a capacity to train five thousand students, yet currently had an enrollment of only seven hundred. These duplications and complications are not the fault of the people, Qadafi stressed, but of the imperialists who kept people in ignorance for so many years.

He stressed again the need for the centralization of agricultural land to assure its maximum productive utilization. He similarly emphasized the need to centralize costs in the reclamation of agricultural land and the need to exploit coastal lands. Many buildings on the coastal lands, he said, may have to be razed so that the lands can be used for productive purposes.

Qadafi also stressed the need to concentrate on the development of the petro-chemical industry and the need to avoid being content to merely sell oil abroad.

The secretary of the congress in Benghazi supported the call of Qadafi and Jalloud for keeping budget requests within the financial and implementation capacity of the country. Similarly, the president of the popular committee of the college of engineering at the university in Fatah emphasized the need to develop the industrial and agrarian bases of the country and the need to increase the productivity of its citizens.

The secretary in Sebha stressed the necessity of reviewing those projects in the plan which have already been executed before deciding to execute new ones. The secretary of the basic people's congress of Tripoli echoed similar thoughts, suggesting that only compatible projects should be added to the plan and that other requests should wait until the plan had been completed.

The secretary in S suggested that the projects be divided into two groups: economic projects and service projects. He further suggested that priorities for the projects must be allocated upon the basis of the true needs of the regions as established by scientific studies. He also suggested directing foreign companies to implement projects in the region of T as well as abolishing the general organization for housing and transferring their services and engineers to the popular committees of the housing districts.

The secretaries of several basic congresses added their voice to the demand that the transformation plan be supported and that self-reliance be stressed.

The secretary in U emphasized his region's support for the revolution and the transformation plan, citing the completion of thirteen hundred dwelling units up to this date. He also stressed the need to concentrate on the execution of the major productive projects scheduled for his region.

Several other people demanded that the plan not be changed and that priority be given to the most important projects, particularly those which would increase productivity.

Qadafi pointed out that the transformation plan had been established by the RCC prior to the establishment of popular authority and that it would terminate in 1980. Additions to the plan suggested by the basic people's congresses totaled 3,500,000,000 dinars this year. He noted that the total of the added expenditures for the two years approached the projected expenditures for the entire five-year plan. In this regard, he stressed that he was not protesting the outcome of direct popular administration, but merely noted that many of the decisions by the basic congresses were the result of inadequate information.

He added that the mission of the general congress was to review the decisions and recommendations of the basic congresses and to give them (a common) form. "It is also upon us," he said, "to single out those projects which fit our financing possibilities and our implementation capacity." He noted that year after year and generation after generation, social consciousness would increase, youth and intellectuals would become members of the basic congresses in the future, and faults in the present application of direct popular administration would be corrected.

He said that the present role of the general congress was to collate all basic congress decisions and sort them out in terms of duplication and feasibility of execution. "All of these decisions," he said, "should be sent to the committee on form, which, in cooperation with the general popular committee, is best able to evaluate them in terms of financial and implementation capabilities."

## The Third Session: Afternoon Meeting

The general congress began with Qadafi requesting the president of the committee on form to outline the final form of the decisions and recommendations relating to the transformation budget for 1979.

The president said that before adding new projects to the plan, it would be necessary to weigh the following considerations:

1. The availability of funds for allocation to the transformation of various sectors of society
2. The implementation capacity of the state as it related to technical and manpower capacity for the preparation, execution, and supervision of the projects
3. Giving priority to projects added to the plan in their final form by the basic congresses in 1977
4. Studying the decisions and recommendations of the General Congress in its third ordinary session for the year 1978, taking into consideration: (1) eliminating duplication; (2) eliminating projects infeasible for technical reasons; and (3) giving first priority to projects designed to increase production, and next priority to projects designed to provide essential services.
5. Including new projects in the plan with the following considerations: (1) projects designed to increase production after ascertaining their economic and technical feasibility; (2) projects relating to essential services, especially those relating to fundamental needs; and (3) transferring to future years projects not congruent with established priorities and fiscal guidelines.

The General Congress shifted to a discussion of Article 10 of the agenda: coastal agrarian lands. The president of the committee on form indicated that 170, or 91.6 percent, of the basic congresses agreed without comment, while 15 expressed reservations. One congress charged the secretariat of agriculture to take whatever steps it felt necessary to implement the article, while another recommended implementation by the secretariat of land reclamation. Other comments concerned preservation of trees and buildings and the need for sound planning.

The president of the federation of *fallahein* ("peasants") spoke about the importance of the area and the need to provide maximum production from the coastal area. He noted that there were many hard-working people there, and raised the question of how they should be divided into productive units.

Qadafi reiterated that 170 basic congresses had accepted the special memorandum on coastal areas without comment, stressing that the general congress was not able to change what the basic congresses had decided.

The discussion turned to Article 8 of the agenda: the areas of competence and authority of the general secretariat. A total of 179 basic congresses had resolved to charge the general congress with the appointment of the president of the high court, its justices, and its prosecutor. Other basic congresses had suggested that the positions be appointed by the secretariat of justice.

In regard to the appointment of the director of the central bank of Libya and his deputy, 170 favored appointment by the general congress. Others suggested appointment by the general popular committee. Two suggested establishment of a general secretariat for appointments.

Other positions included on the special memorandum on appointments included: controller, a committee to supervise the granting or withholding of citizenship, and an administrative committee to supervise oil resources. The terms suggested in the special memorandum were accepted in total by approximately 170 basic congresses, with the others suggesting slight modifications.

At this point, Qadafi indicated that the matters outlined in this memorandum were administrative in nature, and they had been handled by the RCC in the past. With initiation of popular authority, however, they had become the jurisdiction of the people.

Qadafi then stressed that henceforth the permanent general secretariat of the general congress would be assigned to revolutionary tasks. As for its other administrative functions, they would be distributed among the general congress and the general popular committee. Qadafi observed that the security apparatus, including the intelligence and the police, would also become part of the public apparatus and would be subject to popular control. He said that "all citizens in the Jumahuriah must be vigilant in preserving the gains of the revolution and the security of the Jumahuriah."

Qadafi pointed out that the state security apparatus was created originally to protect a government whose only goal was to remain in power. "Now," he continued, "the ruling authority is the authority of the people. It is the people who operate their apparatus and everyone in the Jumahuriah finds himself responsible for the protection of himself, his country, his possessions, and his revolutionary gains against enemies who wish to spy on the country or steal its gains."

Article 9 was discussed, the memorandum relating to the creation of an armed citizenry. The president of the committee on form indicated unanimous support (187) for this memorandum. Many secretaries expressed support, but some were concerned about providing military training for women. Qadafi replied that he rejected the view that only men mattered and stressed that the true practice of democracy made it essential that women participate completely and say their piece on matters presented for discussion. He said that democracy was not for half of society alone. A series of speeches supporting the creation of a citizen army followed.

*The Fourth Day: Morning Session*

The discussion began regarding Article 11: relations with Malta. This memorandum was supported by 185 basic people's congresses, or 98.9 percent. Qadafi mentioned that 98 percent of the basic congresses had agreed to more economic investment in Malta and the building of an educational institution there.

The discussion then turned to Article 16: ratification of agreements with other countries. Qadafi noted that this article provided the masses with the ability to direct the foreign policy of the Jumahuriah. The special memorandum for Article 16 had been agreed on by 178 basic people's congresses, many of whom added comments, such as suggestions to make beneficial loans to friendly countries. Qadafi stressed that it was essential to help anti-imperialist nations and states opposed to the enemy.

The discussion next turned to Article 17, which related to aid for the African strugglers. A total of 186 (99.5 percent) agreed to support the African struggle. Comments ensued regarding the need to use foreign aid to build bilateral ventures between Libya and the progressive African states. Some suggested that Libyan aid should be used to strengthen the cause of Islam in Africa. Others recommended aiding only those African liberation movements that have cut their ties with Israel.

Qadafi indicated that support for Africa was of particular importance to the Arab and Islamic causes and to the general fight against racist imperialism. He noted that "the traitorous recognition of Israel by the defunct regime in Egypt might cause some African states to consider establishing diplomatic ties with Israel," and that this tendency had to be countered.

The discussion moved to Article 12: the employment of teachers during the summer recess. It was indicated that 127, or 67.1 percent of the basic people's congresses accepted the principle of summer work for teachers, whereas 59 congresses expressed reservations. Qadafi asked those with reservations to explain the reasons, despite the fact that the decision to require summer work for teachers had been made. Several secretaries spoke, but Qadafi reaffirmed that there could be no salaries or allowances for teachers unless they completed their summer work on projects important to the masses.

Article 14, relating to the creation of revolutionary agricultural advisors or extension workers, was discussed next. A total of 168 basic people's congresses supported the memorandum; one expressed reservations. The leader of the agricultural union indicated that some branches of the union approved agricultural advisors, believing that it referred to the traditional concept of agrarian advisors or extension workers. He noted that the idea of revolutionary agricultural advisors was more general and inclusive than the traditional concept, and that the mission of the new advisors was to seize agrarian production establishments and to contribute to agricultural production and self-sufficiency.

The general congress then reviewed Article 13, which related to the mission of the revolutionary medical profession. All basic congresses agreed to the memorandum. The secretaries of various basic congresses, unions, and associations asked the medical profession to make sacrifices to increase the level of public health. The secretary of health spoke of the need to revolutionize health and praised the decisions of the congress of health workers for meeting demands and for reflecting sensitivity to the great Fatah revolution. He also spoke of the need to revolutionize medical education in the universities and to change the medium of instruction into the Arabic language. In this regard, he mentioned that the college of medicine had considered establishing a college of Arab medicine, but was overwhelmed by oppressive bureaucratic behavior. "The medical instruction at the college," he said, "continues to be in a foreign language."

Next, they returned to discussing Article 17, on foreign policy; the memorandum of which was supported by all the congresses. The discussions that followed stressed the need to pursue a vigorous foreign policy designed to strengthen Islam and to enlighten the world as to the third universal theory, that is, *The Green Book.*

The general congress then moved to consideration of Article 15, relating to the supervision of public administration. Some basic people's congresses suggested opening branches to supervise the bureaucracy at the municipality level, and adding, revolutionary elements to support the central apparatus in controlling the bureaucracy. Others suggested giving the secretariat general the authority to take whatever measures it deemed necessary. Some proposed restrictions on bureaucratic behavior, while still others suggested giving the general popular committees at the municipal level the responsibility for supervising the bureaucratic projects in their respective areas.

*Fourth Day: Evening Session*

The session began with consideration of Article 7, a memorandum reviewing the organization of the sector of information and culture. It was indicated that 183 basic congresses had accepted the memorandum. The general import of the lengthy discussion that ensued between the secretaries of the congresses, Qadafi, and Jalloud was that the Libyan media was more than adequate by world standards, but that it had failed to keep pace with the revolutionary transformation of Libyan society. As a socialization agent, it had been a failure. Jalloud suggested that this failure was one cause for Libya's low levels of agricultural and industrial production. Proposals for reorganization of the information and cultural sector centered on the establishment of a special high popular committee for broadcasting and, perhaps, the establishment of popular committees for broadcasting at the municipal level.

Qadafi expressed his regrets to those congresses which did not understand the organization and division of coastal lands, and he assailed the revolutionary committees in these congresses for failing in their role as instigators and guides for the revolutionary reforms. Similarly, he said he was sorry that the teachers were unable to build a congress and that they were, accordingly, unable to attend the congress and study the formation of revolutionary groups, such as the revolutionary farmers and health professions. He also expressed his regrets that some basic congresses particularly those in which instructors predominated, had requested that teachers not be asked to serve the revolution during the summer holiday in return for their summer allowances. Finally, Qadafi expressed regret over the absence of women at the people's congresses, in spite of the fact that they had received their political rights. He added that women must decide their own fate and not allow others to serve as their representatives. They must become educated, he said, and be able to participate in the transformation of society. They must not be transformed into economic goods as has happened in capitalist societies.

The leadership of the revolution congratulated the congresses of students, agriculturalists, and medical workers on the application of the sayings of Colonel Qadafi relating to the establishment of revolutionary medical and agrarian professions.

Next, Qadafi indicated that the present general congress marked the end of the three-year term of the current popular committees. At the conclusion of the fourth congress, he said, the selection of new ones would begin. He said it was possible for the basic congresses to retain all or part of their present popular committees, and that the presidents of the new committees (at the zone level) would constitute the general popular committee at the municipality level. This committee would also include the presidents of the specialized popular committees (at the municipality level) for agriculture, industry, health, and such. These presidents, in turn, would form the specialized popular committees for agriculture, industry, and health at the national level. A president would be selected for each of the specialized popular committees at the national level. Finally, the presidents of the specialized popular committees at the national level would become the secretaries (ministers) of the general popular committee. He went on to say that after the initial selection of the general popular committee in this manner (which would take place immediately), he would convene the General People's Congress in two or three months again to select a (new) general popular committee. It would be permissable, Qadafi said, for the masses to retain any members of the general popular committee they believed to be successful in fulfilling their obligations. And, he added, it would also be possible for the masses to select a president for the current general popular committee.

Qadafi stated that over the next three months, he would establish a general secretariat for the general congress from among its current members, and that the congress could select some of the current secretaries from the general popular committee to serve as members of the secretariat general. The members of the revolutionary leadership (who may be serving on the current general popular committee) would be precluded from selection to the new secretariat, because revolutionary authority had now become distinct from popular authority.

Qadafi stressed, however, that the dissolution of the permanent secretariat (the revolutionary leadership) and its replacement by a new secretariat selected by the general congress did not mean that the leadership was abandoning its revolutionary mission. "That is our cause," he said, "and it does not mean that there will be any opportunity for opportunists to spread destruction in the country." "This," he continued, "will not happen for we [the revolutionary leadership] will work to protect all of the new revolutionary fronts." "We will bear responsibility," he said, "for pushing the masses to the forefront in order to insure that the total socialist transformation of Libyan society will be achieved, to insure that exploitation will end and to insure that the people will live in freedom."

Qadafi continued by saying that "we will intervene against all who attempt to deviate from the revolutionary line and its initiatives, from the path of total social transformation, or from the cause of Arab unity." He added that, "the responsibilities of authority and administration had preoccupied the revolutionary leadership in the past and prevented them from concentrating on the true revolutionary causes." "Such causes," he said, "included Palestine and the protection of Islam and Muslims."

He announced that "the greatest achievement of the great Fatah revolution (September 1) was the transfer of total authority to the people," adding that, "the revolutionary committees which are now spreading everywhere are, in reality, the counterparts of the RCC."

*The Final Session*

The last session met to hear the final form of the decisions and recommendations. After opening speeches, the Secretary General called upon the president of the committee on form to present the recommendations and decisions reached by the basic congresses. The results closely mirrored the majority positions outlined during the general discussion of the various agenda items surveyed. Budgetary and agenda items requiring complex legislation were presented in special appendixes not covered by the press.

In its closing remarks, the leadership of the revolution praised the congresses of the medical, farmer, and student groups for taking the initiative in defining a revolutionary role for themselves. Also, it expressed again its extreme disappointment at the failure of the teachers to establish a professional congress and to become part of the revolutionary movement, and urged them to do so immediately.

The revolutionary leadership similarly expressed its deep regret over the position taken by many basic congresses regarding the nationalization of the coastal lands and their failure to comprehend the importance of the coastal lands to the revolution's goal of self-sufficiency. Particular criticism was directed toward the revolutionary committees of those congresses opposing the nationalization of coastal lands, for failing in their role as revolutionary guides.

# 10 The Dynamics of Total Transformation: Projections for the Second Decade

Chapters 8 and 9 examined the parameters within which the Libyan revolution will operate during its second decade and outlined the broad guidelines established for Libya's transformation into a socialist state governed by the precepts of direct popular democracy. The objectives of this chapter are to examine the structural modifications evident in Libya's latest socialist and political transformations and to speculate on their ability to increase the mobilization capacity that eluded the revolution during its first decade. We will also attempt to illustrate how many of the behavioral problems reviewed in earlier chapters continue to plague even the most recent structural innovations of the revolution. Observations are based on the Libyan press, interviews with a variety of public officials and members of the people's congresses, and personal observations of the proceedings of the Fifth General People's Congress convened on March 1, 1979. In terms of format, political reforms will be surveyed first, followed by a discussion and critique of the economic reforms.

## The Political Institutions: 1979 Structural Reforms

The fundamental structural units of the system of direct socialist democracy were described in chapter 7 and do not warrant repetition at this point. Our comments, accordingly, will be limited to a brief analysis of the formal structural modifications in Libya's system of direct socialist democracy instituted by the Fourth General People's Congress, and their underlying logic in terms of solving the operational problems that beset the revolution during its first decade.

In this regard, three structural modifications in the political system are of particular importance: the revolutionary committees, the withdrawal of the RCC to "revolutionary" concerns, and the establishment of general popular committees at the municipality level.

### Revolutionary Committees

The establishment of revolutionary committees within both the basic people's congresses and the professional people's congresses (unions) was

197

designed to counter three behavioral problems: (1) the absence of sufficient revolutionary fervor among the masses, many of whom remained at least partially wedded to the past, (2) the timorousness of the masses, leading to a reluctance to impose revolutionary programs on members of the traditional elite structure, and (3) the tendency of many basic people's congresses to pursue the specific interests of their own regions without adequate concern for the general good of the country. This latter problem was clearly illustrated by the excessive budgetary demands presented by the basic people's congresses at the Fourth General People's Congress. It was also evident in the reluctance of many basic people's congresses to reallocate their coastal lands.

The revolutionary committees, as Colonel Qadafi has pointed out, originally possessed no formal authority. They consisted of self-proclaimed zealots encouraged by Qadafi's call for "revolutionary committees in all places." They exercised their responsibilities by: (1) bringing to the attention of the basic people's congresses those issues that may have been overlooked in their deliberations; (2) suggesting that certain decisions or recommendations made by a basic people's congress be reconsidered in light of those national priorities stressed in Colonel Qadafi's speeches, and (3) focusing the attention of the masses on the recalcitrant behavior of various individuals and groups, including officers of the basic people's congresses and members of the popular committees. The members of the revolutionary committees were to become the true cadres of the revolution.

In the weeks prior to the March 1, 1979, meeting of the Fifth General People's Congress, however, the revolutionary leadership suggested that these committees should, indeed, exercise some formal authority. They would henceforth be responsible for conducting elections at the level of the basic people's congresses, a subject to be discussed shortly. More significantly, the revolutionary committees had rapidly become Colonel Qadafi's direct link with the masses. They now report to Colonel Qadafi directly, with no intervening steps. At times, he convenes the revolutionary committees en masse. At other times, he visits them individually. It should be noted that revolutionary committees exist in virtually all government departments and agencies in addition to their presence in the basic people's congresses and the professional people's congresses.

*Municipal General Popular Committees*

The establishment of general popular committees at the municipal level, turning to a second structural innovation, was proposed by Colonel Qadafi and approved by the people's congresses as a means of decentralizing the national bureaucracy and bringing it under the direct scrutiny of the masses at the municipal level.[1] The general popular committee at the national level, it will be recalled from chapter 7, approximates the cabinet in most political systems and consists of the secretaries of the major administrative departments. Under the decentralization proposal, a network of regional or municipal secretaries would be created to assume authority for the implementation of the decisions of the general people's congress as they pertained to their respective areas. The secretaries of the major departments, in their role as the general popular committee at the national level, would only be responsible for setting national directions and coordinating the efforts of the secretaries at the municipal level. A very interesting administrative structure has thus been created in which communications flow from the secretaries (general popular committee) at the national level to (1) the corresponding secretaries (general popular committee) at the municipal level, and (2) the popular self-management committees which manage all productive enterprises. This process was described in some detail by Colonel Qadafi in the transcripts of the Fourth General People's Congress discussed in chapter 10. All popular committees, of course, are subject to the scrutiny and supervision of the people's congresses at their respective levels.

Formation of the municipal general popular committees begins at the level of the basic (branch) people's congresses, with the nomination of candidates to serve on specialized sector committees (or as the sector representative) at the municipal level. A sector committee or agent corresponding to the major administrative departments in the general popular committee at the national level is to exist in each branch of that municipality.[2] The nomination process is supervised by the revolutionary committee of the basic people's congress which "opens the book" on the professional and revolutionary credentials of individuals standing for nomination for sectorial posts. The basic people's congress also elects an ordinary popular committee for the branch (or municipality, in the case of small municipalities without branches), a process described in chapter 7. These elections are also supervised by the revolutionary committee. Nominees for the sector committee who are not selected as the sector agents for the municipality serve as the sector agents for their respective branches.

The sector agents collectively serve as the general municipal popular committee. One of them is selected by the leadership committee for the municipality to serve as the chairman of the municipal general popular committee. Agents for each sector at the municipal level automatically become candidates for the post of secretary on the general popular committee at the national level, a position equivalent to that of a cabinet minister. This selection is made by the members of the General People's Congress.

The terms of the members of the general popular committee are three years. If one of the members of the general popular committee at the municipal level is selected to serve on the general popular committee at the national level, his position is filled by one of the agents at the branch level. The members of the municipal general popular committee are responsible to both their counterparts in the general popular committee (national) and to the basic people's congress within the scope of its jurisdiction. The general popular committees at both the national and municipal levels currently contain sixteen members, but the number fluctuates.

*Popular versus Revolutionary Authority*

Clearly, the most profound change in the institutional structure of the Libyan political system was Colonel Qadafi's announcement that the present permanent general secretariat of the General People's Congress, the remnants of the RCC, would give way to a general secretariat elected by the General People's Congress. The general popular committee (cabinet) would also be elected by the General People's Congress.

By elevating the RCC to the revolutionary level, the path has been cleared for the emergence of an elite based on technical competence rather than revolutionary credentials to assume the revolution's technical administrative positions. In the analysis of the elite in chapter 3, it was seen that the overwhelming majority of secretarial positions during the early years of the revolution were filled on the basis of revolutionary rather than technological consideration. Such infusions of technical talent are clearly essential if the revolution is to achieve its developmental objectives. The increased participation of technocrats and intellectuals is also perceived by Qadafi as a means of enhancing the overall credibility of the revolution and its programs. Libya's intellectuals may no longer have the option of deserting the revolution.

Nevertheless, in his roles as revolutionary guide and protector, Colonel Qadafi will undoubtedly remain the preeminent figure within the Libyan political system. Indeed, it might be suggested that the decentralized system of direct democracy will make his role as the solitary guide of the revolution assume even greater significance, for he will increasingly become the single most reliable source of information and behavior cues concerning national directions available to the local congresses. As noted in the budgetary discussions of the Fourth General People's Congress, one of the technical problems to arise from the basic congress system was the fact that each congress operated more or less in a vacuum vis-à-vis the actions of the other 187.

**Transformation and Mobilization:**
**Critique of the 1979 Political Reforms**

*Municipal General Popular Committees*

Having examined the major structural transformations of the socialist era, our next objective is to evaluate these modifications in terms of their capacity to solve the mobilization problems that have beset the Libyan revolution during its first decade, and to facilitate attainment of the revolutionary objectives outlined in chapter 8.

In this regard, the addition of general popular committees at the municipality level was designed to serve several revolutionary goals, the foremost of which was to breathe life into Libya's moribund bureaucracy and to bring its penchant for waste and corruption under control. The second goal was to fight tendencies toward excessive centralization and the creation of a new bureaucratic elite that the people might find difficult to control. And finally, the decentralization decision was designed to help the bureaucracy become more effective in implementing the broad range of projects added to its burden by the need to coordinate the workers' self-management programs.

Since the decentralization program is in the implementation stage, it is difficult to evaluate its success. One would certainly expect a brief period of difficulty in sorting out lines of authority and responsibility among the various administrative levels. Such difficulties are inherent in any reform, and are particularly inherent in reforms of grand design. Yet to be ironed out, for example, is the precise relationship between the secretaries at the municipality level and those at the national level. Clearly, if the secretaries in the general popular committee at the national level possess the authority to issue direct orders to their counterparts at the municipality level, their job will be far easier than if they are expected to coordinate and bargain with them. If the latter situation is the case, the secretaries at the national level might find themselves so embroiled in negotiations that they will be totally unable to provide an overall sense of direction to their assigned areas of specialization, be it agriculture, industry, or education. Moreover, if the secretaries at the municipality level do play a major role in policy making — and one must note that the objective of the program was to promote decentralization, and that the municipality secretaries are elected by the municipality and are not beholden to the corresponding national minister — it would mean that a large number of secretaries would be involved in the decision-making process. Decisions relating to the commercial processing of agrarian products, for example, might involve the national secretaries of agriculture, industry, planning, agrarian reform, and finance as well as the forty-five corresponding ministers in each area. This alone would directly involve 230 more or less autonomous individuals in the decision-making process.

We will note, however, that the recent selections for positions on the municipal general popular committees have consistently repudiated the original popular committee-ASU leadership. Individuals elected in March, 1979, were reminiscent of the modernizing administrators discussed in chapter 5. In the municipality of Benghazi, for example, five members of the current municipality general popular committee hold Ph.Ds.

*Revolutionary Committees*

The upgrading of the revolutionary committees by placing them in charge of elections at the basic congress level and by establishing their direct access to Colonel Qadafi should markedly increase the linkage-mobilization capacity of the revolution in a variety of ways.

First, the more or less self-selected, zealous nature of the revolutionary committees has provided Colonel Qadafi with the best available roster of those individuals most supportive of his programs. He thus has a starter core in the process of cadre building. The members of the revolutionary committees are his people.

Second, the presence of the revolutionary committees "in all places," including government agencies, serves an important communication function. It was noted earlier, for example, that the revolutionary leadership had been forced to place excessive reliance on the mass media as a means of providing cues or guidance for the masses. The direct link between Colonel Qadafi and the revolutionary committees now assures Colonel Qadafi that major concerns will be discussed on a one-to-one, word-of-mouth basis throughout Libyan society. In the same vein, the revolutionary committees should also be useful in channeling feedback from the masses to the revolutionary leadership. One might anticipate, however, that the masses may feel a certain reticence about speaking openly in the presence of members of revolutionary committees.

Third, the presence of zealous revolutionary committees should serve as an important control mechanism. The Libyan revolution is not free of its internal detractors, a problem that may have been exacerbated in the short run by the severity of recent socialist economic reforms and the near elimination of the new capitalist class. It is hoped that the revolutionary committees may be able to reduce the level of corruption and related economic crimes discussed in chapter 9. The revolutionary leadership, however, must take care to assure that the revolutionary committees do not become overly active in their watchdog role. The overzealous hunting of antirevolutionary elements could potentially lead to severe decreases in regime support.

Fourth, the revolutionary committees will increasingly serve a "gatekeeper" function at the level of the basic people's congresses by means of their "critiques" of various candidates standing for office. It is important to note, in this regard, that the revolutionary committees, following Colonel Qadafi's urging, did facilitate the election of technically competent people to the municipal general popular committees. If this trend continues, it could be an important factor in achieving the goals of the revolution.

**Economic Transformations: Structure**

The decisions of the Fourth and Fifth General People's Congresses have also served to transform Libya into a totally socialist state. May 1, 1979, for example was scheduled to mark the end of all forms of private enterprise in Libya excepting those farms or firms owned and operated by a single individual as the sole source of his income. Henceforth, all enterprises requiring the paying of wages will be operated by worker self-management committees in partnership with the state. Farmland not used for production is currently nationalized by the state. The effective size of a private Libyan farm has thus been limited to the area one man can cultivate.

In a related move, all members of the Libyan labor force must now be classified as members of one of four categories: farmers, professionals, employees, or laborers. In contrast to the earlier pattern, it is no longer possible for Libyans to operate farms and businesses in addition to holding professional or government positions. Henceforth, an individual will be restricted to a single source of income. Farmers are those individuals who derive their income from farming; employees are individuals who draw salary from the government; laborers are individuals who operate former public and private corporations under the worker self-management system or who work for the oil companies. All members of the former consumer or service occupations — drivers, coffee-fetchers, waiters, shopkeepers, contractors, traders, and so forth — must find work in one of the four productive categories.

**Economic Reforms: Critique**

This brings us to our speculations on the likely results of the economic reforms decreed by the Fourth General People's Congress and given expression by the Fifth General People's Congress. Basically, the transformation to total socialism had three objectives: to destroy the new capitalist class, to break the rentier state pattern by forcing all Libyans to be productive, and to strengthen distributive support for the revolution by assuring that all Libyans receive an adequate standard of living.

In terms of the above objectives, the elimination of the capitalist class was largely achieved under the economic programs discussed in chapter 7. The decision to eliminate all forms of private enterprise requiring the services of wage labor merely provided the coup de grace. All economic activity will henceforth be conducted through worker self-management through worker self-managed cooperative societies, or through other state agencies.

In line with our comments provided in chapter 7, we will reiterate that the decision to force all former members of the consumer class to become effective and enthusiastic producers may be difficult to enforce. There might well be an extended period of foot-dragging and subtle sabotage by members of this group. This would be particularly unfortunate, for members of the new capitalist class represent a majority of Libya's entrepreneurial and technical talent.

On the positive side, the elimination of the new capitalist class will eliminate the problem of capital leaving the country (access to bank accounts has been severely restricted) and might eliminate the opportunity for quick business fortunes. We would point out, however, that most of Libya's transformation budget of several billion dollars will continue to be used to purchase the goods and services of foreign firms, and that personal contacts will remain crucial in the granting of very lucrative contracts. The elimination of the capitalist class, accordingly, has not eliminated the primary source of Libya's problems with "economic crimes."

The transformation of Libya into a totally socialist state in which the citizens are classified as farmers, employees, laborers, or professionals seems to guarantee that the masses will become directly involved in their economic system and that the rentier state pattern might well be broken.

The economic problem that will confront the revolutionary leadership during the coming decade will not be the inordinately large number of individuals involved in the consumer sector although the bureaucracy continues to grow in size, but the quality of the work that occurs in the productive sector. We have already noted that the members of the recently abolished new capitalist class may be somewhat lethargic in the execution of their duties and that this is particularly unfortunate since they do possess a preponderance of Libya's available technical and managerial skills.

Libya's productive enterprises, as Colonel Qadafi has pointed out, can and will be operated by worker self-management committees. The committees, he has acknowledged, will need time to acquire the necessary technical and managerial skills. The cost of industrialization may be high, Colonel Qadafi has stated repeatedly, but the price will be paid. Libya will become an industrialized socialist state.

The type of behavioral problems Libya's self-managed socialist economy is likely to encounter over the next decade are of three varieties:

1.  insufficient technical skills;
2.  perseverance of nonproductive cultural attitudes, including low innovation and low motivation;
3.  conflicting managerial dynamics within the democratically organized, self-management committees.

All three types of behavioral problems are illustrated in the following paraphrased excerpt from a symposium sponsored by the Libyan press. Note that this and other quotes used throughout the book argue well for the vitality of the Libyan press.

> Janzour's establishment represents one of Libya's important industrial establishments. Its problems are roughly similar in character to those of other industrial establishments. For these two reasons, it was used as a point of departure for our inquiry.

> The most dangerous problem, in my opinion, that confronts this establishment is the declaration by the producers that they are not responsible for marketing, and their willingness to produce only what is demanded from them. This means that they are relinquishing their responsibility as producers and as partners in production—not just hirelings. This is a matter that no one who believes in the revolution can afford to tolerate or accept. Such an acquiescence could be interpreted as saying, "We would rather remain hirelings than wage the production battle to the end."

> As brother S.M. indicated toward the end of his speech, the concern of this symposium is to . . . find solutions to all of the problems and bottlenecks that impair production in this plant. It is not reasonable to construct factories in which the people invest millions of dinars and then leave their output stacked in the warehouses, as is the case at this and other plants. It is imperative to find solutions for these problems and obstructions, lest they turn into a conspiracy against the revolution.

> It is true that there were flaws at the establishment [in the production of uniforms]. Nevertheless, the police did not cooperate with us [and cancelled their orders]. The armed forces cooperated with us during the initial years, and purchased a large proportion of our production. Later they reduced their orders. Thus the plant faced a production and surplus problem.

> Engineer F.K. then reviewed a number of solutions that represented his view of how to deal with the problems this plant was facing. His suggestion included improving the quality of the plant's products in conformance with the suggestions of consumers (general and individual), and the convening of regular working sessions with departmental representatives to listen to their observations concerning both technical questions and exporting schedules. "Our side," he said, "admits some negligence, and is open for criticism." "But," he said, "we demand some encouragement also . . . Consumers ought to bear the burden of encouraging the newly born national industry by disregarding some mistakes and mild flaws . . . in order for it to develop . . . and for the plant not to cease production for lack of demand of its products."

> The general consumer is the candidate to hold out a helping hand to the newly born domestic industry. Accordingly, the General Popular Committees, and the Secretaries of Industry, Commerce, Exchequer, and Planning have provided this industry with all the guarantees necessary to encourage the transaction of its business. In spite of all these measures, some circles blink at them and circumvent the decrees protecting domestic production.

Among the schemes deployed is the requirement of high specifications which the local producer cannot meet. These circles surprise the establishment by announcing an arbitration for the importation of items produced locally, and may require deliveries within a certain month. Given the difficulties confronting the national establishment in importing raw materials, utilization of resources, obstruction encountered with ports of entry, and bank accounts, the national establishament cannot take part in this arbitration.

Under these conditions, the plant produces fourteen million meters of cloth a year, while it was scheduled to produce eighteen million meters. The plant is about to further reduce its output due to the continuation of these conditions. The establishment's products remain stockpiled for a period of two years due to the attitudes of the merchants, and to the renouncement of some agencies to their obligations, and due also to the inability of the establishment to reduce its prices sufficiently to compete with imported products.

It may soon become economically feasible to pay the workers salaries without producing . . . The financial loss would be less! We hope that will not happen!

Janzour's establishment must overcome its current bottlenecks. Reports indicate that wages and social security regulation represent sixty-five percent of the total costs . . . this indicator is relatively high. The solution to this problem is to utilize the working body in a more efficient way . . . especially as this indicator shows that employees are not working effectively. Some reports affirm . . . that absenteeism is thirty percent and that the annual job turn over is approximately thirty-seven percent.

The nationalism of the individual consumer is not reliable, for he can not be depended on to purchase an expensive domestic article when he can buy an identical, inexpensive imported article. Unfortunately, he is more concerned with his pocket than with his nation.[3]

In addition to the quality of labor problems, Libya's experiment with socialism must take care not to become stagnated by administrative entanglements. The precise lines of supervision and coordination between the various productive and administrative units are still being worked out. Potential conflicts between the democratic decisions of the self-management units and the demands of the relevant ministers at the municipal and national levels might well arise. The advent of total socialism might also suffer from the overall malaise of the Libyan bureaucracy.

Finally, the classification of all Libyans into one single productive pursuit may cause particularly severe shortages in the agrarian area, for very few Libyans were full-time farmers. In one former tribe of approximately five thousand individuals, for example, only eleven individuals qualified as farmers. In the short run, the resultant dislocations of this program may result in a greater need for imported foodstuffs and for higher levels of government price supports. Recognizing this problem, the government has recently added some flexibility to the program.

Although these problems are severe, the chances of the socialist experiment succeeding are heightened by the fact that Libya is in the fortunate economic position of being able to afford to make mistakes.

Turning to the desire of the revolution to provide all Libyans with an adequate standard of living, a process that is essential to the eventual institutionalization of the revolution, we will only note that the provision of an adequate standard of living for all Libyans is well within the economic capacity of the revolutionary leadership. The goals of the revolution as described in the *Green Book: Part II,* however, call for an adequate but not excessive standard of living for all Libyans. This leads us to suggest that within a relatively short period of time, all Libyans will be receiving approximately the same level of renumeration for their efforts, regardless of what they do or how much they produce. Certainly one step in this direction has been the severe limiting of private bank accounts. Should this occur, it would represent a marked change in the workers' self-management programs which previously allowed workers to share the profits of their organizations. The government would thus be eliminating an important incentive for increased production and would have to resist already marked tendencies toward low productivity, low innovation, and minimal consumer service.

# 11 Political Development in Libya: An Interim Assessment

In chapter 1, it was suggested that political development involved three fundamental components: control, mobilization, and change adaptation. Control, as we have used the term, is a passive concept. It implies the absence of overt resistance to the regime. We have also suggested that control was a necessary but not sufficient requirement for the economic, political, and social modernization of a state. Modernization, for example, is unlikely to occur in an environment of political chaos. It is equally unlikely to occur in an environment in which regime control is maintained through the perpetuation of illiteracy and tribalism.

Mobilization, as we have used the term, is an active concept. It involves the ability of the political leadership to harness the human resources of the state to its modernization (or other) goals. As such, mobilization involves two distinct components: motivational capacity and organizational capacity. The motivational or behavioral component of mobilization involves inducing individuals to engage in behavior supportive of regime goals. Under the rubric of motivational capacity would fall such traditional political science concepts as legitimacy, institutionalization, and political community. Clearly, the more a citizenry of a state believes its political institutions and leaders to be legitimate, and the more it perceives itself to be a member of a political community, the more readily it can be mobilized in support of a regime's development objectives by symbolic appeals. Motivational capacity would also appear to depend upon the extent to which the predominant social, cultural, and economic values of a society's members are compatible with the developmental goals of the regime. The more members of a society remain tradition-bound, the more difficult they will be to motivate in support of developmental goals.

The organizational aspect of mobilization refers to the ability of the state to organizationally direct and coordinate the efforts of its citizens in the achievement of regime goals. Certainly, several key factors would be the capacity of: the political system to make clear decisions relating to its priorities, the bureaucracy to execute those decisions, the regime's political apparatus to link the public to those decisions, the political system to shape the core attitudes of the population into line with regime goals, and the regime to enforce its decisions.

The organizational and motivational components of mobilization are not fully independent. The ability of political leaders to motivate their population, for example, often depends to a large degree upon their organizational capacity to shape mass behavior through the press, education system, and other socialization mechanisms. It also depends upon their organizational capacity to build regime support through the efficient distribution of the state's economic resources. Finally, the motivational capacity of the regime would also appear to be markedly influenced by its coercive capacity to assure its supporters that it can and will enforce rules and that they can rely upon the long-term stability of the regime. It is truly difficult to make an emotional or even a rational commitment to a regime that is on the verge of collapse.

The third component of political development involves the ability of the political system to survive the social dislocations generated by its mobilization programs. Far too often, political leaders have been successful in disrupting the traditional, social, and cultural foundations of their societies only to find that they are unable to control the forces thus unleashed.

The objective of this, our final chapter, is to briefly evaluate the Libyan revolution in terms of control, mobilization, and change adaptation.

## Control

In terms of the control variable, there can be little question of the fact that Libya's revolutionary leadership appears to be in firm control of its human and material resources. If control is measured by the absence of civil disorder, for example, we can state that in recent years the revolution has experienced neither strikes, riots, hostile demonstrations, or any other visible manifestations of well-organized resistance. If control is measured in terms of passive acceptance of revolutionary programs, we can also state that all revolutionary institutions, whether people's congresses or worker self-management units, do meet as scheduled. We will also note that the revolutionary leadership remains in control of the political system in spite of its enactment of programs that have attacked the very core of Libyan society. Tribes have been abolished, the economy is being totally socialized, and the traditional practice of Islam focusing on the figure of Mohammed has been radically transformed into a revolutionary practice of Islam centering on the popular, self-revealed interpretation of the Koran.

## Mobilization: Organizational Capacity

Turning to the organizational dimension of mobilization, we must credit the revolution with considerable success. The efforts of Libya's revolutionary leaders to devise an organizational structure capable of penetrating all segments of the population have been delineated throughout earlier chapters. They include the experiment with modernizing administrators, the Arab Socialist Union, the popular committees, and the various combinations of popular committees and ASU branches, ultimately culminating in the system of basic people's congresses and professional people's congresses described in chapters 7 through 10. Virtually all Libyans currently belong to a basic people's congress. Moreover, these congresses do exercise real authority. Through their popular committees, they regulate the daily life of Libya's citizens and allocate the resources of their regions. The Libyan masses can ignore the people's congresses and popular committees only at their own risk. Colonel Qadafi has made it abundantly clear that individuals who do not participate in the basic people's congresses have no recourse from their decisions. The stakes for nonparticipation, then, are high. This is particularly so in an era of total social and economic transformation. In terms of achieving the goal of penetrating the Libyan masses, the basic congress structure has clearly been a success.

The revolution has also been successful in organizing the masses militarily, and in assuring their attendance at politicization camps designed to build revolutionary cadres. In military terms, for example, most youths of both sexes undergo military training for at least a limited period. In most instances, one member of every family serves in the militia. Moreover, older Libyan males of military age during the Italian era have been formed into the Mujahadein, an armed adjunct to the army complete with its own officer corps. On October 7, 1978, an estimated 400 thousand armed mujahadein marched in Tripoli to demonstrate their support of the revolution. If the basic people's congresses accept the proposition of a civilian army as outlined in the discussions of the Fourth General People's Congress, the blanket of military involvement will become total.

The revolution's organizational capacity is also apparent in the network of professional unions, federations, and associations which cap every professional and social group, including farmers, students, doctors, lawyers, electricians, and such. In cooperation with the people's congress system, each union or association makes rules governing its members. The student association, for example, recently urged that the academic year be shortened to six months and that the remaining six months be devoted to serving the revolution by working in productive enterprises. As in the case of the basic congresses, professionals who do not participate in the congresses of their association run the risk of being totally without input into the rules guiding their occupation. The General People's Congress only recognizes the input of the designated professional congresses. Alternative avenues for professional expression do not exist.

The politicization camps, as noted in earlier chapters, were established in 1973 and have grown steadily since that time. Specialized camps now exist for students, farmers, workers, and professionals. Intensive leadership training camps have also been tailored for the secretaries and assistant secretaries of the people's congresses and for the members of the popular committees. It is estimated that approximately 90 percent of the members of the popular committees will attend the camps and that all Libyan citizens will attend a politicization camp at least once during their lifetime.

The revolution has succeeded, then, in organizationally penetrating the Libyan population and has demonstrated a clear capacity for mobilizing it for participation in the basic people's congresses, in the various branches of the military, and in a variety of popular manifestations of support for the revolution and its leaders. Its organizational capacity, as noted in chapter 10, has also been markedly enhanced by the system of revolutionary committees "in all places."

Two facets of the organizational phase of mobilization continue to pose difficulties for the regime: the media and the bureaucracy. The Libyan media, as Colonel Qadafi has indicated, has failed to play a crucial role in shaping the behavior and values of the Libyan masses. Clearly, the media provides full coverage of revolutionary accomplishments and has tried hard to focus public attention on nonrevolutionary activity. The media does not, however, convey a particularly inspirational tone. Colonel Qadafi's discussion of the media during the Fourth General People's Congress, for example, almost went so far as to suggest that newspapers have been written off as an avenue of socialization and that, henceforth, they will exist for the sole purpose of providing more or less technical information for occupational and social groups, such as farmers, students, or workers. Libyan radio and television, in turn, will increasingly stress the *Green Book* and the popular interpretation of the Koran. They will also provide a crucial link in Colonel Qadafi's ability to disseminate information to the members of the approximately 187 basic congresses and to stimulate a sense of direction and uniformity in their decisions.

Turning to the problem of bureaucracy, one faces the conceptual choice of viewing the bureaucracy as either a formal control and regulatory arm of the executive or as an organizational apparatus capable of building regime support through the distribution of goods and services. In regard to the former, the Libyan bureaucracy has inherited the formidable task of coordinating virtually all economic activity in Libya, much of it generated by the decentralized system of worker self-management. In terms of the latter, the bureaucracy is directly responsible for education, housing, health care, price supports, and all other vital services affecting the Libyan population. How well these and related services are provided, obviously, has a direct bearing upon mass support for the revolution and its programs.

Our earlier analysis of bureaucratic development in Libya left little doubt that the bureaucracy was the revolution's weakest link in relation to both its ability to regulate and control Libya's resources and to build regime support through the distribution of goods and services. How well increased reliance upon popular committees will ease the bureaucratic bottleneck is difficult to anticipate.

In summary, then, the revolution has made tremendous strides in its organizational ability to mobilize mass participation in Libya's revolutionary system of direct democracy and workers' self-management. It remains to be seen how effective the new institutional structures will be in terms of increasing regime support through the production and efficient distribution of goods and services.

## Mobilization: Motivation

This, then, takes us back to the discussion of mobilization in terms of active behavioral support. It will be recalled that many of the structural innovations instituted by the revolutionary leadership had failed to produce the desired behavioral results both in motivating active support for the revolution and in upgrading the quality of that support. Indeed, it is in the areas of achieving the necessary modifications in supportive behavior that the fate of the regime's revolutionary transformations may ultimately rest.

To make the system of direct popular democracy effective, several modes of political behavior apparently lacking during the revolution's first decade clearly must be strengthened. First, the system of people's congresses must become institutionalized in the minds of the people. Just getting people to show up, although an important first step, is not enough. People must learn to believe in the system; to take pride in its operation and be willing to defend its prerogatives against internal and external enemies. The political system must, in short, be made legitimate. As things currently stand, it is Colonel Qadafi, and not the political institutions of the state, that is the focal point of mass attention in Libya. Political institutions do not have legitimacy except through his blessing. The people simply have not had time to catch up with the rapidity of institutional changes or to fully appreciate their complexity.

Secondly, members of the basic people's congresses must develop a broader sense of political community both within the confines of their respective congresses and within the country as a whole. In regard to the former, the deliberations of the basic people's congresses continue to reflect vestiges of tribalism, deference to social status, and the tendency to use new-found popular powers to settle old parochial scores. Moreover, most basic people's congresses are timid. They have not become sources of innovation or creativity. At the national level, their decisions and their claim upon national resources must be mitigated by some sense of national priorities and fiscal restraint. The latter problem was particularly evident in the budgetary demands they presented to the General People's Congress outlined in chapter 9.

The revolutionary leadership, of course, is well aware of these problems. The formation of revolutionary committees was both a recognition of their existence and an attempt to take corrective action. Efforts were also made to bolster the efficiency of the basic groups by providing them with tangible authority in broad areas of policy-making, perhaps at the expense of national coordination and efficiency.

In terms of long-range political and economic development, manifestly political attitudes may pose less of a problem than the continued presence of the social and cultural attitudes judged by many of the theorists discussed in chapter 1 to be antithetical to the revolution's modernization efforts. The continued presence of traditional and transitional behavior patterns among large segments of the Libyan population poses the very real danger that they will continue to impair the routine administrative activities of popular committees and the workers' self-management units. All local administration and all industrial management, it must be stressed, are now in the hands of popular committees selected either by the basic congresses, or by the management committees, as the case may be. Three attitudinal-behavioral dimensions must be considered. The first constitutes what we earlier defined as traditional behavior: fatalism, parochial family and tribal orientations, atomism, and other variables relating to mass motivation. Quite clearly, local or managerial administrators manifesting these and related bahavior patterns are likely to jeopardize the performance of the revolutionary goals outlined earlier. The second set of behavioral problems relate to what might be termed transitional attitudes and behavior, the foremost manifestation of which in Libya has been the profound public reliance on government handouts and the pervasive public tendency to roll with the tide of events without becoming ideologically or emotionally committed. Such tendencies, of course, threaten not only the administrative capacity of the popular committees, but undermine progress toward the institutionalization of the congress system as well. One must also expect, at least initially, the passive resistance and myopic performance of merchants and other members of the consumer class transferred forcibly into the "productive" sector of the Libyan economy.

A third area of behavior problems relates to the low levels of technical and administrative skill available at the lower-level popular committees. For the most part, formal technical and administrative training among popular committee members has been minimal. Some delays and confusion will inevitable ensue until these skills can be upgraded. This, more than anything else, appears to be a matter of time.

Having discussed control and mobilization, we now come to the topic of change adaptation. This is a particularly difficult process to evaluate, for the revolution has moved with such rapidity in such a short space of time that there has been little opportunity for the dust to settle. We will, however, make the following observations. First, the revolution has been particularly effective in destroying the foundations of traditional Libyan society without suffering notable resistance from the Libyan masses. It was generally assumed, for example, that the tribal system was inviolable; that any attacks on this venerable form of social structure would lead to direct armed conflict. The conflict did not occur. Even more dramatic has been Colonel Qadafi's attacks on Libya's religious leaders and on Mohammed as the symbol of Islam. Any tampering with traditional religious practice, it was assumed, would lead to an instantaneous mass uprising. The uprising did not occur. As days passed, people more or less shrugged and said "let Mohammed take care of it." In terms of the Libyan experience, then, social theorists might wish to reevaluate their views on the strength of traditional institutions when confronted with a modernizing regime supported by a strong military force.

Secondly, the Libyan revolution has been far more successful in breaking the social institutions of the traditional past than in transforming the traditional attitudes and behavior patterns. The predominant attitudes and behavior of Libyans remain very traditional.

Third, the revolution has been far more effective in liberating the Libyan population from the institutions of the past than in reintegrating them into the institutions of the revolution. People participate in the people's congresses and in the unions, but many have yet to become believers. They watch and wait.

# Notes

**Chapter 1**
**The Political Development of Libya**

1. C.L. Taylor and M.C. Hudson, *World Handbook of Political and Social Indicators,* 2nd ed. (New Haven, Conn.: Yale University Press, 1972).

2. Benjamin Higgins, *Economic Development: Problems, Principles and Policies,* rev. ed. (New York: Norton, 1968), p. 26.

3. Gabriel A. Almond and Sidney Verba, *Civic Culture* (Boston: Little, Brown and Co., 1963); Talcott Parsons, *Structure of Social Action* (Glencoe: The Free Press, 1949); Gideon Sjorberg, "The Rural-Urban Dimension in Preindustrial, Transitional, and Industrial Societies," in *Handbook of Modern Sociology,* ed. Robert E.L. Faris (Chicago: Rand McNally, 1964), pp. 127-59; Ferdinand Tonnies, *Community and Society Gemeinschaft and Geslschaft,* trans. and ed. C.P. Loomis (East Lansing: Michigan State University Press, 1947); F.X. Sutton, "Social Theory and Comparative Politics," in *Comparative Politics,* eds. Harry Eckstein and David E. Apter (Glencoe, Ill.: The Free Press, 1963), pp. 67-82; Gideon Sjoberg, "Folk and Feudal Societies," *American Journal of Sociology,* 58 (November 1952): 231-39; Hehmet Beqiraj, *Peasantry in Revolution* (Ithaca, N.Y.: Cornell University Press, 1966); Everett E. Hagen, *On the Theory of Social Change* (Homewood, Ill.: Dorsey Press, 1962), pp. 68-69, 124-157; John C. McKinney, *Constructive Typology and Social Theory* (N.Y.: Appleton-Century-Crofts, 1966); Helio Jaguaribe, *Political Development: A General Theory and a Latin American Case Study* (New York: Harper and Row, 1973). W.W. Rustow, *The Process of Economic Growth,* 2nd ed. (N.Y.: W.W. Norton and Co., 1952, 1962); Joseph A. Kahl, *The Measurement of Modernism: A Study of Values in Brazil and Mexico,* Latin American Monographs, No. 12 (Austin, Tex.: Institute of Latin American Studies, University of Texas, 1968); David Horton Smith and Alex Inkeles, "The OM Scale: A Comparative Socio-Psychological Measure of Individual Modernity," *Sociometry* 29 (December 1966): 353-77; Kalman H. Silvert, ed., *Expectant Peoples* (N.Y.: Random House, 1963); Kuswin Nair, *Blossom's in the Dust* (London: C. Duckworth, 1961); George Dalton, ed., *Economic Development and Social Change: The Modernization of Village Communities* (Garden City, N.Y.: The Natural History Press, 1971); Samuel P. Huntington, *Political Order in Changing Societies* (New Haven, Conn.: Yale University Press, 1968); S.N. Eisenstadt, "Convergence of Modern and Modernizing Societies: Indications from the Analysis of the Structuring of Social Hierarchies in Middle Eastern Societies," *International Journal of Middle East Studies* 8 (1977): 1-27; David E. Apter, *The Politics of Modernization* (Chicago: University of Chicago Press, 1965).

4. Almond and Verba, *The Civic Culture.*

5. Kahl, *Measuring Modernism:* Smith and Inkles, "The O-M Scale."

6. David C. McClelland, *The Achieving Society* (Princeton, N.J.: D. Van Nostrand, 1961).

7. For example, see: Dean C. Tipps, "Modernization Theory and The Comparative Study of Societies: A Critical Perspective," *Comparative Studies in Society and History* 15 (March 1973): 199-225.

8. For an excellent review of literature on the elite, see: Robert D. Putnam, *The Comparative Study of Political Elites* (Englewood Cliffs, N.J.: Prentice-Hall, Inc., 1976).

9. Monte Palmer, *Dilemmas of Political Development,* 2nd ed. (Itasca, Ill.: F.E. Peacock, 1980).

10. For examples of this argument, see: H.D. Graham and T.R. Gurr, eds., *Violence In America: Historical and Comparative Perspectives* (New York: Bantam Books, 1969).

11. W.F. Ilchman and N.T. Uphoff, *The Political Economy of Change* (Berkeley: University of California Press, 1969); A. Etzioni, *Political Unification* (New York: Holt, Rinehart and Winston, Inc., 1965).

12. For an interesting attempt to use the concept of identity in political analysis, see: Lucian Pye, *Personality, Politics and Nation Building: Burma's Search for Identity* (New Haven, Conn.: Yale University Press, 1962).

13. David Easton and Jack Dennis, *Children in The Political System* (New York: McGraw Hill, 1969).

14. Ibid.

15. See note 10.

16. Ferrel Heady, *Public Administration: A Comparative Perspective,* 2nd ed. (New York: Marcel Dekker, Inc., 1979).

17. Almond and Verba, *The Civil Culture.*

18. D.E. Smith, *Religion and Political Development* (Boston: Little, Brown and Co., 1970).

19. Max Weber, *The Theory of Social and Economic Organization* (New York: Macmillan Co., 1947).

20. Monte Palmer and William Thompson, *The Comparative Analysis of Politics* (Itasca, Ill.: F.E. Peacock, Inc., 1978).

**Chapter 2**
**Libya: The Historical, Economic, and Social Milieus**

1. House of Commons Debates, January 8, 1942, vol. 377, cols. 77-78, quoted in M. Khadduri, *Modern Libya: A Study in Political Development* (Baltimore: Johns Hopkins University Press, 1963), p. 35.

2. Ibid., pp. 57-58. See also *Jaridat Benghazi* (Benghazi), 7 August

1945, where al-Kikhya's letter was supported and considered a representation of Cyrenaican's opinion.

3. Khadduri, *Modern Libya,* p. 58.

4. Ibid., pp. 92-94.

5. Ibid., p. 129.

6. *New York Times,* 19 May 1949; Khadduri, *Modern Libya,* p. 132.

7. See Articles 2, 3, and 36-49 of the Libyan Constitution.

8. See chapters 5 and 6 of the Constitution; Khadduri, *Modern Libya,* appendix B; Elizabeth R. Hayford, "The Politics of the Kingdom of Libya in Historical Perspective" (Ph.D. diss., Tufts University, November 1970), pp. 220-23.

9. Hayford, "Politics of the Kingdom," p. 226.

10. Ibid., p. 227.

11. Henry Serrano Villard, *Libya: The New Arab Kingdom of North Africa* (Ithaca, N.Y.: Cornell University Press, 1956), p. 42.

12. Ruth First, *Libya: The Elusive Revolution* (Baltimore: Penguin Books, 1974), p. 151.

13. Khadduri, *Modern Libya,* pp. 237-38; Hayford, "Politics of the Kingdom," pp. 248-49; *Times* (London), 6 February 1954; Salaheddin S. Hasan, "The Genesis of the Political Leadership of Libya, 1952-1969: Historical Origins and Development of Its Component Elements" (Ph.D. diss., The George Washington University, June 1970), p. xv.

14. Khadduri, *Modern Libya,* pp. 240-43; Hayford, "Politics of the Kingdom," p. 440.

15. Hasan, "Genesis of Leadership," pp. 286-90, 298-312, 314-17; Hayford, "Politics of the Kingdom"; Wright, pp. 237-42.

16. Hayford, "Politics of the Kingdom," p. 259; *Christian Science Monitor,* 27 January 1964; *Maghreb Digest* (February 1964), p. 14.

17. Hayford, "Politics of the Kingdom," p. 262; *New York Times,* 22 March 1965; *African Diary* 7 (August 6-12, 1967): 515.

18. *Christian Science Monitor,* 29 April 1968; Hasan, "Genesis of Leadership," pp. 447-48; Hayford, "Politics of the Kingdom," pp. 265-66.

19. Hasan, "Genesis of Leadership," pp. 440, 448, xv.

20. Ibid., p. 448.

21. An example of corruption is "the occidential oil concessions" case where two Libyan ministers became involved in bribery and disclosure of cabinet secrets. See *Wall Street Journal,* 8 February 1973; see also Leonard Mosley, *Power Play: Oil in the Middle East* (New York: Random House, 1973), pp. 328-333.

22. First, *Libya,* p. 78.

23. Richard F. Nyrop, et al., *Area Handbook for Libya* (Washington, D.C.: U.S. Government Printing Office, 1973), p. 159.

24. See Lewis and Gordon, "Libya After Two Years of

Independence," *Middle East Journal* 8 (Winter 1954): 41-53; Lewis, "Libya: An Experience," *Current History* (August 1955): 102-109; Hayford, "Politics of the Kingdom," p. 235.

25. John Wright, *Libya,* (New York: Praeger 1969) p. 260.

26. Benjamin Higgins, *Economic Development: Problems, Principles, and Policies,* rev. ed. (New York: W.W. Norton, 1962), p. 819.

27. Nyrop, *Area Handbook,* p. 3.

28. Benjamin Higgins, *Economic Development: Principles, Problems and Policies* (New York: W.W. Norton, 1959), p. 26.

29. William Zartmen, ed., *Man, State, and Society in the Contemporary Maghrib,* (New York: Praeger Publishers, 1972), p. 345.

30. Hayford, "Politics of the Kingdom," p. 457.

31. R. El-Mallakh, "The Economics of Rapid Growth: Libya," *Middle East Journal* (Summer 1969): 308.

32. Ali A. Attiga, "The Economic Impact of Oil on Libyan Agriculture" in *Libya: Agriculture and Economic Development,* eds. J.A. Allan, K.S. Mclachlan, and E.T. Penrose (London: Frank Cass, 1973), pp. 9-18.

33. Ministry of Planning, Libyan Arab Republic, *National Accounts, 1962-1972* (Tripoli: Government Press, 1973).

34. First, *Libya,* p. 145.

35. H. Mahdavy, "The Patterns and Problems of Economic Development in Rentier States: The Case of Iran" in *Studies in the Economic History of the Middle East from the Rise of Islam to the Present Day,* by M.A. Cook (London: Oxford Press, 1970), pp. 428-67.

36. Wright, *Libya,* p. 259.

37. Robert Mabro, "La Libye, Un Etat Rentier?" in Project 39, quoted in First, *Libya,* pp. 149-50.

38. Nyrop, *Area Handbook.*

39. Monte Palmer, *The Dilemmas of Political Development: An Introduction to the Politics of the Developing Areas* (Itasca, Ill.: F.E. Peacock Publishers, 1973).

40. Hasan, "Genesis of Leadership."

41. Ibid., p. 192. In his valuable study, Hasan succeeded in tracing origins and backgrounds of the families which practically run Libya during eighteen years of monarchy.

42. Ibid., p. 49.

43. N. Ziyada, *Libya* (Beirut: The American University Press, 1948), p. 12. quoted in Hasan, "Genesis of Leadership," p. 91.

44. *Shulat al Hurriyya* (Tripoli), 11 February 1951, quoted in Hasan, "Genesis of Leadership," p. 91.

45. Nyrop, *Area Handbook, p. 115.*

46. *The International Bank for Reconstruction and Development, The*

*Economic Development of Libya* (Baltimore: The Johns Hopkins University Press, 1960), p. 8.

47. Nyrop, *Area Handbook,* p. 116.

48. Ministry of Planning, Libyan Arab Republic, *The Development of Education in Libyan Arab Republic* (Tripoli: Government Press, April 1973), p. 44.

49. Nyrop, *Area Handbook,* p. 5.

50. Ibid., p. 57.

51. Ibid.

52. PA2, Oblique. Listwise deletion of cases. N-503. Intercorrelations between factors did not exceed 350.


## Chapter 3
## Revolution and Revolutionary Elites

1. M. Khadduri, *Modern Libya: A Study in Political Development* (Baltimore: Johns Hopkins University Press, 1963); Henry Serroho Villard, *Libya: The New Arab Kingdom of North Africa* (Ithaca, N.Y.: Cornell University Press, 1956); Elizabeth R. Hayford, "The Politics of the Kingdom of Libya in Historical Perspective" (Ph.D. diss., Tufts University, November, 1970); Salaheddin S. Hasan "The Genesis of the Political Leadership of Libya, 1952-1969" (Ph.D. diss., The George Washington University, June 1970).

2. Ibid.

3. An interesting picture of Heikal's mission is found in: M. Heikal, *The Road to Ramadan* (London: W. Collins Sons and Co., 1975). No mention, however, is made of this rumor.

4. Ruth First, *Libya: The Elusive Revolution* (Baltimore: Penguin Books; 1974); Heikal, *Road to Ramadan,* chapter 10.

5. First, *Libya.*

6. Monte Palmer and William Thompson, *The Comparative Analysis of Politics* (Itasca, Ill.: F.E. Peacock Publisher Inc., 1978), chapter 4.

7. Heikal, *Road to Ramadan,* chapter 2.

8. Muammar Al Qadafi, *The Green Book,* (Ministry of Information and Culture, Libyan Arab Republic, n.d.)


## Chapter 4
## Consolidation of the Revolution

1. Ruth First, *Libya: The Elusive Revolution* (Baltimore: Penguin Books, 1974; Richard F. Nyrop, et al., *Area Handbook for Libya*

(Washington, D.C.: U.S. Government Printing Office, 1973).

2. Salaheddin S. Hasan, "The Genesis of the Political Leadership of Libya, 1952-1969" (Ph.D. diss., The George Washington University, 1970); Elizabeth R. Hayford, "The Politics of the Kingdom of Libya in Historical Perspective." (Ph.D. diss., Tufts University, November 1970).

3. E.E. Evans-Pritchard, *The Snusi of Cyrenaica* (London: Oxford University Press, 1949).

4. *Hayford,* "Politics of the Kingdom". *Hasan,* "Genesis of Leadership."

5. This rumor has been widely circulated in Libya. M. Heikal's *The Road to Ramadan* (London: W. Collins and Sons, 1975) makes no mention of it.

6. Max Weber, *The Theory of Social and Economic Organization* (New York: Macmillan Co., 1947), p. 328.

7. *Ibid.,* p. 361.

8. Monte Palmer, *Dilemmas of Political Development,* 2nd ed. (Itasca, Ill.: F.E. Peacock, 1980), chapter 4.

9. Nevitt Sanford, "The Dynamics of Identification," *The Psychological Review* 62 (March 1955): 106-7; Kenneth V. Gergen, *The Concept of Self* (New York: Holt, Rinehart and Winston, 1971).

10. Jerome Kagen, "The Concept of Identification," *The Psychological Review* 65 (September 1958): 296-305.

11. David E. Apter, "Nkrumah, Charisma and The Coup," *Dendalus* 97 (Summer, 1968).

12. Palmer, *Dilemmas,* chapter 4.

13. Ibid.

14. S.M. Ghanem, *The Pricing of Libyan Crude Oil* (Valletta, Malta: Adams Publishing House, 1975).

15. Heikal, *Road to Ramadan,* chapter 10.

16. John Waterbury, *Egypt* (Bloomington, Indiana: University of Indiana Press, 1978), pp. 235-75.

17. Ibid.

18. E.E. Evans-Pritchard, *The Sanusi of Cyrenaica.*

## Chapter 5
## Mobilization and Modernization

1. See note 3 in chapter 1.

2. The "experts" were interviewed independently of the Zawia survey.

3. Omar Fathaly and Monte Palmer, "Political Development Among Rural Libyans" in *Political Development and Bureaucracy in Libya,* by Fathaly, Palmer, and Chackerian (Lexington, Mass.: Lexington Books, D. C. Heath, 1977), pp. 46-70.

4. Possible scores of the mayor performance scale ranged from 4 through 16, with a score of 4 indicating total approval of the mayor's performance, scores of 16 indicating total rejection. Scores ranging from 4 through 6 were considered excellent evaluations of the mayor's performance; 7 through 9, "good"; 10 through 12, "poor"; 13 through 16, "bad." Possible scores on the administrator performance ranged from 4 through 8, with scores of 4 indicating a positive evaluation on all items; a score of 8 indicating a negative evaluation. Scores of 4 were considered "excellent" evaluations of the administrator's performance; 5 and 6 "good"; 7, "poor"; 8, "bad."

5. Possible scores on the agricultural satisfaction scale ranged from 3 through 12, with 3 indicating high satisfaction on all items, and 12 indicating nonsatisfaction on all items. Scores of 3 were considered "excellent"; 4 and 5, "good"; 6 and 7, "poor"; 8 through 12, "bad." Possible scores on the health satisfaction scale ranged from 2 through 8, with 2 indicating the highest possible satisfaction, 8 the least. Scores of 2 or 3 were considered "excellent"; 4, "good"; 5, "poor"; 6 through 8, "bad." Possible scores on the housing-transportation satisfaction scale ranged 3 through 12, with 3 indicating the highest level of satisfaction, 12 the lowest. Scores ranging from 3 to 5 were considered "excellent"; 6 and 7, "good"; 8 and 9, "poor"; 10 through 12, "bad." Possible scores on the education satisfaction scale ranged from 2 through 8, with 2 indicating maximum satisfaction and 8 indicating minimal satisfaction. Scores of 2 and 3 were considered excellent; 4, good; 5, poor; and 6 through 8, bad.

6. The discussion of the organizational structure of the ASU is based on a variety of ASU documents provided by the ASU. An extended but uncritical review of the structure of the ASU may also be found in Henry Habib, *Politics and Government of Revolutionary Libya* (Ottawa, Ontario: Le Cercle du Livre France, 1975).

7. John Gerassi, *Ernesto Che Guevara, Venceremos! The speeches and writing of Che Guevar,* (New York: Simon and Schuster, 1968), pp. 205-206.

8. Habib, Politics and Government.

9. E.E. Evans-Pritchard, "Arab Status in Cyrenaica under the Italians," *The Sociological Review* 36 (January 1944): 13-113; A.J. Cachia, *Libya Under The Second Ottoman Occupation, 1835-1911,* Trans. Yussef al Assali (Tripoli, 1946).

10. Based upon responses to questionnaire items not contained in the 1973 Zawia survey.

11. See note 1, chapter 3.

12. The International Bank for Reconstruction and Development, *The Economic Development of Libya* (Baltimore: The Johns Hopkins University Press, 1960).

13. Estimates of the exact number of Libyans employed in these oc-

cupations varies widely. See, for example, Qadafi's statement on the subject appearing on page (ooo).

14. *El Vehad,* 9 July, 1976.


### Chapter 6
### Mobilization Stage Two

1. Ruth First, *Libya: The Elusive Revolution* (Baltimore: Penguin Books, 1974), pp. 160-62.

2. Socialist Popular Libyan Arab Jamahiriya, *Fact and Figures,* (1977) p. 143.

3. Libyan Arab Republic, Department of Information and Culture, *The Human March in The Libyan Arab Republic,* (1976), p. 190.

4. First, Libya, pp. 160-62.

5. Ibid., p. 162.


### Chapter 7
### Mobilization Stage Three

1. Muammar Al Qadhafi, *The Green Book: Part One* © London: Martin, Brian and O'keeffe, 1976, pp. 9-11. Reprinted with permission.

2. Ibid., pp. 13-17. Reprinted with permission.

3. Ibid., pp. 23, 24. Reprinted with permission.

4. Ibid., pp. 27, 28. Reprinted with permission.

5. *The Political Weekly* (in Arabic), Tripoli, 22 October, 1977.

6. Ibid.

7. *The Political Weekly* (in Arabic) Tripoli, Fall, 1977. (date obliterated).

8. Jean-Jacques Rosseau, *On the Social Contract,* ed. Roger D. Masters, trans. Judith R. Masters (New York: St. Martins Press, 1978).

9. Muammar Gheddafi (Qadafi), "Speech delivered on the occasion of the Sixth Anniversary of the Libyan Revolution," Arab Socialist Union, Tripoli Libya.

10. Ibid.

11. *The Political Weekly,* 22 October, 1977.

12. Ibid.

13. Muammar Gheddafi (Qadafi), "Speech delivered on the occasion of the Sixth Anniversary of the Libyan Revolution," Arab Socialist Union, Tripoli Libya.

14. Socialist Popular Libyan Arab Jamahiriya, *Facts and Figures,* (1977).

15. *El Jehad,* 5 July 1976.

## Chapter 8
### The Coming Decade

1. Muammar Al Qadhafi, *The Green Book: Part Two* © London: Martin Brian and O'Keeffe Ltd., 1978), p. 13. Reprinted with permission.

2. Ibid. Reprinted with permission.

3. Ibid., p. 10. Reprinted with permission.

## Chapter 9
### Implementation of the New Socialist Transformation

1. A transcript of the agenda may be found in *El-Fajer El-Jadeed,* 17 October 1978.

2. Adapted from the transcript of the first session, Fourth General People's Congress appearing in *El-Fajer El-Jadeed,* 17 December 1978.

3. A reference to the Egyptian-Israel treaty negotiations.

4. Minor place names have been omitted.

5. Adapted from the transcript of the second session, Fourth General People's Congress appearing in *El-Fajer El-Jadeed,* 18 December 1978.

6. Adapted from *El-Fajer El-Jadeed,* 19 December 1978.

7. Adapted from *El Fajer El-Jadeed,* 20 December 1978.

## Chapter 10
### The Dynamics of Total Transformation

1. Socialist Popular Libyan Arab Jamahiriya, *Decision of the General Secretarial of the General People's Congress No. 1, for the year 1979 Relating to General Popular Committees in the Municipalities.*

2. S.B. Maskoula, *Popular Administration* (in Arabic) Mimeo, College of Law, Garunis University, Benghazi.

3. *The Political Weekly* (in Arabic) Tripoli, 11 December 1978.

# Index

# About the Authors

**Omar I. El Fathaly** received the Ph.D. in political science at Florida University in 1975, and is currently chairman of the Department of Strategic Studies at the Arab Development Institute, Tripoli, Libya.

**Monte Palmer** received the Ph.D. in political science from the University of Wisconsin in 1963, and is currently chairman of the Department of Government at the Florida State University.